Tearing Apart the Land

Tearing Apart the Land

ISLAM AND LEGITIMACY
IN SOUTHERN THAILAND

Duncan McCargo

Cornell University Press

Ithaca and London

First published 2008 by Cornell University Press

Printed in the United States of America

Library of Congress Cataloging-in-Publication Data

McCargo, Duncan.
   Tearing apart the land : Islam and legitimacy in Southern Thailand / Duncan McCargo.
     p. cm.
   Includes bibliographical references and index.
   ISBN 978-0-8014-4527-9 (cloth : alk. paper)
   ISBN 978-0-8014-7499-6 (pbk.: alk. paper)
   1. Thailand, Southern—Politics and government.   2. Legitimacy of governments—Thailand, Southern.   3. Islam and politics—Thailand, Southern.   4. Political violence—Thailand, Southern.   5. Muslims—Thailand, Southern—Political activity.   6. Malays (Asian people)—Thailand, Southern—Politics and government.   7. Insurgency—Thailand, Southern.   8. Thailand—Politics and government—1988-   I. Title.
   DS588.S68M34   2008
   959.3—dc22

2008010483

Contents

Illustrations

Preface

In June 2006, I sat in a Yala village chatting to four very ordinary youths who had taken part in some extraordinary events. Early in the morning of April 28, 2004, these unassuming young men—in their late teens and early twenties—had been roused, made their morning prayers, and had been given some unusual-tasting tea to drink. Carrying kitchen knives they had borrowed from home the previous evening, they set out on motorcycles in small groups. A trusted local Islamic teacher, Ustadz Soh, had told them to attack two nearby security installations and steal some weapons. They were never told what to do with the weapons, or where to meet after the attacks. Within a few minutes, their leaders and most of their group had been shot dead by armed Thai security personnel. These four had managed to escape; after surrendering to the authorities, they had now returned to relatively normal life in the village. They could give no convincing explanation to why they had joined a war against the Thai state, a war they claimed they never understood. On that same day, 105 fellow "militants" perished in a series of simultaneous attacks, 32 of them when the Thai Army stormed the historic Kru-Ze Mosque where they had taken refuge. Ustadz Soh disappeared without trace. A low-intensity civil war is still under way in Southern Thailand, a war about which there remain more questions than answers. Even those who have participated in the violence, like these youths, seem unable to account for it.

A common but troubling reading of the Southern Thai conflict uses the tropes of "Islamic violence" and the global "war on terror" to frame the violence within larger notions of a civilizational clash between Islam and the West.[1] According to this perspective, popularized by terrorism specialists such as Rohan Gunaratne and Zachary Abuza, the Thai conflict forms part of a pan–Southeast Asian network of radical Islamic violence. Viewing Thailand as a Western-aligned democratic nation, terrorism specialists tend to regard Malay Muslim resistance to the Thai state as animated by a worldwide resurgence of radical Islam aimed at overturning democracy and instituting some form of caliphate. In a damning indictment, Michael Connors has shown that Gunaratne's writings are riddled with embarrassing errors of fact and interpretation: Connors advocates a "war on error" to counter the ill-informed, sensationalist, and muddle-headed work too often published by members of the "insecurity industry."[2] Terrorism experts frequently know very little about the countries on which they write, constructing arguments on the basis of news clippings, internet sources, and (if they are lucky) confidential briefings from security sources. Outside the United States, a backlash against such work is currently under way.[3]

The idea of a coherent and expansionist radical regional Islamist movement is, as John Sidel has cogently argued, deeply flawed.[4] He advocates a much closer examination of the interplay among Islam, radicalism, and violence in Indonesia, the Philippines, Malaysia, and Thailand, to provide a "fully elaborated" understanding of recent developments, one that traces how Islamist political groupings across the region have experienced "demobilization, dissension, disappointment and disentanglement from state power."[5] Radicalization has taken place largely in response to specific setbacks, declines, and defeats, often associated with challenges to religious authority and identity. Overall, the strength of radical Islamist movements in Southeast Asia actually declined significantly between 2000 and 2007. The pronouncements and performance of security agencies in Southeast Asia need to be exposed to much greater critical scrutiny.

This book aims to offer just such a full elaboration of the Southern Thai conflict, rooting that conflict in Thailand's persistent failure to establish legitimate participatory rule in the Malay-Muslim majority provinces of Pattani, Yala, and Narathiwat. Thailand's security forces are treated here not as the primary agency for the solution of the conflict but as a core component of the problem. Islam is viewed as a rhetorical resource selectively invoked by militant groups in the Thai South rather than the source of their core motivation. Echoing the title of the International Crisis Group's first report on the Southern Thai conflict, this is a study of an insurgency, not a jihad.

But is the war essentially a "separatist" conflict? Previous waves of violence in the South from the 1960s onward had been perpetrated by clearly defined separatist groups, most notably the Patani United Liberation Organization (PULO) and Barisan Revolusi Nasional (BRN), both of which later splintered and assumed new forms. The failure of any group to make public claims of responsibility for the renewed violence led to some initial skepticism that the militants were pursuing explicit political goals. Over time, a consensus has emerged that the violence is animated by demands for an independent state, or at least an autonomous region, in the deep South of Thailand. The nature of the militant movement, however, continues to be a source of controversy: Is there a clear command structure? Some analysts insist that the movement is essentially a reconfigured version of earlier groups such as BRN Coordinate (BRN-C, descended from BRN), while others see the movement as a shadowy and largely ad hoc network.

The renewed violence did not begin, as is often popularly assumed, in 2004. From December 2001 onwards, militants in the Southern border region resumed regular and sophisticated attacks on the security forces, including a series of large-scale raids on police posts. Six security personnel were killed in coordinated raids on December 24, 2001; and five marines died in coordinated attacks on their bases in Narathiwat and Yala on April 28, 2003. These incidents were played down by the Thailand government as banditry or localized interest-group conflicts, and received relatively little media attention.[6] Security analyst Anthony Davis argues that these incidents demonstrated the emergence of a revitalized militant movement, one that had been re-grouping and re-organizing under BRN-C leadership after PULO was "decapitated" by the 1997 arrests of its main leaders in Malaysia.[7] Whatever the precise nature of the movement's leadership, Davis is surely right to suggest that the spectacular violence of 2004 was long in the making.

The Southern Thai conflict has been largely invisible to the outside world, little reported in the global media. By the end of April 2008, 3,002 people had been killed and 4,871 injured.[8] There were 1,850 incidents in 2004, 2,297 in 2005, 1,815 in 2006, 1,861 in 2007, and 241 in the first four months of 2008. While the large-scale fatalities of April 28 and October 25, 2004, were not surpassed,[9] numbers of shootings never dropped below 40 per month in the forty months after January 2004, and often exceeded 80; in seven of these months there were more than 100 shootings. Most people who died were shot in ones or twos. Bombs, both thrown and remotely triggered, were also commonly used in the conflict: military patrols were often targeted to deadly effect, and bombs were also planted in markets, cafes, government buildings, and other commercial locations. However, explosive devices rarely caused large numbers of casualties; their impact was usually more psychological. Coordinated attacks, in which as many as sixty targets were hit simultaneously, were staged quite regularly; again, casualties in these attacks were often quite low. Some victims of violence were beheaded after being killed.

While soldiers and members of the security forces regularly topped the casualty lists, in the first six months of 2007 farmers were the largest category of victims, traders the third largest, and factory workers the fifth largest.[10] The war took an increasingly ugly turn, as the violence became less focused and less controlled. Large numbers of teachers and school staff—in many areas, the frontline of the Thai state—were killed and injured in the violence. The conflict was a murky one, since the militant groups involved made no public statements of responsibility and articulated no demands. Many victims were Muslims, who were fingered as *munafik* (traitors to their religion) because they either worked openly for the Thai side or were regarded as undercover informers. Most attacks were carried out by small groups of youths who quickly disappeared back into their communities. Some of those who died were killed extrajudicially by the authorities, while others were victims of revenge killings. Other killings were just dry runs: young militants often attacked civilians to test their skills and courage before hitting harder security targets. Some supposedly insurgency-related incidents were actually ordinary crimes motivated by personal conflicts, of the kind that claim many lives across Thailand every day.[11] Just what proportion of incidents were militant violence, extrajudicial violence, and ordinary crime was a source of considerable controversy. My own view is that between 70 and 80 percent of incidents were carried out by militants (almost two thousand killings), between 10 and 20 percent were linked to the authorities, and around 10 percent were essentially criminal. During 2006 and 2007, the number of extrajudicial killings seemed actually to be increasing, despite official claims to the contrary.

Partly because foreigners were not targeted in the violence, international media interest was very limited.[12] More than a thousand kilometers from Bangkok, Pattani had no regular foreign correspondents in residence. It was visited mainly by well-intentioned "parachute journalists" writing somewhat predictable stories, typically citing the same well-worn informants favored by local fixers. The Thai authorities were keen to play down the Southern unrest, discouraging diplomats and international organizations from enquiring too deeply into the conflict. Most ambassadors to Thailand never visited the region, ostensibly for security reasons. Following the October 25, 2004, Tak Bai incident, the Foreign Ministry briefed the diplomatic community in Bangkok, far from the tragic events themselves; at the Association of Southeast Asian Nations (ASEAN) summit in Vientiane, Laos, later that year, Prime Minister Thaksin Shinawatra threatened to walk out if Tak Bai or other abuses in the South were raised by his counterparts. When the secretary general of the Organization of the Islamic Conference (OIC), Professor Ekmeleddin Ihsanoglu, visited Thailand in 2007, he confined his stay to Bangkok.[13] Thai officials viewed interest in the conflict by ASEAN, the OIC, and UN agencies with intense suspicion, fearing that international attention could lead to pressures for Aceh-style autonomy or an East Timor-style independence referendum. They were also concerned that if the scale of the conflict—an average of almost 700 deaths annually from 2004 to 2007—became widely understood, the lucrative Thai tourist industry, much of it focused around Southern beach resorts such as Phuket, could be adversely affected. As so often, Thais were preoccupied with saving face and presenting a positive image to the outside world, however incomplete or misleading.

The conflict was a source of tension between Thailand and Malaysia. An unknown but sizeable number of Malay Muslims in the Southern provinces held dual Thai and Malaysian citizenship, and Thailand-based voters undoubtedly helped keep the opposition party Parti Islam SeMalaysia (PAS) in power in neighboring Kelantan. While the United Malay National Organisation (UMNO)–led Kuala Lumpur government had nothing to gain from violence and instability on Malaysia's borders, most Malaysian Malays felt considerable residual sympathy for Patani Malays, viewing them as a kindred and repressed minority. Thaksin's government—and many officials in the Southern border provinces—tended to believe that Malaysia was "behind" the Southern conflict. Certainly, many members of the old separatist groups were based on the Malaysian side of the border, but this was a far cry from demonstrating the active complicity of the Malaysian state in the ongoing violence. The full story of the conflict's "Malaysian connection" has yet to be written and is outside the scope of this book. But a peaceful resolution of the conflict was strongly desired by elites in both Kuala Lumpur and Singapore, who feared a contagion of Islamic radicalism and irredentism along the Malay Peninsula. In this sense, Southern Thailand was a significant regional issue.

In public at least, the United States has adopted a hands-off approach to the conflict; former premier Anand Panyarachun, asked by an American journalist what his country could do to help with the conflict, responded, "Tell them to stay the hell out of here."[14] Matt Wheeler, after a careful review of the evidence, argues that despite its interventionism in the Middle East, the United States has adopted a measured and restrained stance toward the Southern Thai conflict.[15] But local suspicions concerning American involvement were widespread and were publicly voiced by figures such as former senators Fakhruddin Boto and Suphon Suphapone, and academic-turned-Democrat-MP Perayot Rahimulla. Despite insisting that the conflict was an internal matter, the Americans grew increasingly alarmed by the incoherence and ineptitude of the Bangkok government's responses to the growing crisis. Because of the sensitivity of the issue, almost any moves by the United States on the South were likely to be counterproductive.

Sources

From the outset, I was skeptical about the value of accounts of this conflict (or, frankly, any conflict or complex political issue) based on secondary sources and determined to do firsthand research. I was able to spend more than a year conducting fieldwork for this project based at Prince of Songkhla University (PSU) in Pattani, building on my existing academic contacts.[16] I had initially planned to base myself in the Pattani town of Saiburi, using ethnographic and participant-observation methods to unpack the politics behind the conflict. Because of the worsening security situation, and based on advice from mentors in Bangkok and colleagues in the South, I opted instead to live on the PSU campus and make regular research forays around the three provinces, mainly in the form of day trips. This approach to fieldwork resulted in a broader study with less depth. Using initial introductions supplied mainly by my academic hosts, often via people I met while attending PSU-organized workshops and seminars, I developed my own network of informants. These included a wide range of local and national politicians, community leaders, National Reconciliation Commission (NRC) members, human rights activists, Islamic teachers, imams, monks, academics, journalists, lawyers, security officials, and both victims and perpetrators of the violence. Much of my research involved conducting around 270 in-depth, semistructured interviews with these informants, typically lasting between thirty minutes and two hours, conducted at their homes or workplaces, at PSU, or at neutral locations such as Pattani's CS Hotel. Most informants were interviewed only once, but some twice or more. The great majority of interviews I myself conducted in Thai;[17] a small number used Pattani Malay, with the aid of a local translator.[18] Around thirty interviews were conducted jointly with Francesca Lawe-Davies, a researcher from the International Crisis Group (ICG);[19] Michael Connors also conducted half-a-dozen interviews with me. I was accompanied by my senior assistant Bhatchara (Pat) Aramsi for a good number of interviews;[20] Pat also carried out a few interviews without my participation.[21] A few additional interviews were conducted in late 2006 and in 2007, in Australia, Sweden, Bangkok, and the South. Around seventy interviews were recorded and later summarized in English by my assistants; others were summarized in notes made during or shortly after the interviews. Apart from a few politicians and public figures who were happy to speak on the record, all my informants are cited anonymously.

In addition to interviews, I also made use of participant observation methods, joining numerous workshops and seminars with groups of local politicians, community leaders, lawyers, and religious leaders on a range of topical issues. In addition, I loitered with intent on the fringes of NRC meetings in November 2005 and February 2006. During the April 2006 Senate elections, I accompanied four candidates in Pattani and Narathiwat on the campaign trail; I also attended a weekend seminar held in Phang-nga by the newly formed Santiphap Party in September 2006.

My fieldwork was a driving project: during my first week in Pattani, I bought a growling 1989 Mercedes (of a kind favored by Malay-Muslim taxi drivers in the deep South), in which I drove more than ten thousand miles during the year that followed. After conducting hit-and-run interviews around the three provinces, I typically tried to return to Pattani town by nightfall (around 7:00 P.M.) to avoid tire spikes and other hazards. On various occasions I experienced mechanical problems, only to be promptly rescued by enterprising and generous locals. Luckily, I never needed to use the car as a getaway vehicle. The Mercedes was a wonderful icebreaker, opening many conversations with local men.

As a European conducting research in a conflict zone, I was initially apprehensive about my reception in the deep South. In this climate of fear and suspicion, occasional rumors linking me to the usual western intelligence agencies were inevitable. I sought to head off skepticism about my activities by identifying myself strongly with my local host, PSU. I gave my PSU name card to almost everyone I talked to at any length (handing out around a thousand cards altogether), displayed a PSU parking permit in my car, and wrote all my interview notes on PSU pads, every page of which featured the university symbol.[22] That I had a desk at the political science faculty and lived in a PSU lecturers' apartment—points I repeatedly mentioned—reinforced my academic affiliation, and so my credibility, with those I contacted.

When traveling to rural areas, I nearly always made appointments with informants in advance.[23] Typically, I drove to these areas alone, presenting myself as an academic researcher who was sincerely interesting in understanding the situation on the ground. I was careful to wear a tucked-in shirt with no jacket and not to carry a bag—all so as to demonstrate that I was not, as Don Pathan puts it, "packing anything" (meaning a gun). Before leaving Leeds, I had momentarily considered buying a bullet-proof vest and taking a course in antiterrorist driving techniques, but soon thought better of these notions. During all my travels, I encountered no overt hostility from informants and experienced an extraordinary amount of kindness and hospitality from the people of both major communities.

As a western academic, I was generally accepted as a neutral outsider who would help inform the wider world about the situation in the three provinces. Those who seemed most suspicious of me were low-level military personnel, who may have regarded me as potentially sympathetic to the Malay cause.

This book is based primarily on my own extensive fieldwork and interview materials.[24] I make no apology for the fact that I have consistently privileged these original materials over secondary sources such as published books, reports, and newspaper articles, partly because I am more confident of their reliability, and also because I want to foreground new materials that are not available elsewhere.[25] I possess a large number of secondary sources in both English and Thai that are not cited here; many of them have nevertheless informed my understanding and interpretation of the conflict. Any serious student of the Southern Thai conflict should read this book alongside the recent invaluable reports by the International Crisis Group and Human Rights Watch, and analyses by other fieldwork-oriented Deep South watchers.[26]

As well as my fieldwork materials and secondary sources, this book also draws on a range of unpublished primary sources, including a collection of more than a hundred anonymous leaflets distributed in the deep South during the period 2004 to 2006; a set of ninety-six essays written by participants in an army-run "surrender camp" in late 2005;[27] and a large number of depositions ("confessions") taken by the security authorities, mainly in 2004 and 2005.[28] I also had access to some lecture materials prepared by security personnel. Anonymous leaflets are particularly important sources: given that the movement has made no formal statements or pronouncements, they are the nearest thing we have to the voice of the militants. All of these written sources are treated with caution, since their reliability is contested; some leaflets have certainly been faked for a variety of reasons, whilst the surrender camp essays are often self-serving, and the depositions may contain information extracted under duress, or feature accounts and interpretations that strongly reflect the mind-set of the questioners.[29] I have used all of these sources critically, and I discounted far more material (especially from the depositions) than I have cited or deployed in the book. Wherever possible, I tried to triangulate materials from these unpublished sources with insights gained from interviews and elsewhere.

I could not have written this book without an extraordinary amount of assistance and support. I have been visiting Pattani regularly since 2000, when Pavinee Chaipark first put me in touch with Dr. Srisompob Jitpiromsri of PSU; in a typical act of generosity, Srisompob kindly invited me to spend several nights staying with him, and introduced me to friends and colleagues, including Dr. Wattana Sugunnasil and Suleeman Wongsuphap. Srisompob, Wattana and Suleeman played lead roles in a British Council–managed, Department for International Development–funded "Higher Education Link" between Leeds and PSU, which funded a series of bilateral academic exchange visits from 2002 to 2006. Our link led to a set of papers on the growing violence, which were presented at the 2005 International Conference on Thai Studies at Northern Illinois University; these were published in a special issue of *Critical Asian Studies* and later an edited volume under the auspices of NUS Press.

Building on the collaborations and friendships created through the link, PSU generously invited me to spend a year in Pattani from September 2005 to help establish a new faculty of political science. I am very grateful to the senior administrators who supported my stay, especially former PSU president Dr. Prasert Chitapong, as well as his successor Dr. Boonsom Siribumrungsukha, former dean of humanities and social sciences Dr. Sontaya Anakasiri, her then deputy Dr. Prathana Kannaovakun, and the founding dean of political science, Piya Kittaworn. It was extremely generous of Dr. Prasert to provide me with a lecturer's flat at PSU Pattani throughout my project. During my fieldwork, I received extraordinary hospitality from Ajarns Srisompob and Wattana (with whom I enjoyed many, many hours of discussion over numerous dinners and coffees), from Ajarn Kusuma (Salma) Kruyai, and Panyasak Sobhonvasu, as well as from Srisompob's indefatigable assistants Anne, Nitnoi, and Fit, and his regular driver Ber Ma. I was also ably supported by fellow coffee-lover Krittaporn Termwanich, the British Council's then Pattani-based project manager.

Research for this book was facilitated by a generous grant from the Economic and Social Research Council, RES-000-22-1344. Thanks to Tess Hornsby-Smith, Helen May, Helene Pierson, and Susan Paragreen for their administrative help. My time away from the School of Politics and International Studies, University of Leeds, was made possible by my very supportive successor as head of school, Hugo Radice, and our school manager par excellence, Caroline Wise.

My ESRC grant allowed me to hire some wonderful assistants, without whom I would quickly have drowned in materials. Bhatchara (Pat) Aramsri was my senior assistant and "secret weapon" for most of 2006; bringing her fabulous journalistic skills and infectious enthusiasm to the project, she tracked down numerous interviewees and documentary sources, all the while generating reams of notes. She was later joined by Kaneeworn (Pim) Opetagon, who deployed her wonderful language abilities in summarizing and translating the mounting backlog of voice files and anonymous leaflets. I owe an enormous amount to them both. Additional materials were translated by Diyaporn Wisamitanan, Pakorn Atikarn, and Piyanut Kotsan; Amornrat Luangpathomchai managed my numerous newspaper clippings. On trips to Malay-speaking areas, Mukhtar and Saronee acted as regular translators.

I am fortunate in having two longstanding and brilliant academic mentors in Thailand, who again helped guide me during this project: Sombat Chantornvong and Ubonrat Siriyuvasak. Chaiwat Satha-Anand was another equally invaluable mentor for the project, whose advice surely saved me from calamity. Other constant friends and allies in (and sometimes out) of Thailand included Kevin Hewison, Patrick Jory, Heike Loschmann, Amporn Marddent, Ukrist Pathmanand, Ora-orn Poocharoen, Jane Vejjajiva, Pacharee Tanasomboonkit, Suranuch Thongsila, and Imtiyaz Yusuf. My oldest Thai friend, Daeng Aounsaard, continues to support all that I do. A series of visitors to Pattani helped me to relax and to keep my project in perspective, including Sumalee Bumrungsuk and Bill Callahan, Michael Connors, and especially Ima Sheeren. In the South, I benefited from a wonderful circle of people who gave generously of their time and thoughts, often providing invaluable introductions. For obvious reasons I will not try to name them all, but those in and around PSU included Worawidh Baru, Ahmad Somboon Bualuang, Sukree Langputeh, and Ibrahem Narongraksakhet. My greatest debt is to the 270-plus interview informants who generously took time to talk to me in depth, and without whom this book could not have been written. I would also thank the hundreds of informants I encountered less formally, many through a series of workshops on decentralization organized by Srisompob Jitpiromsri.

This book was largely written during my year-long appointment as a visiting senior research fellow at the Asia Research Institute (ARI), National University of Singapore, 2006–7. Warm thanks are due to director Anthony Reid, and religion and globalization cluster leader Bryan Turner, for inviting me to a place where I had no responsibilities other than my own writing: a rare privilege. At ARI, I was supported by a wonderful group of administrative staff and academic colleagues, including Michael Feener, Bina Gubhaju, Noorhaidi Hasan, Gavin Jones, Laavanya Kathiravelu, Pattana Kitiarsa, Hee-sun Kim, Yasuko Kobayashi, Windel Lacson, Michael Laffan, Jiang Na, Mahua Sarkar, Ardeth Thawnghmung, and Mika Toyota. Many other NUS colleagues, notably Goh Benglan, Vedi Hadiz, Suzaina Kadir, Alex Mutebi, and Terry Nardin, helped sustain me during my writing up. Beyond NUS, Qamaruzzaman Bin Amir, Pavin Chachavalpongpun, Joseph Liow, Sakulrat Montreevat, Sim Chi Yin, and Eugene Tan made me most welcome. May Tan-Mullins was a great friend and regular critic. Singapore was much enlivened by the company of Mike Montesano, with whom I endlessly discussed Thailand, the South, and other great issues of the day, and who magnanimously housed me in his spare room well beyond the formal end of my stay at Kent Vale.

I have benefited from the chance to give conference and seminar presentations drawing on this research across four continents: I'm very grateful to the many people who made and supported these invitations, including John Funston (ANU), Trudy Jacobsen (Griffith), Peg LeVine (Monash), Phil Hirsch (Sydney), Sripan Rattikalchalakorn (Macquarie), and Anthony Bubalo (Lowy Institute); Mustafa Ishak and Laila Suriya Ahmad (UUM) and Sumit Mandal (UKM); Claudia Merli and Jan Ovensen (Uppsala), Soren Ivarsson (Copenhagen), and Mette Kjaer (Aarhus); Joern Dosch (EUROSEAS, Naples); Justin McDaniel (AAS), Samson Lim and Thak Chaloemtiarana (Cornell), and Meredith Weiss (East-West Center, Washington); Haydon Cherry (Yale), Jim Della-Giacoma (SSRC), Michael Laffan (Princeton), Ardeth Thawnghmung (UMass Lowell), and Bridget Welsh (SAIS, Johns Hopkins). Thanks also to Jim Ockey for sharing his unpublished papers on Pattani history and politics, and to David Fullbrook for his thoughts on security issues.

Another set of debts are owed to my fellow international deep South watchers, especially the inexhaustible Francesca Lawe-Davies, formerly of International Crisis Group—with whom I've spent hundreds of hours exploring these issues, including numerous joint forays to dodgy conflict zones, and meetings in five different countries—and also Don Pathan of *The Nation*. Others include Marc Askew, Tony Davis, Michael Jerryson, and Sunai Pasuk. Michael Connors has been amazingly generous with his time and friendship in supporting my research. In this field, armchair analysts abound, but the researchers who really make a difference are those prepared to experience conflict zones for themselves; for these rare people I have boundless respect, even when (as often) our methods, interpretations, and conclusions differ.

Most important, I must thank all those who have spent considerable time reading draft chapters or versions of the manuscript. Michael Laffan, Michael Nelson, and Don Pathan kindly read and commented on individual chapters or sections; Mike Montesano, May Tan-Mullins, and Pat Aramsri commented on all the main chapters in draft, while Francesca Lawe-Davies and Michael Connors read the entire manuscript. Pat Aramsri also checked all the Thai-language references and proper names, as well as worked on the glossary and the abbreviations list, for which I offer more thanks. In every case, their dedication went way beyond the call of duty, and the final text has benefited immensely from their detailed attentions. The same applies to the two very thorough anonymous readers for Cornell University Press, who responded in record time, and senior editor Roger Haydon for his own exceptionally meticulous comments. Karen Laun did an excellent job of finalizing the manuscript.

My father, Graham McCargo, died suddenly as I was finishing this manuscript. A teacher, a humanist, a conversationalist, and an internationalist, he will always remain an inspiration.

Abbreviations

BIPP	Barisan Islam Pembebasan Patani, Islamic Liberation Front of Patani (formerly known as BNPP)
BRN	Barisan Revolusi Nasional, National Revolutionary Front
BRN-C	Barisan Revolusi Nasional Coordinate
CIA	Central Intelligence Agency
CNS	Council for National Security (name of the post September 19, 2006, military junta)
CPM 43	Civil-Police-Military joint command
CPT	Communist Party of Thailand
GMIP	Gerakan Mujahideen Islam Pattani, Pattani Islamic Mujahideen Movement
HRW	Human Rights Watch
ICG	International Crisis Group
ICJ	International Commission of Jurists
ISOC	Internal Security Operations Command
JI	Jemaah Islamiyah
NAP	New Aspiration Party
NCCC	National Counter Corruption Commission
NE(S)DB	National Economic (and Social) Development Board
NIA	National Intelligence Agency
NLA	National Legislative Assembly
NRC	National Reconciliation Commission
NSC	National Security Council
OIC	Organization of the Islamic Conference
PAO	Provincial Administrative Organization

PSU	Prince of Songkhla University
PULO	Patani United Liberation Organization
RKK	Runda Kampulan Kecil (small fighting units used by the militants, sometimes wrongly assumed to be the name of an organization)
SBPAC	Southern Border Provinces Administrative Centre
SBPPBC	Southern Border Provinces Peace Building Command
TAO	Tambon (Subdistrict) Administrative Organization (sometimes referred to as "SAO")
TRT	Thai Rak Thai Party
UN	United Nations

Timeline of Major Events

2001

January 6 — Thaksin Shinawatra's TRT Party wins a landslide election victory

December 24 — Five police officers and one defense volunteer shot dead in attacks on five police posts in Pattani, Yala, and Narathiwat

2002

March 23–24 — Five police officers killed in attacks on police posts in Pattani, Yala, and Narathiwat

May 1 — Thaksin government abolishes SBPAC and CPM 43, puts police in charge of Southern security

2003

April 26 — Two border patrol police intelligence officers beaten to death by a mob in Rangae, Narathiwat, after being taken hostage

July 3 — Five policemen and one civilian killed in coordinated raids on three checkpoints in Pattani

2004

January 4 — Large-scale militant attack on army base in Joh-Ai-Rong signals renewed outbreak of hostilities

April 28 — Simultaneous attacks on twelve security checkpoints culminate in storming of Kru-Ze Mosque, 105 militants, 5 security personnel and 1 civilian killed

October 25 — Mass demonstrations at Tak Bai, Narathiwat: 7 demonstrators shot, 78 apparently die of suffocation during transportation in army trucks

November 29–30	Thaksin threatens to walk out of ASEAN summit in Vientiane if Tak Bai is raised

2005

February 6	TRT wins a second election victory, but loses all its constituency seats in the three border provinces
February 17	First ever car bomb in Thailand kills six in Sungai Kolok
March 1	Thaksin sets up the National Reconciliation Commission chaired by Anand Panyarachun
April 3	Bomb at Hat Yai airport kills one
July 14	Wave of coordinated attacks in Yala town
July 19	Thaksin government announces plans for new emergency legislation for use in the South
September 20–21	Following shooting of two villagers at a teashop, two marines are taken hostage and killed at Tanyong Limo, Narathiwat
October 16	Monk and two temple boys killed at Wat Phromprasit, Panare, Pattani
October 26	Coordinated attacks on sixty-three locations
November 16	Muslim family of nine killed in suspicious circumstances, Bo-ngor, Narathiwat
November 24	Provincial Islamic council elections: Narathiwat president is ousted, Pattani president is strongly challenged

2006

January	Anti-Thaksin demonstrations escalate
April 2	Snap general election held, with opposition boycott; courts later annul election; TRT MPs fare very badly again in the South
April 19	Senate elections; Buddhist businessman tops Pattani polls, while former terrorist suspect wins in Narathiwat
May 19	Two female Buddhist teachers taken hostage and beaten at Tanyong Limo, Narathiwat; one later dies from her injuries.
June 5	Anand publishes the NRC's report, which is largely ignored
June 15	Forty simultaneous bombs targeting government buildings
August 6	Caretaker Narathiwat senator Fakhruddin Boto shot, though he survived
August 31	Simultaneous bombing of 22 banks in Yala
September 19	Military coup led by army commander Sonthi Bonyaratkalin ousts Thaksin from power and abrogates 1997 constitution
October 1	Surayud Chulanont becomes prime minister
November 1	Surayud apologizes for Tak Bai incident

2007

February 17–18	71 separate violent incidents over Chinese New Year weekend
March 9	Rangers shoot dead a Muslim youth and raid a nearby pondok at Ta Se, Yala
March 14	Eight Buddhist civilians shot dead in an attack on a commuter van in Yaha, Yala
April 9	Village defense volunteers shoot dead four Muslim youths in Banang Sata, Yala
May 22	Suspected rangers shoot dead four members of a family, allegedly raping one of the women
May 30	Constitutional Tribunal dissolves Thai Rak Thai Party for violating election laws in 2006
May 31–June 4	Mass demonstrations against abuses by the security forces at Pattani Central Mosque
June 14	Four Muslim TAO members shot dead in a suspicious ambush in Mai Kaen, Pattani
August 19	New constitution approved in Thailand's first ever referendum
December 23	General election held to restore parliamentary rule. Pro-Thaksin People's Power Party (PPP) tops the ballot, but gains only two of the twelve constituency seats in the three Southern border provinces

2008

January 29	PPP leader Samak Sundaravej becomes prime minister, heading a six-party coalition government
March 15	Car bomb at CS Pattani Hotel kills two and injures fourteen including hotel owner and newly appointed senator Anusart Suwanmongkol

Tearing Apart the Land

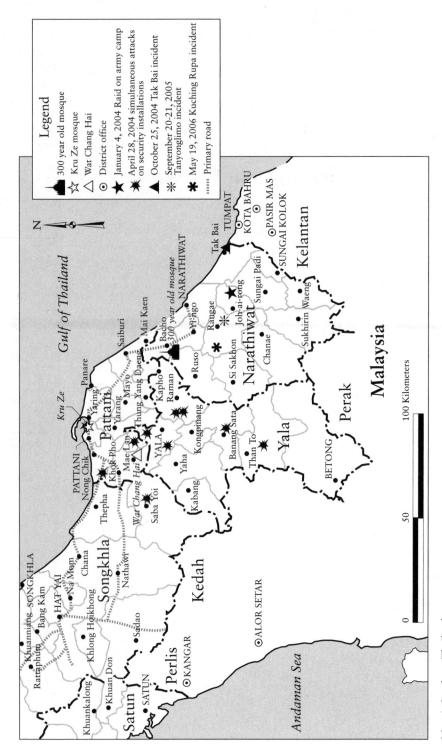

Map 1 Southern Thailand

INTRODUCTION

An English-language sign outside the historic Kru-Ze Mosque in Pattani (which I photographed in 2006) was riddled with bullet holes. One bullet had passed through the second "t" in the word "Pattani," so changing the spelling of the word to "Patani." There is no way of knowing how this happened: Was the bullet fired randomly by Thai security forces on April 28, 2004? Or did militants deliberately shoot up the sign, in order to make a political statement? Spellings can be highly political: Pattani is the name of a modern Thai province, whereas Patani alludes to an older and larger area, and may carry Malay nationalist connotations. In places here, I have used the term *Patani,* sometimes following my sources, to invoke (rather than necessarily to commend) a wider imagined or historical region than that described by Pattani. In the highly charged world of Thailand's Malay-Muslim provinces, small details count.

Like many other modern nation-states, Thailand has rather arbitrary borders that reflect a variety of historical accidents.[1] Many of these arose from the era of British and French colonialism in Southeast Asia. Prior to the late nineteenth century, Siam (as Thailand was formerly known) claimed jurisdiction over large swathes of mainland Southeast Asia—but this jurisdiction was expressed largely in terms of tribute and allegiance paid by local rulers. The Malay state of Patani paid tribute to Buddhist Siam, yet was largely self-governing.[2] However, during the twentieth century this area was forcibly incorporated into the Thai state. Thailand is a highly centralized political order, in which all provinces are administered by unelected governors—sometimes characterized as a form of "internal colonialism."[3]

The three "Southern border provinces" of Pattani,[4] Yala, and Narathiwat have an ambiguous status within Thailand. Officially part of Siam from 1909, the region roughly corresponds to the former Malay sultanate of Patani. The area remains around 80 percent Malay-speaking and Muslim, and has never been properly incorporated culturally or psychologically into predominantly Buddhist Thailand. Bangkok has largely pursued a policy of assimilation and standardization, making few concessions to the distinctive history and character of the region. Like the rest of Thailand, the Southern border provinces are administered mainly by officials dispatched from the distant capital. The region has a long tradition of resistance to the rule of Bangkok, and political violence has emerged at various junctures in modern history. Some of this violence was perpetrated by the Thai state. Landmark events included the 1948 Dusun-nyor incident (in which dozens, perhaps hundreds, of Malay-Muslim villagers were killed in Narathiwat); the 1954 arrest and disappearance of prominent Islamic teacher Haji Sulong, at the hands of the Thai police; and mass demonstrations at the Pattani Central Mosque in late 1975, triggered by the extrajudicial killing of some Malay Muslim youths.

Radical "separatist" elements began waging a guerrilla war against the Thai state in the 1960s: fighting was most virulent during the late 1970s and early 1980s. The most important groups behind the fighting included the Patani United Liberation Organization (PULO) and the Barisan Revolusi Nasional (BRN). By 1980 as many as a thousand insurgents were carrying out regular attacks in the South and had even staged bombings in Bangkok. But the Prem Tinsulanond governments (1980–88) successfully reined in the violence, granting amnesties to former militants and setting up new security and governance arrangements in the area, coordinated by the Southern Border Provinces Administrative Centre (SBPAC). Prem's policy was to co-opt the Malay-Muslim elite through a combination of political privileges and development funds, much of these brokered by the army. Though far from perfect, these policies were broadly effective in muting the violence for around two decades. The Prem-era policies were the product of a "semi-democratic" period, during which the military and the palace played a leading role in shaping the country's politics. After the February 1991 military coup and the May 1992 "prodemocracy" demonstrations (which the army suppressed violently), Thai politics moved into a more open period in which elected politicians gained increasing power. The 1997 "people's constitution" confirmed the trend toward the institutionalization of parliamentary politics, paving the way for the emergence of Thailand's most popular and powerful civilian prime minister, police officer turned telecommunications tycoon Thaksin Shinawatra, and his Thai Rak Thai Party.

During Thaksin's first term (2001–5), however, the security situation in the South deteriorated sharply.[5] An overconfident Thaksin dissolved the Prem-era special administrative arrangements and placed the highly unpopular police force in charge of security in the deep South. These politically motivated policy blunders coincided with a sharp rise in militancy and the reemergence of violent resistance to the Thai state, which was evident from December 2001 onwards. On January 4, 2004, more than fifty militants raided a Narathiwat army camp, seizing a large cache of weapons and scoring an enormous propaganda victory. In the four years that followed, nearly three thousand people were killed in political violence in the region. The two worst days of violence were April 28, 2004—when more than a hundred men died in simultaneous attacks on a series of security posts, culminating in a bloody siege at the historic Kru-Ze Mosque—and October 25, 2004, when seventy-eight unarmed protestors died in Thai military custody, apparently mainly from suffocation, following mass arrests at Tak Bai, Narathiwat. These two incidents greatly undermined the legitimacy of the Thai state and boosted the militant movement. As Tamara Loos notes, the tensions of 2004 had historical precedents dating back to the beginning of the twentieth century.[6]

Whereas earlier political violence in the region used mainly "separatist" rhetoric drawing on notions of Malay identity and history, some anonymous leaflets circulated since January 2004 have invoked explicitly "jihadist" sentiments. Most analysts of the conflict remain skeptical about claims that the Southern Thai violence is linked with transnational networks such as Jemaah Islamiyah (JI); the causes of the conflict seem overwhelmingly home grown. This book starts from the premise that the Patani conflict is a complex political problem centered on questions of legitimacy.

Identity

In many respects, Patani was a center of diversity and cultural riches, a primary nexus of what Montesano and Jory term "the plural peninsula."[7] Montesano has demonstrated the longstanding importance of Pattani as a trading center and a centuries-old focus of Sino-Thai capital flows.[8] The region was also the cradle of strong Buddhist traditions, epitomized by the legendary Wat Chang Hai in Pattani; Buddhist and Muslim cultures have been enriched by extensive interactions and borrowings. During the 1960s, the National Economic Development Board (NEDB) sought to boost the Buddhist population of the region through schemes to encourage migration into the area.[9] Alongside other bureaucratic moves, such as dividing the region arbitrarily into three provinces in 1931, and assigning four districts with large Malay Muslim populations to neighboring Songkhla, the NEDB schemes reflected Thai government attempts to manage and dilute the Muslim population of the region and so promote greater assimilation. Pluralism in this peninsula was partly a matter of accident and partly a matter of design.

Malay Muslims in Thailand's Southern border provinces are very proud of an identity that they consider highly distinctive, as Malays (*Melayu;* in local dialect, *nayu*), as Muslims, and as people of Patani, an ancient kingdom and center of Islamic learning and culture. These three identity markers clearly distinguish Patani people from the rest of Thailand's population. At the same time, Patani identity has an ambiguous relationship with the modern nation-state and with notions of citizenship. Almost all Patani people are citizens of Thailand, but for many of them this citizenship is a flag of inconvenience, a formal identity that they are obliged to adopt for pragmatic reasons. Numerous Malay Muslims, especially those living along the border between Kelantan and Narathiwat, hold flexible dual Thai and Malaysian citizenship.[10] For many Malay Muslims, Malaysia offers an alternative to Thailand: a place to work, a place to earn additional income, and potentially as a land of refuge or exile.

As one former resident of the region told me: "Scratch a Malay Muslim and you find a separatist underneath." This exaggeration contains a kernel of truth, a widespread sense among ordinary Malay Muslims that their externally imposed identity as Thais resembles an ill-fitting suit of clothes, one they would not be wholly averse to casting off if an alternative outfit were on offer. At the same time, many Malay Muslims—especially the better-educated middle classes—have thrown in their lot with Thailand, believing that they should obey the Prophetic tradition that says, "Whoever learns the language of a people, he will be saved from their cunning."[11] While rejecting assimilation, this Malay-Muslim elite has pursued a strategy of pragmatic accommodation with Bangkok, seeking to carve out political space for themselves in a wider order framed primarily by Thailand.

Patani Malay historians have advanced various claims about Patani history, which have formed the basis for a resurgent Malay nationalism since the mid-twentieth century.[12] Their key assertion is that Patani used to be an independent sultanate, until either 1785 or 1902. By contrast, conservative Thai historians have argued that Patani was always a vassal state of Siam. The truth may lie somewhere in between: Davisakd Puaksom has argued that Patani was generally held within Ayuttaya's grasp, though at times only weakly.[13] Before the creation of modern nation states in Southeast Asia, small states paid tribute to a range of larger ones, and independence was essentially a question of degree. Other contested issues include the extent to which the former Patani sultanate could be seen as an Islamic state—for which there is little evidence—and the question of how "Malay" Patani was.[14] Nevertheless, it is clear that the Thai state has sought at different junctures—notably during the reign of King Chulalongkorn and the hypernationalist premiership of Field Marshal Phibun—to suppress Patani's distinctive identity and history. The hyperbole of some local historical claims has reflected a fundamental imbalance of power relations between Bangkok and Patani.

Malay-Muslim society in the three Southern border provinces differs significantly from wider Thai society. Malay Muslims are in an ambiguous position, forming the majority group within their own region (close to 80 percent of the 1.8 million or so residents of Pattani, Yala, and Narathiwat), yet constituting a small minority within Thailand as a whole—under 2.2 percent of the country's population.[15] Accordingly, they combine a very strong sense of their own identity with an uneasy relationship to the wider world. One Malay Muslim informant facetiously compared the region to a "dinosaur island," a cultural Jurassic Park, which adjoined both Thailand and Malaysia, and yet was far removed from both neighbors in terms of worldview.[16] Srisompob Jitpiromsri suggested that Malay Muslims had their own "virtual reality," a way of seeing themselves in religious, social, and historical terms that was largely disconnected from the way they were viewed by others.[17]

The area was characterized by an intense regional pride and a profound religiosity. Viewing themselves as an in-group, Patani Malays were deeply mistrustful of outsiders, a mistrust bred from their own understandings of their history.[18] If the daughter of a Patani Malay family married a Muslim from central Thailand, her family might almost feel that she had married outside the religion.[19] Patani Malays tended to view Muslims in other parts of Thailand as insufficiently devout and too deeply insinuated into Thai society. Historically, there was a deep resistance to studying the Thai language, viewed as a language of oppressors; associated with this resistance was a rejection of the state education system, which has been viewed as an agent of assimilation intended to eradicate Malayness. In many communities, school attendance was haphazard.[20]

Explanations

A range of explanations and causes have been advanced for the Southern Thai conflict. The popularity of various explanations has waxed and waned. In the period immediately after January 2004, Thaksin and many government figures blamed the violence primarily on banditry and lawlessness—

conforming to cultural stereotypes of hot-headed southerners running amok.[21] More elaborate versions of this argument posited the existence of conspiracies involving organized criminals, government officials, and local politicians who were engaged in "incident creation" for the purpose of "benefit seeking." According to these readings, the Thai authorities themselves were largely responsible for violent attacks, including the January 4, 2004, weapons seizure. Such interpretations have been reviewed by Marc Askew:[22] while containing beguiling nuggets of truth,[23] they fail convincingly to account for a violent conflict in which over three thousand people have been killed, many of them members of the security forces, government officials, and Malay Muslims who could be portrayed as supporting or collaborating with the Thai state. These theories also conveniently absolved ordinary Malay Muslims of involvement or complicity in the violence, which was portrayed as an elaborate elite game.

Another area of explanations centers around the idea of grievances: violence is a response to economic deprivation and social exclusion, or is inextricably linked to contests over resources. The National Reconciliation Commission (NRC), a independent body appointed by the Thaksin government to propose solutions for the Southern conflict, flirted with such ideas, which locate the origin of the problem in broader socioeconomic structures, and again play down the agency of Malay Muslims.[24] A more sophisticated version of the grievance explanation links socioeconomic issues with questions of identity, ethnicity, culture, and religion, arguing that Thai attempts to suppress or marginalize Malay-Muslim identity have laid the ground for violent rebellion. But, as Srisompob Jitpiromsri has cogently argued, grievance-based explanations completely fail to explain the upsurge of violence in the South in the new millennium—at a time when rubber prices were high, when many Malay Muslims were better off than ever before, and when identity issues were nothing new.[25]

A third area of explanations located the conflict within wider political developments in Thailand, notably the clash between the Thaksin Shinawatra government and forces loyal to the monarchy during the 2004–6 period.[26] Domestic politics explanations that fingered Thaksin were popular among Malay Muslims—again, partly because they did not focus on the agency of militant groups or support for those groups from some local communities. While domestic politics–based interpretations have been criticized for evading the question of agency, they were never meant as a comprehensive explanation of the violence; rather, they sought to explain how Thaksin created new political space for the militant movement.

A fourth area of explanations emphasized external factors, variously arguing that international jihadist networks,[27] such as JI,[28] or foreign-funded agent provocateurs (variously backed by the CIA, the OIC, or the

Singaporean government, for example, depending on the source) were behind much of the violence.[29] The jihadist explanations favored by some commentators chimed with Bush regime rhetoric about the global war on terror. Speaking at the National University of Singapore on November 16, 2006, George W. Bush referred apocalyptically to groups whose "stated goal is to establish a totalitarian Islamic empire stretching from Europe to Southeast Asia."[30] But for many Malay Muslims it was the United States and her regional lieutenants who had imperial designs on Southeast Asia; some informants were extremely ready to believe that the violence in Patani was part of a great power chess game. While both the pro- and anti-American versions of these "clash of civilizations" conspiracy explanations were compelling, there was precious little evidence to support either of them.

The fifth and most persuasive core explanation is that the violence was animated by broadly the same "separatist" aspirations that underpinned early waves of conflict in the region.[31] While other explanations were widely favored soon after January 2004, by mid-2006 I found my Malay-Muslim informants generally accepted that a ruthless and well-organized militant movement was responsible for most of the violence taking place in the Southern border provinces. The remaining challenge was to understand the nature of that movement: What conditions had created it? How was it organized and who supported it? Was it an essentially political movement, and how much Islamist or jihadist thinking, rhetoric, or overtones had it incorporated into its rhetoric?

Monarchy

Building on earlier work, this book views the deep South as an important site for "network monarchy."[32] Contrary to much conventional wisdom, Thailand is not a constitutional monarchy, and the highly respected King Bhumibol (Rama IX, who has reigned since 1946) is not "above politics." Rather, the King is a major political actor in his own right, who generally—though not invariably—favors ideas of virtuous rule over either representative or participatory rule. At crucial junctures—notably in May 1992—he has made interventions in the political process that have helped shape outcomes. Usually, however, he prefers to operate as a deus ex machina, guiding Thailand's politics from behind the scenes. He is aided in this by an extensive network of lieutenants and supporters, led since the early 1980s by former prime minister and later Privy Council president General Prem Tinsulanond. In earlier decades, the network was dominated by military figures. However, after the military was discredited by the violence of May 1992, a more liberal, civilian-led wing of network monarchy rose to prominence, informally led by another ex–prime minister and royal confidante, Anand Panyarachun. The liberal wing of network monarchy secured royal support for a process of political reform that culminated in the historic "people's constitution" of 1997. The underlying purpose of the 1997 constitution was to institutionalize a form of representative politics, so as to avert a political crisis on Bhumibol's death.

The 1997 constitution paved the way for the rise of an extremely powerful prime minister, the former police officer and billionaire telecommunications tycoon Thaksin Shinawatra.[33] Thaksin was able to use his considerable wealth to gain power through unrivalled control of Thailand's "money politics," creating his party by buying electable parliamentary candidates on an unprecedented scale. Electoral politics had provided a strong challenge to earlier modes of military, monarchical, and bureaucratic dominance since the 1980s and was now firmly in the ascendant. For the first time since the 1950s, Thailand had a prime minister of boundless energy and ambition and, crucially, one who was unwilling to defer to the monarchy. Support for Thaksin and the "populist" programs of his Thai Rak Thai Party from the rural poor, especially in the North and Northeast of the country, challenged the monarchy's monopoly of virtuous rule; and this at a time when the King, now nearly eighty, was growing weaker. Thaksin won two landslide election victories in 2001 and 2005 before his power began to unravel early in 2006. During his time in office, Thaksin created his own elaborate and extensive support network, which began to rival that of the palace. He was finally ousted in a military coup staged by royalist officers led by army commander General Sonthi Boonyaratkalin on September 19, 2006, and replaced as prime minister by a member of the Privy Council, former army commander General Surayud Chulanont. The coup group, calling itself the Council for National Security (CNS), pledged to hold fresh elections by the end of 2007, once a new constitution had been written and ratified.[34]

In many respects, politics in the deep South from the 1980s onward were a microcosm of the wider power struggles affecting Thailand. Political violence was greatly curtailed by a set of political and security arrangements brokered by Prem and network monarchy, based around the SBPAC—in effect, the center for virtuous monarchical rule. Establishing the legitimacy of the Chakri dynasty in the deep South became a crucial test for the *barami* of King Bhumibol: Could he win the hearts of people who did not see themselves as ethnically or culturally Thai?[35] In the 1970s, Malay Muslims were largely indifferent to the visits of the "raja Si-yae" (king of Siam), as they called him,[36] but through an extensive propaganda campaign led by Queen Sirikit during long annual visits to the Narathiwat palace, the

Thai monarchy was able to establish greater acceptance, among at least some elements of the local population. In the deep South, the monarchy worked largely through a network of Buddhist government officials and Fourth Army officers, most of whom supported the Democrat Party, along with a group of Muslim leaders who threw in their lot with the Thai state, notably the prominent Saiburi Islamic school owner Nideh Waba. At the same time, by co-opting leading Malay Muslims, the SBPAC also sapped their legitimacy at a time when the gulf between ordinary villagers and the Malay elite was expanding, opening up new space for rekindled militant recruitment in the 1990s.

When Thaksin came to power in 2001, he was frustrated by his Thai Rak Thai (TRT) Party's inability to win seats in the Democrat-dominated upper South; by contrast, the Southern border provinces, where Yala politician Wan Muhammad Nor Matha's Muslim Wadah faction was preeminent, offered a window of electoral opportunity. Thaksin set out to incorporate the Southern border provinces into his own network, which meant displacing the Democrat-network monarchy alliance that controlled the region.[37] He did so by normalizing security arrangements in mid-2002, placing the police in charge of law and order, and abolishing the SBPAC. In effect, Thaksin staged a frontal assault on the legitimacy of the palace, unraveling the mode of virtuous rule that had been somewhat successful in curbing an earlier wave of "separatist" violence in the region. But violence had actually begun rising again in 2001, and the advisors who had assured Thaksin that these incidents were mere banditry and incident creation by unscrupulous local politicians were woefully mistaken. Senior police officers loyal to Thaksin moved to eliminate former separatists who had long served as key informants for military intelligence, sometimes under the cover of the controversial 2003 "war on drugs," an officially sanctioned policy of extrajudicial murder. By 2004, Thaksin's administration faced extensive and violent rebellion across the three provinces, and responded with repressive measures that played into the hands of a resurgent militant movement. His actions culminated in TRT losing all its seats in the border provinces in the February 2005 general elections. Thaksin had undermined virtuous monarchical rule in the South but had nothing with which to replace it, other than the flawed "representative rule" of Wan Nor and other Wadah politicians who abandoned their own communities to mouth progovernment lies and platitudes.

In March 2005, Thaksin was obliged to set up the National Reconciliation Commission under former premier Anand Panyarachun, following critical statements by the King and members of the Privy Council. This was an apparent victory for the forces of network monarchy, but in practice

Thaksin had no intention of following the recommendations of the high-level commission. Reporting in June 2006, Anand made a series of modest proposals for improving the quality of justice, security, and governance in the deep South—proposals that Thaksin proceeded to ignore. The NRC's proposals were considered too progressive by most government officials but did not go nearly far enough for most Malay Muslims. The NRC refused to engage seriously with ideas of substantive decentralization—such as electing provincial governors in the area—let alone any proposals for different forms of autonomy. The NRC's failure to grasp the prickly nettle of autonomy marked a lost opportunity to come up with bold proposals with real potential to head off the growing political violence. The NRC report demonstrated that network monarchy liberals had little new thinking to bring to the Southern crisis. Anand and his colleagues were ready to accommodate Malay Muslims on some identity issues and to distance themselves from hard-line assimilationist policy stances. Yet they were not willing openly to debate Thailand's overarching structures of power.

The problem was further illuminated when network monarchy conservatives seized power from Thaksin in the September 19, 2006, military coup. The military-installed government quickly apologized for Thaksin's excesses, notably for the Tak Bai incident, and began talking about amnesties for militants and dialogue with their leaders. But it quickly became clear that there was nothing on the table: like the NRC before them, the CNS and privy-councilor-turned-premier Surayud Chulanont had no intention of offering the Southern border provinces substantial control over their own affairs. Immediately after Surayud's Tak Bai apology, violent incidents surged. Thaksin's use of repression and the NRC-CNS discourse of "reconciliation" amounted to two sides of the same coin: not one inch of Thai territory would be given up and any form of autonomy was viewed by Bangkok simply as a dangerous step in the direction of a separate Patani state.

Rebels

Most analyses of civil wars, ethnic conflicts, and "separatist" movements are highly case specific, offering little by way of systematic comparative perspectives. Where comparisons are invoked, they are often superficial to the point of glibness. A rare exception is Mohammed Hafez's extremely lucid book, *Why Muslims Rebel,* which offers a set of broadly applicable conceptual insights.[38] Though strongly grounded in case studies of Egypt and Algeria, Hafez also looks carefully at what he terms "Muslim rebellions" in Kashmir, the Southern Philippines, Chechnya, and Afghanistan.[39] His conclusions are clear, compelling, and highly relevant to the Thai case.

First, Hafez insists that socioeconomic explanations are inadequate to account for these rebellions.[40] Structural grievances are ubiquitous, but very few of them lead to violent militancy, and so a focus on socioeconomic and related issues will fail to explain why Muslims rebel. Rather, he advocates a "political process" approach which examines the "political environment" within which militants operate, the "mobilization structures" they use to obtain resources, and "the ideological frames with which Islamists justify and motivate collective action." He suggests that analysis of conflicts should focus on the core resources needed for a militant struggle: material and organizational resources (activists, funds, shelter, weapons), legitimacy and identity resources ("moral authority to command commitments and sacrifices from activists, sympathizers and supporters based on perceived primordial ties; shared historic experiences; or possession of special knowledge, wisdom, or charisma"), and institutional resources (public office, elite support, access to political platforms). Hafez insists on the "primacy of process over structure"; militant movements do not respond to conditions mechanistically but engage in a "dynamic of interaction, adaptation, and intended and unintended consequences."[41] The process by which a movement becomes rebellious involves a combination of institutional exclusion and state repression, a process that generates radicalization and the formation of exclusive mobilization structures by militant movements. These movements then begin to engage in increasingly irrational anticivilian violence.

Hafez finds that political exclusion is often a feature of mass insurgency but is not a sufficient condition to create it (65). However, "when institutional exclusion is combined with indiscriminate repression after an extended period of mass organizing and mobilization, large-scale rebellion is likely to occur" (104). Movements go to great lengths to create what Hafez terms "antisystem ideological frames," which provide a legitimating rationale for increasingly irrational violence directed against civilians (191–92). Hafez advocates maximizing formal institutional political participation for those willing to engage in mainstream politics, while employing a "selective repression" of violent elements that refuse accommodationist overtures. This strategy involves a delicate balancing act and can only be pulled off by astute leaders.

Although Hafez makes no mention of the Southern Thai conflict, his argument provides a blueprint for the interpretation of that conflict offered here. I will argue that the militant movement in the South forms part of a political process, abetted by the Thai state's initially successful but ultimately corrosive attempts to enlist the Malay Muslim elite through a process of cooptation and coercion. Thai offers of greater political participation were gradually seen as a systematic program for excluding Malay Muslims from effective involvement in the management of their own affairs. Moderate leaders in the deep South were captured by the Thai state, thereby losing their own credentials and legitimacy. Repressive state actions, particularly a series of brutal missteps by the first Thaksin Shinawatra government, allowed militants to discredit moderate leaders and claim moral legitimacy for a violent struggle. The militants forged a new form of exclusive mobilization structure and engaged in a propaganda struggle to justify their increasingly rapacious anticivilian violence. Combating this movement would require a combination of a bold strategy for political inclusion—probably, the offer of some form of autonomy—coupled with firm action against the perpetrators of violence. Only such a two-pronged approach could hope to weaken the militants and bring them to negotiations.

Several possible "lessons" are suggested by the application of Hafez's analysis to the Patani conflict. One is that socioeconomic grievances are not at the root of the militant activity, and so aid and development projects will do little to curtail the violence. While Hafez may overstate his case in places, my informants persistently failed to offer socioeconomic explanations for the Southern crisis, instead emphasizing political and identity issues. Second, although triggered largely by state repression, the conflict is not essentially about "justice," and easing state repression will not itself end the conflict: the repression of 2003 to 2004 provides a continuing reservoir of moral legitimacy for the militants. A third point is that without competent and effective security forces, a resolution is not likely to be achieved. A fourth point highlights the essentially exclusionary nature of the political bargain Thailand offered Malay Muslims in the 1980s and 1990s, and the failure to create truly participatory and representative structures in the deep South. In all this, Islam is not a distinct "cause" of political violence, but an ideological frame, a legitimating resource that has gradually been seized by those of a militant orientation. As John Sidel writes of political violence in Indonesia, insurrection capitalizes on rising popular mobilization by making assertive claims "articulated in the idiom of Islam."[42] Where states are able to monopolize or at least to dominate legitimacy and identity resources, broad-based rebellion is impossible; but when a significant proportion of these resources can be exploited by antisystem actors, the conditions for rebellion are met.

Accordingly, this book devotes two chapters to the question of legitimacy and identity resources, and associated matters of institutional resources—focusing on issues of Islam and politics—before moving on to a consideration of repression and the shortcomings of Thailand's security apparatus, and only then to a detailed discussion of the mobilization structures of Patani's shadowy militant movement.

Legitimacy

Most discussions of legitimacy are quite narrowly focused on procedural issues of political representation and participation, and the threshold for defining a legitimate regime is set quite low. Where there is little or no political violence, and especially when citizens actively participate in elections organized by the regime, a broad degree of legitimacy is often inferred. But in areas where legitimacy and identity resources are highly contested, such as Thailand's deep South, such indicators may be misleading. As one Narathiwat local politician, who was unable to persuade even his own relatives to vote for him, explained: "Actually, the movement would be happy if people didn't vote at all, but since they don't want their supporters to be suspected because they never vote, they get them to go along and spoil their ballot papers, or else choose a weak figure."[43] According to one successful candidate in the 2001 parliamentary elections in Yala, around eight thousand ballots had been spoilt in his constituency, mainly by voters drawing small pictures of a tiger on the ballot paper.[44] Participating in elections could imply offering legitimacy to a given regime; but in rural areas where electoral participation was closely monitored, voting could also provide a convenient cover, a mode of everyday resistance that operated on more than one level. By playing nonspeaking parts in the regime's elections, militant sympathizers could even be engaging in acts of ritual mockery.

In a volume focused on political legitimacy in Southeast Asia, Muthiah Alagappa moves beyond narrow procedural understandings to sketch out a multifaceted concept of legitimacy, analogous to Hafez's conception of legitimacy as a resource.[45] After an extensive literature review, Alagappa adopts a wide-ranging definition of legitimacy, as "the belief by the governed in the ruler's moral right to issue commands and the people's corresponding obligation to accept such commands."[46] He breaks legitimacy down into four major components: "shared norms and values, conformity with established rules for acquiring power, proper and effective use of power, and consent of the governed" (15). Crucially, Alagappa concedes that legitimacy is not simply present or absent, but amounts to a matter of degree: What constitutes "consent" on the part of the governed, especially when policies that receive consent from the majority of the population are opposed by minority groups? Such questions come to the fore when a government uses force: "A massive use of force reflects the ineffectiveness of coercion and the weakness of the government's legitimacy" (19). In the context of a "minority" region such as the deep South, a government such as Thaksin's could undermine its legitimacy with local Muslim populations through a use of force that was tolerated or even applauded in the rest of Thailand—and even by Buddhists in the same region. Faced with Muslim rebellions, non-Muslim governments could experience a double standard in terms of legitimacy. The widening gap between "Thai majority" and "Malay Muslim minority" legitimacy created new political space for militants who were trying to expand the perception gap between the two sides, so securing their own hold over identity and legitimacy resources in Patani.

Alagappa also distinguishes between two forms of allegiance: allegiance of the elites, and allegiance of the masses. He suggests that elite allegiance is particularly crucial for "authoritarian, totalitarian, and monarchical systems" (30), while mass allegiance is more important in a participatory system. This begs the question of how to characterize Thailand's recent political system. While Thailand was widely seen as a democratic system headed by a constitutional monarch, in practice democratic ideals were often in contestation with monarchist propaganda and rhetoric, and there were regular monarchical interventions in the political order. For a variety of historical reasons, Bangkok's approach to Patani centered on securing the allegiance of Malay Muslim elites to the Chakri dynasty. Bangkok consistently relied on local elites to deliver the allegiance of the Malay Muslim masses to the Thai state, exemplified in the creation of the SBPAC in the early 1980s. It will be argued here that successive Thai governments failed to move beyond securing the allegiance of elites; as the Malay Muslim elites gradually became alienated from their own communities, so the Thai state lost legitimacy and moral authority in the deep South. While monarchical aspects of government were often less apparent in the rest of Thailand, in the Malay Muslim majority provinces, the paternalistic hand of royalism was ever present.

In the context of Islam, ideas of political legitimacy have an extra dimension: for radical Muslims, "God alone has sovereignty (*hakimiyya*) over the world, and...has provided Muslims with what amounts to a complete (*kaffah*) ethical model for social and political life."[47] According to radical traditions, only just rulers are entitled to obedience: "Disobedience and revolution against those who are deemed unjust are justified."[48] In other words, Islam raises the bar for legitimate government, arguably setting higher standards than other belief systems in relation to matters of justice and the appropriate use of force. These higher standards offer an additional legitimacy and identity resource that can be appropriated by an antisystem militant movement. *Ulama* (respected Islamic scholars) "fervently deny that the authority of the elected representatives of the people extends, even in principle, to all areas of public or religious life": the legitimacy of the secular state is tightly delimited.[49] The question of how a Muslim minority negotiates its relations with a host state raises a set of issues of recent interest to Islamic jurists: How far can any non-Muslim state offer a fully legitimate source of rule?[50] Although prominent Indian ulama Wahid al-din Khan has argued that Islamic traditions crafted on the basis of Muslim dominance need to be rethought by Muslim minorities in societies such as modern India, Islamists call for the increased political mobilization of Muslims to defend their identity.[51]

Alagappa also observes that questions of legitimacy are foregrounded at crucial "politically defining moments" characterized by "high political consciousness that can generate deep emotion and galvanize enormous support for a cause."[52] While defining unjust rule is a problematic issue, blunders such as the deaths in custody of 78 Tak Bai protestors in October 2004, could amount to grounds for rebellion. Alagappa also distinguishes between "legitimacy strain," a persistent but not acute problem of legitimacy, and a "legitimacy crisis."[53] David Beetham similarly distinguishes between various problems of legitimacy: one where power suffers from a "legitimacy deficit," or weakness, and another, more severe problem where the ruled withdraw their consent, which he terms "delegitimation."[54] While Thai rule over Patani suffered from legitimacy strain, or deficit, for much of the twentieth century, legitimacy crises in the region were much more episodic; after January 2004, the severe crisis amounted to a form of delegitimation.

As a general proposition, the more political space the majority population of a given nation-state grants to a minority group, the more legitimate the nation-state will become in the eyes of that minority group. Questions about legitimacy, political institutions, and political process in the Southern border provinces need to be understood in relation to three different conceptions of legitimacy, which might be termed virtuous legitimacy, representative legitimacy, and participatory legitimacy. These three forms of legitimacy form overlapping threads of a legitimacy continuum that ranges from completely authoritarian or monarchical rule at the far end of the "virtuous" mode, to complete decentralization at the opposite end of the "participatory" mode.[55] Historically, the Thai state has sought to secure its legitimacy while offering the most limited possible degree of political space to minority groups such as Malay Muslims.

The first conception of legitimacy is based on ideas of virtuous rule, which can be traced back to notions of virtuous Buddhist kingship, or *dhammaraja*.[56] According to this construct, rule is legitimate if the ruler is good. The idea that politicians and other leaders may be divided into "good" and "bad" people is a pervasive one in Thailand and has been framed by the moralistic tutelary discourse that characterizes speeches by King Bhumibol and his network. Michael Connors has theorized the implications of this stance as "royal liberalism," which he relates to the Thai concept of *rachaprachasamasai*.[57] This approach was particularly explicit during the turbulent events of 1992, during which popular discourse and the media classified politicians as either "devils" (aligned with the military and forces of dictatorship) or "angels" (aligned with the opponents of dictatorship). The 1997 constitution reflected systematic attempts by its architects to create a framework within which good people could enter politics. A similar discourse followed the September 2006 military coup, which framed Thaksin Shinawatra as a "bad" figure, in contrast with the "good" royal servants generals Sonthi and Surayud. According to this notion of virtuous rule, those endorsed and supported by King Bhumibol were held to be dedicated to the best interests of Thailand as a whole. In the specific context of the Southern border provinces, advocates of virtuous rule argued that there was no fundamental problem with the way political power and representation was organized in the region. So long as good people were sent to administer the area on behalf of the Thai state and monarchy, all would be well. This approach was represented by the SBPAC, a Prem-era initiative that was closed by Thaksin and then reopened by Surayud. The SBPAC undertook to transfer "bad" officials out of the border area, since according to notions of virtuous rule, "bad" individuals were the only shortcoming of Thai administration.

Unfortunately, Thai Buddhist notions of virtuous rule relied on appeals to what Alagappa calls "shared norms and values," which were not in fact shared by Malay Muslims. Thai virtuous rule was predicated on the shibboleth "Nation, Religion, King," but Malay Muslims understood all three of these elements differently from Thai Buddhists. Mutuality between King and people did not work properly in the deep South. For this reason, virtuous rule did not provide a sustainable basis for the legitimacy of the Thai state in the Southern border region. Some people—including "royal liberal" Thai bureaucrats and moderate Muslims—tried to equate Thai notions of *dhammaraja* with Islamic ideas of just rule.[58] This approach underpinned much of the thinking behind the 2006 NRC report. But following the "defining political moment" of Tak Bai, the rupture between Thai Buddhist and Malay Muslim understandings of virtue and justice was plain for all to see. For Surayud, to issue an apology for Tak Bai was to reassert virtuous rule in the South; but for Malay Muslims, the failure of the Surayud government to bring those responsible for Tak Bai to justice demonstrated a fundamental insincerity. Malay Muslims were no longer willing to take on trust Thai claims about the paternalistic benevolence of rule from Bangkok; Thai suzerainty over Patani needed new and more robust sources of legitimacy.

Representative rule was another potential source of legitimacy for the Thai state in the deep South. Representative rule could have two broad components: representative bureaucracy and representative politics. Representative bureaucracy meant that government officials administering the area would be drawn substantially or mainly from the Malay Muslim population, a demand first articulated in Haji Sulong's 1947 seven points, one of which called for 80 percent of government officials to be Malays.[59] Yet such an idea was considered too radical even for the NRC, sixty years later. The insincerity of the Thai state in addressing this issue was illustrated by the fact that no proper data on the religious composition and provincial origins of government officials in the Southern border region has ever been published, making discussion about the extent to which the bureaucracy is or is not already representative very difficult. Broadly speaking, there are significant numbers of Malay Muslims in the lower echelons of government service and very few in key decision-making positions in the agencies where such representation really matters: the Interior Ministry, the police, and the army. The Thai state tends to rely on virtuous tokenism, holding up a small number of "representative" individuals such as the Malay Muslim Yala governor Theera Mintrasak as exemplar figures within structurally unrepresentative agencies.[60] After the events of 2004, this approach was no longer credible in the eyes of many Malay Muslims.

Another source of legitimacy actively promoted by the Thai state was representative politics. Because most MPs from the Southern border provinces by the 1990s were Malay Muslims, so the argument went, the minority population was well represented at the national level. The quality of this representation was enhanced by the bargaining power of the Wadah group, which had held a number of ministerial positions: junior ministries for Den Tohmeena and Ariphen Utarasint, and major posts including Parliament president, communications minister, and interior minister for Wan Muhammad Nor Matha. Even Muslim political leaders from outside the border provinces, such as former Democrat foreign minister Surin Pitsuwan and CNS leader General Sonthi Boonyaratkalin, were also sometimes portrayed as "representing" Malay Muslims. In reality, however, Malay Muslims were such a small minority that their elected or appointed representatives could make little impact within a highly centralized political order such as Thailand's; in a memorable phrase, Den Tohmeena described such MPs as "ornamental plants."[61] After the pivotal events of 2004, which saw Wan Nor and his Wadah colleagues conspicuously co-opted by the Thaksin government, representative politics as a source of legitimacy for the Thai state was exposed as a sham. The same applied to parallel arguments positing the existence of another form of representation, an alliance between the Thai state and virtuous Islamic leaders from the Southern border provinces. Muslim leaders who took leading roles in the Islamic school system, were elected to the Thai senate, or were appointed to bodies such as the NRC or the National Legislative Assembly soon lost their legitimacy to speak on behalf of Malay Muslims.

In theory, provincial, municipal, and subdistrict elections offered a range of opportunities for representative politics; empowered by the political reform and "decentralization" processes of the 1990s, Malay Muslims controlled most of these elected bodies across the three provinces. Yet in practice many ordinary Malay Muslims were skeptical about local electoral politics, seeing it as a means by which the Thai state had sought to subvert and divide their communities. Ultimately, elected Malay Muslim politicians had little freedom of maneuver, since real control of local government in Thailand remained firmly in the hands of the Interior Ministry and the Bangkok state, and linked to well-oiled networks of vote canvassers. In the eyes of many Malay Muslims, "decentralization" amounted to yet another legitimacy scam perpetrated by the Thai state. Discussion of real decentralization in the South—even the question of electing governors, let alone any form of autonomy—remained firmly off the table. The NRC never even mentioned it in their report. Representative politics for Malay Muslims could only operate within a structurally unrepresentative, Bangkok-driven, top-down Thai political order. Nothing else was on offer.

Largely missing from Thai constructs of legitimacy in the deep South are mechanisms to ensure the active participation of Malay Muslims in their own affairs: in short, participatory legitimacy. A participatory bureaucracy, run by and for Malay Muslims with real local accountability, remains apparently beyond the imagination of the Thai authorities. So is a thoroughly participatory political order, such as some form of autonomous region in the deep South. Such participation as is permitted is always framed by Thai structures, priorities, and agendas. Provincial Islamic councils are elected by local imams, for example, but political parties and state agencies actively intervene in the election processes. In the early years of its original incarnation, the SBPAC employed relatively effective mechanisms for consulting local leaders, but these participatory mechanisms were always framed by Thai paradigms of paternalist virtuous bureaucracy. Given the persistent failure of virtuous rule and the structural shortcomings of representative rule exposed by the defining political moments of 2004, the best hope for Bangkok is further to enlarge political space by embracing some form of participatory rule, giving Malay Muslims a much greater say in running their own affairs, within the broad umbrella of the Thai nation-state.

1

ISLAM

What does the violence in Southern Thailand have to do with Islam? Anonymous leaflets purportedly issued by militant groups often contain some jihadist language. Many young militants received training and indoctrination from Islamic teachers, some of which took place within Islamic educational institutions. The perpetrators of some incidents used Sufi-style rituals, swearing ceremonies, and "magic spells" intended to protect them from harm. It is tempting to see the Southern Thai violence as a form of Islamist militancy, testifying to the strength of Malay Muslim beliefs and the determination of local people to resist the Thai state on religious grounds. Some commentators have linked the militant movement in the South with "Wahhabi" or Salafist teaching, and with a "fundamentalist" resistance to secular modernity. In fact, such attempts to read Patani through Western images of Osama bin Laden are profoundly unhelpful. Islam in the Southern border provinces remains predominantly Malay in character; Salafism is a relatively new arrival in Thailand. Islam in the region has been weakened and divided by doctrinal differences, divisions that have been exploited by the Thai state for political purposes. The history of Islam in the deep South since the 1960s, and especially since the 1980s, is largely a tale of Thai successes in undermining the traditional system of Islamic education—through converting *pondoks* (Islamic boarding schools) into private Islamic schools that offer the standard Thai curriculum—and refining mechanisms for controlling imams and provincial Islamic councils. External interventions have indeed destabilized Islam and undermined the legitimacy of Islamic leaders in Patani, but these interventions have emanated largely from Bangkok, rather than from Saudi Arabia or elsewhere in the Muslim world. The upsurge of violence reflects fragmented, weak, and insecure Islamic institutions in the deep South, but is not primarily animated by religious tensions or grievances. Rather than demonstrating a resurgent, aggressive Islam, wielding arms with a confident flourish, the renewed violence reflects a disappointed, dissenting, and divided Malay-Muslim community, whose most capable leaders have been captured by Bangkok. Where Malay Muslims have turned to militancy, it has been because Thai rule no longer appears legitimate, and because their own leaders have experienced a parallel loss of spiritual, moral, and political authority.

Traditionally, Malay Muslim communities had been viewed as relatively tight-knit and resilient, and as firmly based on two core religious institutions, mosques and pondoks. This portrayal may have been a romanticization; in any case, by the beginning of the twenty-first century, these strengths had eroded significantly. Islam itself was broadly divided into traditionalist and new school wings. As a result, mosques had multiplied and were left weakened and divided. Imams had suffered a loss of standing and were increasingly incorporated into power plays initiated by provincial Islamic councils and national-level politicians. Starved of funds, traditional pondoks were being gradually marginalized, while the owners of modern Islamic private schools formed an emergent elite, tied to the Thai state through political and financial networks. The result was a crisis of leadership within Malay Muslim communities. This chapter explores the issues behind the loss of direction that afflicted Muslim society in the three provinces following the turn of the millennium.

Sects

As elsewhere, Southern Thailand's Malay Muslims were commonly classified in terms of "modernist" and traditionalist tendencies: the "new school" (*khana mai* in Thai, or *kaum muda* in Malay) and the "old school" (*khana kao* in Thai, *kaum tua* in Malay). This shorthand distinction was a useful heuristic device at a certain level but could not be pressed too far.

Traditionalist Islam in Patani had syncretistic elements, influenced by Hinduism, Buddhism, and local spirit beliefs; these included the use of magic charms, spells, and offerings. The elderly abbot of Wat Srisudachan in Panare, Pattani, had a regular stream of visitors most afternoons. He specialized in dispensing herbal medicines, blessing powerful amulets designed to protect the wearer from danger, and dehexing those who believed that they had been cursed. Many dehexing customers were Muslims, who believed that a Muslim spell was best removed by a powerful Buddhist.[1]

In Khota Baru, Raman, Yala, Muslims make offerings at the su-san (*kubo*), a set of graves belonging to former rulers, or *jao muang*.[2] To support a special request, locals recommend taking a white chicken to the grave and releasing it.[3] Informants admitted that chicken offering was not strictly Islamic and that some imams and *ustadz* (religious teachers, literally "masters") had tried to forbid the practice—but the tradition was centuries old and reflected the immense local pride of Khota Baru people in their distinctive history. Releasing chickens was only done as a last resort, they insisted, but added that the practice remained very popular. Chinese and Thai Buddhists in the area lit joss-sticks at the same site.

In Saiburi, Pattani, fisherfolk offered prayers to the goddess of the sea and lit firecrackers before setting out in their boats, until they were forced to stop by khana mai religious authorities in the early 1990s. In nearby Yaring, I attended a midnight session on the beach, at which a Muslim fisherman-turned-soothsayer made predictions of the future revealed to him by spirits. My consultation with the master was brokered by a local Sufi-inclined taxi driver.[4] More mundane practices, such as sprinkling holy water on new vehicles, are widespread and persistent Muslim adaptations from Buddhist rituals. Some Muslim teenagers were not averse to throwing water over people during the Thai Songkran festival and went into Narathiwat town from outlying areas especially for this purpose.[5]

By no means do all "khana kao" Muslims dabble in outright syncretism, but traditional Malay Islam was much less doctrinaire and prescriptive than newer forms. Successive waves of reformists had sought to standardize and regularize the Islam practiced in the Thai south. Haji Sulong exemplified this trend as early as the 1920s, preaching against traditional practices and having no truck with the mystical rituals that characterized the Dusun-nyor "rebellion."[6] Former Narathiwat senator Umar Tayib, who graduated from Al-Azhar University, in Egypt in 1964, put his finger on the problem: those who used to be considered "new school"—like himself—had already been surpassed by new waves of thinking and were now viewed as "old school."[7] The original idea of the "new school" dated back around seventy years, and the teachings of this school had long since become a standard view of Islam among more educated people, though often not by ordinary villagers. Umar argued that "most villagers are still in the old school mindset. Most imams and Islamic Council members are not exactly in the old school kind of thought, but they didn't want to make it known, fearing decreased popularity."[8] The theme of a social, educational, and cultural gap between a "new school" Muslim elite and a traditionalist Muslim community was a highly persistent one. While Haji Sulong represented an earlier form of khana mai, and Umar's 1960s generation formed a second wave, most prominent Muslim academics in Patani were broadly aligned with the stricter reformism associated with Ismael Lutfi Chapakia, a Saudi-educated preacher and the founder of Yala Islamic College. When he returned to Thailand in the 1980s, Lutfi was a Salafist firebrand, inspiring a new generation of teachers and academics. His return coincided with a new emphasis on "proper" Islamic dress (many khana kao women traditionally wore loose headscarves, readily removing them when working in the fields, for example), rigorous performance of prayers, an emphasis on systematic Koranic teaching, and a questioning of old-style ceremonies. These included the *mawlid* celebrations held to commemorate the birthday of the Prophet and various practices commemorating the dead. In khana kao households, married couples would pray separately, but some new school couples prayed together. Khana kao practitioners tended to place a lot of emphasis on extended Koranic readings and prayers at dawn, whereas khana mai practices were normally less elaborate.[9] Lutfi was initially renowned for his hard-line inflexibility: in some villages fights actually broke out between traditionalists and reformist in disputes over religious issues.[10] Initially, Lutfi's outspoken stance was widely rejected by local Muslim society, and he was actually unable to travel to some parts of Narathiwat for fear of being killed.[11] Over time his positions became slowly mainstreamed, partly because they had won greater acceptance, and partly because Lutfi had moderated some of his views. Traditionalist rituals such as parading newly circumcised boys through the village or eating three colors of sticky rice at wedding ceremonies, gradually waned under khana mai influence.[12]

The College of Islamic Studies at Prince of Songkhla University (PSU), founded in 1989, was in religious and intellectual terms an outpost of Yala Islamic College. Most of the academic staff there regarded Lutfi—rather than the college's director, the low-profile Ismail Ali—as their inspiration or mentor. For Lutfi's detractors, he and his followers were not simply khana mai, but "Wahhabi," a word carrying negative associations with ideas of inflexibility and intolerance, as well as implicit accusations of sympathy for anti-Western thinking, a stance that could be conflated with support for violence. Imtiyaz Yusuf bluntly referred to Lutfi's Yala Islamic College as a "Wahhabi outfit," but the term "Wahhabi" was highly contentious, rejected by Lutfi himself, and by most of his supporters.[13] "Wahhabi" was a problematic category, given its association with the formal rejection of established schools of jurisprudence.[14] Most Patani Malay Muslims identified themselves as Shafi'i. As one informant explained, "We are khana kao, but we are more modern. . . . Nobody accepts himself as a Wahhabi."[15] Another informant actually announced that he was happy to call himself "Wahhabi:" Wahhabism was the most authentic, original form of Islam and had nothing to do with violence at all.[16] A more gnomic response came from an academic who said, "Wahhabi? I'm not sure whether I'm Wahhabi or not."[17] His institutional affiliation might make him appear "Wahhabi," but he was not comfortable with the term. Scholars such as Noorhaidi Hasan prefer to use the term *salafism* rather than Wahhabism; Noorhaidi argues that in the Indonesian context, "the contemporary Salafi movement can be called a form of reconstituted Wahhabism."[18]

On one level, "Wahhabi" could be seen as a term of abuse used opportunistically by more traditionalist-inclined religious teachers and politicians. When Umar stood for the senate in 2000, anonymous leaflets were circulated accusing him of being a "Wahhabi"—but he was elected regardless.[19] But Umar stressed the need for Islamic Council members with different perspectives to possess a good knowledge of Arabic, otherwise scholars of Wahhabist inclinations could "seize" the Koran and claim a monopoly on the right to interpret the text. Supporters of Lutfi's approach saw themselves as engaged in a gradual and long-term process of intellectual dominance. Since these ideas were now pervasive among leading Muslim scholars in the region—and were near-hegemonic within the two main bastions of higher Islamic learning, the Yala Islamic College and PSU's College of Islamic Studies—they believed it was only a matter of time until traditionalist understandings of Islam withered away. While the khana mai included most well-known Muslim academics in the South, the khana kao had little real leadership: it was backed by leading politician Den Tohmeena (the son of Haji Sulong), the provincial Islamic councils, and by a dwindling number of prominent *babors* (pondok schoolmasters) and popular preachers, based in the traditional pondoks.[20] Yet despite its weak leadership, the khana kao remained overwhelmingly dominant in numerical terms and comprised somewhere between 70 and 90 percent of the Muslim population. One typical nonacademic informant explained that she found the ideas and practices of the khana mai incomprehensible.[21]

The clearest symbolic distinction between the two khana could be seen at weekends. On Saturday mornings at ten o'clock, the well-known traditionalist preacher Ismael Sapanyan taught at the Pattani Central Mosque, drawing huge crowds; at the same time on Sundays, he preached at the Yala Central Mosque. In recent years, Lutfi had begun a rival operation, preaching on Saturdays from 9.30 to 10.30 at the Bamrung Islam School on the main Pattani-Yala road, and on Sundays at the original Yala Islamic College campus, close to the Malayu-Bangkok intersection outside Yala.[22] Significantly, Ismael Sapanyan operated from the central mosques, with the blessing of the traditionalist Muslim elite; Lutfi preached from his own educational institutions, illustrating the source of his learning and spiritual authority. While Lutfi's gatherings were serious affairs, addressed mainly to an audience of educated, middle-class Muslims, including many government officials, Ismael Sapanyan's sermons at Pattani Central Mosque took place in a festive and friendly atmosphere, as men in sarongs and women wearing bright-colored headscarves picnicked on fruit under the trees around the grounds.[23] Lutfi's Sunday sermons were broadcast live on the INN radio station, while his Saturday preaching was relayed to local shops and houses through a closed circuit television network; Ismael Sapanyan, by contrast, had declined offers from INN to broadcast his preaching, insisting that the faithful should attend in person.[24] Khana mai Muslims disparaged pondok-educated Ismael Sapanyan's technophobia and complained that his teachings—full of superb metaphors and artfully delivered in a lyrical local Malay that ordinary villagers found easy to grasp—were not based on a deep, scholarly understanding of Islam.[25] But locals who had attended his sermons would often continue discussing their content after returning to their villages.[26]

Fig. 1.1 Crowds of worshippers leaving Pattani Central Mosque (Charoon Thongnual)

Yet the divide between old and new schools had limited salience. People had been washed back and forth by different waves of "new" belief and practice, distinctions between new and old had become blurred, and informants had great difficulty locating themselves within the resulting spectrum. Though Lutfi was a dominant figure, his followers were not synonymous with khana mai. Many people considered themselves "in between" the two schools; one informant described himself as *khana patjuban*, or "contemporary school." For some people, this intermediate category was actually a hybrid Thai-Malay identity; their "Thai" education and working experiences (sometimes outside the region) made them unable to locate themselves according to standard local categories. A research report done by a local team identified five groups of Muslims in the South: khana kao, *klum sunah,* Shi'ite (a very small minority in Thailand), Dawah Tabligh,[27] and Sufi.[28] These categories coyly dodged the term *khana mai* (let alone "Wahhabi"), instead substituting the fuzzier phrase *klum sunah.*[29] One academic familiar with the study was highly critical of this approach, suggesting that a more sure-footed form of classification would use the names of leading figures in each group (for example, the Lutfi group, Ismael Sapanyan group, or Zakaria group).[30] Yet while designating groups by the names of their *ulama* had the advantage of avoiding hard-and-fast labels, it also had considerable heuristic drawbacks; on one level, it was simply another cop-out. Distinguishing between the old and the new was fraught with practical as well as theological difficulties, and in practice many Malay Muslims embraced hybridized beliefs, practices, and identities. An informant I met by chance at Lutfi's Yala sermon had previously accompanied me to a *mawlid* ceremony at the Pattani Central Mosque—a practice Lutfi rejected. In theory, khana mai men wore white caps, whereas as the khana kao favored black Malay caps: but many of those sporting white caps would not identify themselves as khana mai. Men from khana kao often touched themselves on the chest or face after shaking hands; but while some khana mai refrained from doing so, personal preference trumped axioms of faith.[31]

Alarmists feared that hard-line modernism was spreading across the Southern provinces, bringing religious and political radicalization in its wake. Lutfi's group was one of the first to come under suspicion.[32] Yet both elements of this fear were questionable. A widespread local understanding was that Arabized ideas from foreign-trained scholars peaked in influence in the early 1990s, before subsequently declining. Scholars returning from abroad were very welcome in the beginning and often received donations from local Malay Muslim businessmen to create new mosques. Then modernization tailed off, fisherfolk stopped wearing impractical

Arab-style dress, and funding new mosques became more problematic.[33] Lutfi's influence was checked by nationalist-oriented Malay traditionalists, who saw his new school as a threat to militant doctrines which increasingly appropriated Islamic rhetoric in support of a quasi-religious separatist ideology.[34] By contrast, Lutfi's stance had evolved into one that was neither separatist nor integrationist, but involved articulating a form of Salafi Islam ("Wahhabi" to his critics), which could carve out its own space within Thailand.[35] Given the minority status of his followers in the region, Lutfi had little to gain from a separate Patani state. The term *Islamists* was too problematic to use in the context of Thailand, but the Lutfi school arguably shared with classic "Islamism" a desire to use religion as a political ideology, with which to embark on negotiations with the Thai state.

Three broad alternative explanations emerged for the apparent "peaking" of Salafist practices and ideas: accommodation, rejection, and suppression. Those from the khana mai perspective tended to talk in terms of a mutual accommodation. This accommodation took place on two fronts: an accommodation with the realities of living alongside Thai society and an accommodation with the Malay traditionalist majority population of the region. An academic informant argued that previously people from the two groups would not pray together or even talk much, and many of the khana mai people had little contact with Buddhists or other groups. This had changed over the last five years or so, as the "new" group had moderated their thinking and become more willing to make common cause with fellow Muslims of different persuasions. He believed that Southern Malay Muslims were operating within a more tolerant framework created by wider Thai society, which influenced the way they thought and acted.[36] Other informants suggested that Lutfi himself had changed; in late 2005, he surprised his colleagues by declaring in an internal meeting that he wanted Yala Islamic College to produce the first ever female Malay-Muslim provincial governor. Lutfi's appointment to the National Reconciliation Commission in 2005, and to the coup group's National Legislative Assembly in 2006, illustrated the lengths to which the Thai state was prepared to travel to embrace him. Yet behind Lutfi's accommodationist perspective sometimes lay an implicit triumphalism, a belief that since the intellectual elite had embraced his teachings, the masses would soon have to follow.

A second explanation was that the Salafi reformists had been forced to retreat.[37] A self-proclaimed *khana kao* Narathiwat local politician suggested that the khana mai had simply faced popular rejection: "I don't know how active this movement was in the past ten years, but nowadays the movement is not active, moreover, the new way of Islam is not accepted by local people."[38]

A third explanation was that tensions between the old and new schools had not gone away, nor had traditionalism triumphed: rather, the wider political situation had suppressed this latent conflict, which was overshadowed by more pressing issues related to the resurgent "separatist" violence.[39] According to this reading, these religious tensions could well reemerge at some future juncture.

Although widely understood locally, questions such as the tension between khana kao and khana mai were little discussed in public. Malay Muslims rarely debated internal religious and political conflicts among themselves, even in academic circles:

> Malay Muslim society is similar to Thai society in the way that people are reluctant to confront their own diversity, divisions, and problems—you don't really have frank discussions with other Muslims about these issues concerning different practices and orientations very much. It's like the Thai idea that you don't talk about politics or religion, otherwise your friendships and relationships with those around you may be jeopardized.[40]

However, this informal taboo was violated in August 2006, when Saudara, a student group at PSU's Pattani campus, published a lengthy statement on the *Prachatai* news website. The statement amounted to a denunciation of khana mai Islam, as practiced and taught by academics at the university:

> Therefore, the expansion of the Wahhabi way of thinking in the College of Islamic Studies, Prince of Songkhla University, Pattani has created irritation among students who are not Wahhabi, and created anxiety amongst the parents of students who were sending their children to enroll in this institution. The thing that the parents were most concerned about was that their children would be forced in a Wahhabi direction.[41]

The statement criticized leading campus Muslims for opposing the holding of *mawlid* and Ashura day ceremonies, and accused them of "looking down on and insulting the traditional pondok education system." They were also accused of helping raise money to build mosques that created social divisions. Members of Saudara came mainly from a group of ten well-known private Islamic schools in the three provinces;[42] in effect, they were hard-line defenders of a Malay nationalist, traditionalist Islam. There were intimate links between certain modes of "old school" Islam and a support for Malay identity. Saudara encouraged an informal student boycott of the Prince of Songkhla University Mosque—which was attended by only a minority of Muslim students on campus—and discouraged applicants from enrolling at the College of Islamic Studies.[43] Rather than providing academic and spiritual leadership for the Muslim students at PSU, the College of Islamic Studies had become an enclave, an "out-group" that did not receive full acceptance from the wider "in-group" of traditionalist Malay Muslim students.

This on-campus tension was a microcosm of a much bigger disparity between the khana mai ulama and the wider traditionalist Malay Muslim society in the three provinces. Never far away was the question of violence: the August 18 statement was a direct response to an earlier *Prachatai* piece, which accused Saudara of having links with the militant movement.[44] Some PSU academics believed that they were seen by those who sympathized with violence as implicitly "blocking" the separatist struggle; by teaching "real" Islam they were holding back the spread of violence, and therefore could be viewed as enemies of the militant movement.[45]

The distinction between traditionalist and "modernist" Islam was a very ambiguous and somewhat unhelpful one in the context of Patani. However, at the risk of terrible oversimplification, educated, khana mai Muslims were more likely to reject the emphasis on Malay identity that offered potential support for separatist ideas. This emphasis on Malay identity was largely the preserve of traditionalists. In other words, whereas in the wider Islamic world "Wahhabi" ideology was often constructed as the handmaiden of political violence, in Patani the opposite arguably held true.[46]

Imams

In Patani, the mosque was the center of village life; men prayed at the mosque five times a day; the imam was a highly respected community elder, supported in his work by a *khatib* and a *bilal*,[47] and by a mosque committee. Such were the essential shibboleths recited in most studies of the region. The realities were somewhat more complex.

By 2006, many villages contained more than one mosque, mosque construction was proceeding apace, and new mosques were not simply to serve a growing population. Other explanations were more common. A young local man came back from studying abroad, perhaps in the Middle East or Pakistan, was unhappy with the way his local mosque was run, and solicited funds to build a new one.[48] Or there was an election for imam, there were two candidates, one popular candidate lost, but he and his followers did not want to support the winner. Underpinning such conflicts usually lay ideological differences concerning divergent understandings of Islam, typically between "modernist" and "traditionalist" schools:[49] "There is a school of thought divide.... Once they lost, all they can do is thinking about building a new mosque, because they have different ideas."[50] Alternatively, a serving imam found himself ousted from the mosque committee. The

Fig. 1.2 Malay-Muslim women at the historic Kru-Ze Mosque, Pattani (Charoon Thongnual)

result was the same: the ousted faction created their own mosque nearby, and the community was split.

The normal approach was "build first, register later." If the Islamic Council approved the new mosque, a much easier procedure in Thailand than in neighboring Malaysia, one village then had two mosques.[51] But because of the laborious paperwork involved in registering mosques, many

communities did not bother, and unregistered mosques—formally designated simply as *suraus,* or prayer places—were legion.[52] In many places,
multiple mosques reflected different schools of Islam; for example, the small
town of Sakom in Songkhla had three mosques: one founded by an imam
who graduated from Pakistan, another headed by a Medina graduate, and
a third connected to the Thamma Wittaya School in Yala.[53] In some places,
there were not enough people to attend all the new mosques created.[54]
Even where the process of creating a new mosque was relatively amicable,
the change divided villagers who had previously prayed together.[55]

One imam explained how heightened conflict was avoided in his community: Originally he did not want to become the imam, but finally assumed the post out of necessity. Despite the existence of a rival candidate,
no election was held. On the day they met at the mosque to select the
imam, he left the meeting so as not to be directly involved. At the meeting,
the people talked another candidate out of standing, because most people
did not want an election, and thought he would be the best choice. He was
from an old family of imams—his grandfather and uncle held the position
before him. People had the idea that elections were not good and created
conflict. They preferred to use a peaceful way of choosing wherever possible, because otherwise the losers might not want to go to the mosque any
more and the community could be split. This had happened in a nearby
village; the election created problems, and the group who lost the election
set up a new mosque.[56]

Electing imams turned them into local politicians, undermining their
status and authority. Communities became fragmented and a single village might now contain multiple mosques, alternative sources of religious
authority. Rival imams, with different Islamic orientations, would criticize
one another, filing complaints about the work of competing mosques with
the district officer and other authorities.[57] Problems were compounded
when contestation between rival mosques mapped onto political conflicts
between headmen, *kamnan* (sub-district chiefs), and subdistrict organizations. Whereas in the past, imams could command immense respect and
loyalty from villagers, many were now regarded with suspicion or even a
degree of contempt. The introduction of elections for imam and mosque
committees, combined with the associated external penetration of village
politics, contributed to a decline in the ability of villagers to govern
themselves.[58]

While Patani was known for religious piety, any notion that nearly all
adult men prayed at the mosque five times daily was naive. Although some
traditions have it that prayers at the mosque count for twenty-seven times

more than prayers conducted elsewhere,[59] one Narathiwat imam admitted that no more than twenty of his hundred-strong Friday congregation
prayed five times on other days.[60] Villagers living close to mosques in Pattani and Narathiwat suggested typical attendance figures might be as low
as 10 percent.[61] Poor mosque attendances had many causes and illustrated
the declining authority of the imam but also reflected the routinized nature of many prayer services. Most traditionalist mosques had a "village
meeting" style of prayers, in which the four essential religious elements
might take little more than a couple of minutes. On Fridays, the rest of
the time was given over largely to public announcements by people such
as the headman or chairman of the subdistrict administrative organization, but on other days there was little to draw a crowd. This contrasted
with the more didactic approach adopted by the khana mai at the mosque
on the PSU campus, for example, where prayers were followed by fifteen to
twenty minutes of serious teaching, drawing on contemporary issues and
events.[62] In communities adjoining pondoks, or private Islamic schools,
locals sometimes attended prayers led by the babor or ustadz rather than
those led by the village imam. Many imams, especially in rural areas, were
poorly educated, had a limited command of Thai, and had often been
selected for reasons other than their level of religious knowledge.[63] Partly
given the formalized and routinized nature of prayers at many mosques,
discussions after prayers, especially in the evening, often assumed great
significance. Groups of men would often linger at the mosque during
the gap (of less than an hour) between the two evening prayer sessions,
maghrib and *isha*, during which they would talk over both religious and
secular matters. This period of the evening was an important moment for
the exchange of political views and ideas.

In theory, all Muslims were supposed to pay *zakat*, a form of taxation
to support the welfare of others. Zakat ought to provide a basic level of
funding for mosques. Yet in practice, very few Malay Muslims in the South
paid zakat systematically. In Narathiwat, the Islamic Council had decreed
that all Muslims should pay 40 percent of their zakat to the local imam
and mosque, and 60 percent to the Islamic Council.[64] But widespread suspicion of the Islamic councils offered an excellent excuse to refrain from
paying zakat. Similarly, mosque committees were often highly politicized
and tainted by allegations of corruption and mismanagement. Some locals
took the easy way out by dispensing zakat to their own poor relations,
or to charitable causes of their own choice.[65] One informant argued that
mosques had lost their way: at the time of the Prophet, mosques were not
just for praying, but also for studying, holding meetings, and economic

activities. They also held funds that could be used to assist people in need. Yet these wider social functions were now being neglected. If imam and mosque committees were able to perform these roles properly, problems in the three provinces would be eased.[66]

Some Muslim community leaders argued that a dependency mentality had set in, whereby villagers expected other people to pay for their mosques, forgetting that giving money was at the heart of Islamic culture.[67] A vicious circle resulted: mosques did not enjoy the confidence of their own community and were therefore unable to solicit proper funding; mosque committees resorted to underhand means to raise money, and their reputations were further tarnished. Imams were paid a derisory salary of two thousand baht a month by the state and had to rely on patronage to cover expenses. One academic argued that most government development projects were misguided and the Thai state would do best simply to invest resources in building and improving mosques, with no strings attached: "It's the easiest way to get to the hearts of Muslim people. The impact can be very strong."[68]

The preoccupation of the Thai state with trying to impose external regulation of mosques was largely counterproductive and reminiscent of the state's attempts to subordinate local forms of Buddhism to central authority.[69] When one Narathiwat imam sought funding from the provincial governor to make improvements to his mosque, a senior official urged him to invite the governor to address a large crowd there.[70] Yet such a quid pro quo would have reinforced a growing negative perception that the imams had been incorporated into the state security structure and were becoming "subordinates"[71] of district officers—some of whom held monthly imam meetings.[72] Certain imams willingly collaborated with the state and the security services; others preferred to keep their distance. Leaflets warned imams not to cooperate and highlighted their alleged hypocrisy. One such text identified the selection of progovernment imams as an integral part of Thai security policy: "Appoint some greedy imams through the Chularajamontri in order for these local imams to take part in solving the problems and respond to various policies issued by the kafir Siam government, the occupier."[73]

When sensitive issues arose, such as the question of whether or not the corpses of those killed in violent incidents should be left unwashed (in other words, treated as *shahid*),[74] imams found themselves on the frontline. Most victims of the April 28 incidents had their corpses left unwashed. The families of some victims insisted that these decisions were made by individual imams.[75] But imams were mindful that their actions might be judged by the militant movement; as this anonymous warning made clear, the decision to wash the corpse of a slain "collaborator" could be just as contentious as leaving a possible *shahid* unwashed:

Attention

To all Toh-imam, Khatib, Bilal,
   Do not wash and pray for the corpses of people that lost their lives in the following causes:

1. Spying
2. The guards for schools of other religions
3. Men and women in the 4,500 baht scheme[76]
4. Civil servants

Be careful!
Whoever takes down this flyer will be included[77]

Imams suffered a considerable loss of standing from the 1980s onward: as founts of religious knowledge, they were increasingly displaced by better-educated babors and ustadz, while as community leaders they were strongly challenged by headmen, *kamnan,* and subdistrict council chairs, all of whom were now elected. The traditional focus of the community was weakened by the proliferation of new mosques. Because imams were often forced to ally themselves with politicians, Islamic Council members, government officials, and military officers, they found their legitimacy and integrity questioned in the eyes of their communities. Yet if they were suspected of siding with the militants, they faced constant official scrutiny and possibly arrest. A number of imams were killed or injured in political violence. Overall, mosques were a declining source of community resilience, partly because of social changes imposed by the Thai state and partly because of infighting within local Muslim society.

Majalis

Mediating between the state and Thailand's Muslim population was an elected bureaucracy, a structure of Islamic provincial councils (*majalis*) linked with a national Islamic Council, which was headed by the Chularajamontri (Thailand's royally-appointed Islamic leader).[78] In the eyes of the Thai state, these councils existed to manage the Muslim population. For Malay Muslims in the Southern border provinces, the councils enjoyed an ambiguous status, and some leading Muslims preferred to shun them. The legal powers of the councils were very limited,[79] dealing mainly with overseeing imams, mosque committees, and arbitration relating to family law and inheritance.[80] But members of the Islamic councils were also advisors to the provincial governor on Islamic affairs; at least some members of the Yala Council were also appointed personal advisors to the Fourth Army region commander. On this basis, the Interior Ministry had sought to involve the councils in security matters, asking them to promote the "proper" teaching of Islam and even to intervene when imams were suspected of lending support to the militant movement. Pattani governor Panu explained that when doubts emerged about a particular imam's loyalty, he would ask the president of the Islamic Council to invite the imam for dinner at his house; Panu himself would attend the meal, talk to the imam directly, and administer an informal warning to him.[81] By implication, the president was made responsible for the behavior of imam in the province. Some Islamic Council members were uneasy with this style of intervention, criticizing the stance of the Thai state toward the Muslim community: "It's like a marriage where the husband is abusive to his wife, but expects her to take care of and respect him, though he does not respect her."[82]

> Effectively...there are two parallel systems: in the three provinces the Islamic Councils are taking care of 80 percent of the people, and the provincial government the other 20 percent, they are the representatives of the Buddhists.... If you see the provincial office as administering Buddhists and the majalis administering the Muslims, we are bigger than them.[83]

In this radical understanding, the Islamic Councils had more legitimacy than the provincial government; by implication, the president of the provincial Islamic Council was a more legitimate leader than the unelected provincial governor. Yet, the Pattani Islamic Council, for example, received a subvention of only around seventy thousand baht to cover its annual running expenses.[84] Although the president of the Pattani Islamic Council held almost twenty different advisory positions, and was almost constantly attending meetings and ceremonies, he received a derisory official allowance of twenty-five hundred baht a month.[85]

In 1997, a group of Muslim politicians, led by Den Tohmeena,[86] introduced a new Islamic Organizations Administration Act, which had the effect of "democratizing" provincial Islamic councils.[87] Whereas previously vacancies on the councils had been filled via an opaque, papal-style selection process by the remaining members, the new legislation provided for council members to be elected by the imams of all registered mosques in a province. Some conservative Muslims defended the previous system as conforming to the idea of a *shura*, or Islamic decision-making process.[88] Pattani, Yala, and Narathiwat had thirty-member Islamic councils, with electorates of between three hundred and six hundred imams per province.[89] On November 24, 2005, the second ever Islamic Council elections were held; the violence in the South had generated considerable interest, and the military, the Interior Ministry, and the political parties all became involved in supporting particular outcomes in the Southern border provinces.

The hotly contested elections highlighted several critical issues. First, because Thai state agencies were dissatisfied with the performance of the existing councils, they encouraged teams or candidates to challenge the serving presidents. The root cause of this dissatisfaction was the refusal of these presidents directly to condemn the violence. A contributory factor was a joint statement issued by the three provincial Islamic Council presidents in 2004, in which they asked the military to behave cautiously and with restraint.[90] Some sources suggested that the military had directly supported the challengers, arguing that Nideh Waba—one of the leading figures on the challenging team in Pattani—was well known for his close military connections.[91] Other sources were skeptical;[92] Nideh himself denied receiving funds from the military,[93] and the ousted Narathiwat president Abdul Rahman Abdul Shamad questioned rumors that the military had backed his rivals: "I've heard of that but there's no concrete evidence to support the notion. There was no reason that they wouldn't support me. I personally don't think it's true."[94]

A second critical issue was the role of national-level politicians and parties in the elections. The Pattani Islamic Council had long been the personal fiefdom of Senator Den Tohmeena, who had supported Waedueramae Mamingchi to become president in the 1999 elections. On the day of the elections, Den (then aged seventy-one) held court at the vote-count from early in the morning until almost 1:00 A.M., personally scrutinizing every single ballot paper held up by the officials overseeing the count. The Pattani contest saw a very strong rival team seek to oust the incumbents backed by Den, with support from networks associated with the Democrat Party. Meanwhile, incumbent president and Den protégé Waedueramae had forged a strong relationship with the secretary general of the Islamic Council of Thailand, Phichet Sathirachawala, a former Thai Rak Thai minister, close Thaksin associate, and Den's nemesis. In typical Thai fashion, Phichet backed both teams: since his ultimate aim was to secure a further term as secretary general, he needed to ensure that the future Pattani Council would be loyal to him.[95] Some sources suggested that Phichet's support was funded by Pojaman Shinawatra, Thaksin's wife.[96] When the incumbents were returned to office in Pattani, Waedueramae assumed the position of representative to the national Islamic Council himself—a post that Den had demanded for his own nephew. Den had been double-crossed. It was widely alleged that the two rival teams had both bought votes and that the challengers led by Nideh Waba had taken more than two hundred imams to a "safe house"—a hotel in Hat Yai—the night before the election.[97] One leading challenger explained that the imams could be divided into three groups of roughly two hundred, one group solidly for the challengers, another solidly for the incumbents, and a third "swing" group who determined the result.[98] In the end, the challengers gained eleven seats to the nineteen held by the incumbents. Waedueramae acknowledged that the election had assumed the character of a sports contest[99] and accused his opponents of using 20 million baht to buy votes in a failed attempt to oust him.[100]

In Yala, however, the military and Thai Rak Thai struggled to find a rival team to oust the existing president and eventually had to give up. While six independents did run against the incumbent team, none was elected. Again, the president assumed the post of central committee representative himself after the election, prompting speculation that Phichet had supported him on this condition.[101]

Narathiwat was the sole province where an incumbent president was ousted. The flamboyant, outspoken Abdul Rahman Abdul Shamad was defeated by former senior members of his own team, who had grown tired of his "one man show" style of "dramatic performance" leadership[102] and his frequent statements to the media.[103] Tensions within the old council had peaked over a controversial deal signed by Abdul Rahman with a Malaysian company, to produce a brand of tomato sauce endorsed by the council. For his adversaries, the deal was evidence that he had lost all sense of direction, though Abdul Rahman insisted that the council needed to diversify its sources of income.[104] In the end, he and two supporters retained their posts, while the challengers gained the remaining twenty-seven seats and control of the council. Abdul Rahman accused his opponents of threatening imams who had planned to support him.[105]

Nideh Waba, who was closely connected with network monarchy, claimed that he had coordinated a plan to oust the sitting Islamic Council presidents and their associates in all three provinces, with military and state support. Though both insisted they were working for peace and cooperating fully with the state, Abdul Rahman and Waedueramae were often spoken of in suspicious whispers by security officials. Whatever the truth behind such claims, the 2005 provincial Islamic Council elections left a legacy of bitterness and division. One academic called them the worst elections in the history of the three provinces and an indictment of Den's attempts to politicize Islam.[106] Another observer expressed surprise that no one had been killed during the elections.[107] The politicization of many leading Islamic figures in the three provinces, along with the extensive use

Fig. 1.3 The flamboyant former Narathiwat Islamic Council president, Abdul Rahman Abdul Shamad, astride a Vespa (Duncan McCargo)

of money and incentives to buy or otherwise extract votes from individual imams, contributed to a further erosion of religious authority in Malay Muslim society.

Pondoks

Traditional pondoks long formed a central element of Malay Muslim culture and identity in the deep South: a system of austere Islamic boarding schools, where mainly male students, usually aged from thirteen to around twenty, resided in simple huts,[108] which they had often built themselves.[109] In principle, a pondok had only one schoolmaster, a highly respected babor, who oversaw all the core instruction personally;[110] in practice, though, he appointed some of the brightest senior students as teaching assistants. Pondoks had no formal curriculum, and the hours of study were not strictly defined.[111] Nor was there a division of students into year-based classes; most pondoks used a simple, three-way split into small, medium-sized, and big pupils.[112] In their pure form, pondoks offered an alternative, unworldly way of life, close to medieval ideals of a university,[113] in which older students mentored younger ones, and long days and nights were filled with prayer, close study, and memorization of the Koran, and lessons in subjects that included Islamic dogmatics, jurisprudence, and the Arabic and Malay languages.[114] Traditionally, pondoks taught *kitab* (religious studies; from the Arabic word for book) on a "lifelong learning" principle; there was no upper age limit for students.[115]

Most pondoks had a conservative and disciplined regime, forbade both females and pet animals from entering their premises (though some pondoks admitted girls), and maintained a curfew, typically of 10:00 P.M. As one babor explained, the philosophy of pondok education emphasized moral training and self-reliance: "This is an exemplary pondok.... It's not only about studying...they know how to do things themselves...and they know how to help people...it's a school that produces students who know how to do good."[116]

While pondok graduates might have excellent morals, they were not renowned for their vocational skills; the only careers for which pondoks offered any direct preparation were those of ustadz or imam. Because the main language of instruction was Pattani Malay, pondok graduates were rarely highly functional in Thai, and so had difficulty entering the wider job market beyond their villages. Pondoks had earlier served as a part-time form of religious education for Malay rubber-tappers and were less effective as a form of full-time schooling. For the Thai state, the pondok system, as the stronghold of Malay linguistic, cultural, and religious identity, was one of the greatest barriers to the implementation of an assimilation policy.

Babors (in Malay, *tok-guru*) were among the most respected members of society in the region. "The term *babor* refers to a person with higher spiritual integrity and nobility,"[117] normally the founder or owner of a pondok. Typically, babors declined leading community roles in order to concentrate on teaching their students, though sometimes they did preach to a wider audience: "There are lots of babor, but really knowledgeable ones are hard to find."[118] Babors were themselves products of the pondok system. While some babors had gone on to further their studies abroad, many lacked higher religious knowledge, simply passing on what they themselves were taught. Part of the respect accorded to babors derived from their knowledge of Islam, but another element derived from their dedication and sacrifice. Babors devoted their whole lives to teaching; since pondoks did not charge any academic fees, their vocation brought few material rewards.[119] Many traditional babors lived rather like ordainees in other religions.[120]

By 2006, there were 319 registered pondoks in the Southern border provinces;[121] an average pondok had around sixty students.[122] Individual communities had longstanding connections with particular pondoks. For example, for the past forty years, youths from one Saiburi fishing village had generally attended the same pondok in Pattani's Muang district, some fifty kilometers away—despite the fact that Saiburi had several famous pondoks of its own. Teachers at one former pondok explained that until recently, most of their students came from the group of "feeder" villages from all around the three provinces.[123] In other words, students often attended pondoks in groups and would typically all return to the same village when they completed their studies. Pondoks were often networked in "pondok families," where the babors were closely related, or were themselves protégés of the same senior ulama.[124]

Following the upsurge in violence of January 2004, the Islamic education system in the Southern border provinces became a focus of intensive state scrutiny. The April 28, 2004, incidents were masterminded by Ustadz Soh, a pondok teacher; many young militants had studied in this system, receiving indoctrination or military training from traditionalist Islamic teachers. Ustadzs were accused of implanting separatist and jihadist ideas; the Thai state became preoccupied with ideas of regulating and managing Islamic education, seeking to ensure that "proper" religious teachings were advanced and suspect teachers removed. Underlying this approach was a moralistic dualism, a desire to separate "good" Muslims from the influence of "bad" Muslims. Central to these ideas were attempts to register Islamic schools and to reform their curricula. These changes applied not only to full-time schooling, but also to *tadika,* part-time schools offering Islamic education mainly to younger children, usually organized by mosques.

During the 1960s, pondoks had been permitted to register with the Thai government, but between 1971 and 2004, no further registrations were permitted.[125] The creation of new pondoks did not cease, however; instead, unregistered pondoks proliferated. In an attempt to bring the sector under tighter official control, the Thaksin government began permitting new

registrations in 2004, and considerable pressure was placed on unregistered pondoks retrospectively to formalize their status. Registered pondoks
were officially known as *sathaban pondok,* or "pondok institutes"; this
title suggested bureaucratization and "Thai-ization," but also reinforced the
idea that pondoks were something other than "schools." For the Thai state,
pondoks were something *less* than schools; for Malay Muslims, pondoks
were something *more* than schools, serving as beacons of religion and
morality. For pondok owners, the new climate of regulation was a mixed
blessing. Underpinning the state's approach was an ill-concealed desire to
transform pondoks into private Islamic schools wherever possible. The
most important difference between a pondok and a private Islamic school
was that while pondoks taught only religious studies (*satsana*), private
Islamic schools also offered a parallel secular (*saman*) curriculum, like that
provided by Thai government high schools. Most private Islamic school
students spent half of the day following a religious course of study, and
the other half following a Thai secular curriculum. Substantial incentives
existed for those pondoks that agreed to become private Islamic schools
offering the state curriculum, since these schools received government subsidies in the form of both capital allowances, and per capita grants based
on the numbers of students.

The first Islamic school to open in Pattani had been established by Haji
Sulong in the 1930s; influenced by his experiences in (newly Saudi) Arabia, Sulong did not believe in a separation between religious and secular
learning, and wanted to raise standards of education and development
in the area.[126] Some of the funding for Sulong's school was provided by
Prime Minister Phahon Phonpayuhasena, who presided over its opening;
the school was also visited by Pridi Phanomyong during his time as interior
minister. Creating Islamic schools was a longstanding area of collaboration between Bangkok and local Malay Muslim elites, despite their mutual
wariness.

Registration could take different forms: as pondoks, or as private Islamic
schools under various categories. Fully operational private Islamic schools
that offered both streams of education were usually registered under Category 15 (1) of the 1982 Private Schools Act. Some others were registered
as Category 15 (2); these were supposed to be aspiring private Islamic
schools, which had not yet fulfilled all the requirements for "15 (1)" status,
since they lacked requisite facilities, such as a science laboratory or a school
clinic.[127] In practice, "15 (2)" schools tend to be viewed with suspicion by
the authorities, who viewed them as having opted for "15 (2)" status as a
"flag of convenience," without really intending to conform to requirements.
While this was true of some such schools, others were genuinely trying to

upgrade to "15 (1)" status. Of the approximately one hundred schools holding these licenses, around half were actually defunct. The other fifty or so included schools that remained pondoks in all but name: though they had permission to open a secular program, they had yet to do so.[128] Many "15 (2)" schools were registered in this category under duress, during the 1969 to 2003 period when pondok registration was not permitted. While "15 (1)" schools received 500,000 baht in annual capital subsidies, those in "15 (2)" received only 50,000 baht.[129]

In the face of growing pressures and incentives from the Thai state, babors had a range of choices. For many, the temptations to mainstream their educational activities and embrace the offering of a secular curriculum were overwhelming. Wider trends in Malay Muslim society supported these moves. Muslim parents were dissatisfied with the quality of teaching offered by government schools, and also uneasy about placing the education of their children in the hands of a de facto Buddhist state. Yet they also recognized the importance of secular learning, and the need for their children to master Thai. The emergence of private Islamic schools offered their children the benefits of a modern education, without the moral and spiritual compromises involved in sending them to a state school.[130] Babors were able to parlay their own religious credentials into a hybridized educational commodity. As a result, enrollments at government schools in the three provinces were in freefall, especially in the secondary sector. Saiburi Jaeng Prachakan School, for example, a large government high school in the middle of Saiburi town with excellent facilities—including the most impressive school hall for hundreds of miles around—and the recipient of extensive royal patronage and official largesse, had seen its numbers drop from a peak of more than seventeen hundred students, to less than five hundred by 2006.[131] The government high school in Thung Yang Daeng, Pattani, enrolled only around ten new students in 2006, while a nearby private Islamic school enrolled about a hundred.[132] Similar stories could be found all over the three provinces.

The financial incentives for converting into a private Islamic school were considerable and went far beyond the official levels of subsidy. It was an open secret that most private Islamic schools operated a system of double accounting. Schools greatly exaggerated the numbers of pupils enrolled, in order to solicit additional per capita subsidies from the state. They also capped teachers' salaries to extremely low levels.[133] In a typical example, during 2004 one of the most famous private Islamic schools in the region was paying Saudi-graduated Arabic language teachers with ten years' experience the derisory salary of four thousand baht month—around half the official rate.[134] The result was that the state subsidies intended solely to support the teaching of the secular curriculum could be stretched to pay the entire salary bill of the school, for teachers covering both religious and secular subjects. In theory, for example, the Thai government might be paying for the secular half of the instruction of two thousand notional pupils at a certain school; but in practice, the overpayments covered both the secular and religious instruction of a thousand real pupils; at the same time, the school owner was also siphoning off sufficient excess funds for new buildings and other projects.

Budgetary manipulation on this scale could only persist with the active involvement and complicity of Ministry of Education officials in the region, who were well aware of the issues of fake pupil enrollments, and the under-payment of teachers' salaries. Indeed, senior education officials shared in the benefits of this system of structural corruption, part of an implicit "so-cial compact" between the Thai state and the Malay Muslim elite that was originally devised during the 1980s and was supervised by the SBPAC.[135] The subsidy system had been urged on the former Democrat government by prominent Pattani Islamic school owner Nideh Waba, who headed the association of private Islamic schools in the three provinces.[136] The au-thorities hoped that by co-opting—or simply by purchasing—support from prominent Islamic teachers, they could neutralize dissent, curb violence, and ensure their "buy in" to wider government objectives in the region.

But a weakness of the policy was that benefits were monopolized in the hands of school owners. In private Islamic schools, instruction was car-ried out mainly by ustadz, many of whom had studied overseas. Often, ustadz were actually better qualified and more knowledgeable in religious terms than those who owned and managed their schools. But because their degrees from countries such as Egypt, India, Indonesia, Pakistan, Saudi Arabia, and Sudan were not recognized in Thailand, those who lacked the resources to open their own schools had to work for the owners of exist-ing institutions.[137] Ustadz were enormously influential social actors, who had direct access to Malay Muslim youth during their formative years; if radically inclined ustadz taught their students about issues such as the historical and religious grievances of the region, their words would reso-nate strongly.[138] Ordinary ustadz often felt exploited and manipulated by the private school system. They were expected to accept poor conditions without complaint, and make personal sacrifices for moral and spiritual goals; but in practice they sometimes felt like ill-used and low-salaried employees, serving the ends of highly profitable private enterprises. It is little wonder that some ustadz were alienated, not just from the Thai state but also from the schools that employed them, and from school owners who enjoyed collusive relations with government agencies.

Precisely because turning a pondok into a private Islamic school meant entering into a Faustian pact with the Thai state, some babors sought to resist this trend. Babors derive their status, prestige, and identity from their relative unworldliness, their detachment from wider Thai society, and their close involvement with the local community. As soon as a babor becomes the owner of a private Islamic school, his standing in the surrounding community subtly declines. Of course, former babors often retained an air of their "past identity," and remained "freeze frame" babors,[139] but once their schools were professionally managed in a modern way, their real baborness had irrevocably changed, and there was a consequent decline in the faith people placed in them. A few prominent private school owners have some characteristics of babors; Nideh Waba was one example, Umar Tayib another, though Umar insisted that he did not consider himself a babor.[140]

As in other Muslim societies, once traditional Islamic schools were deserted by the political and religious elite, they were limited to recruiting poor, rural students and underwent a gradual decline.[141] Many traditional pondoks faced looming collapse, as pupils increasingly switched to private Islamic schools; only babors who commanded considerable popular faith could be sure of continuing enrollments.[142] But pondoks that clung to their traditional status faced suspicion and close scrutiny from the security forces, which tended to see them as "holding out" against the authority of the Thai state. Some babors sought ways of negotiating their identity, which would enable them to retain their venerated status in the community yet form necessary accommodations with the Thai state so as to permit their continuing survival. One alternative was to allow either the Nonformal Education Department or the government's Vocational Training Department to offer vocational training at their pondoks.[143] The Nonformal Education Department would fund the construction of buildings for this purpose; but since the department was notoriously inefficient, babors could accept these "free" buildings in the knowledge that there would be few strings attached. By having accepted the involvement of a government agency in the teaching provision of the pondok, the babor would reduce suspicion of his pondok on the part of the Thai state.

Most pondoks, however, chose a simpler strategy: conform to the registration requirements but keep all interaction with the authorities to a minimum. Many babors were happy to let the 319-member Association of Pondoks of the Three Southern Border Provinces apply for registration on their behalf.[144] This organization, set up on the initiative of Nideh Waba and Wan Nor, was headed by a committee of pondok owners led by Babor Panya and based at the Office of the Government Inspectorate in Yala. Two civil servants from that office, both pondok graduates, had effectively been seconded to work for the association, and all records were maintained there. By locating its offices within a government building and referring all enquiries to government officials, the association legitimized its activities and emphasized its loyalty to the Thai state. The association did not produce a newsletter, apparently because it had no desire to call attention to itself. The fifteen-member committee of the association met every two or three months, but general meetings of the babors were only held in response to invitations for government agencies: the babors much preferred to avoid all meetings. The association was closely linked with Nideh Waba, forming an important extension of his political network.[145]

Other categories of Islamic schools also had their own associations, which functioned as intermediaries between school owners and the state. The most prominent of these was Nideh Waba's 129-member Associa-tion of Private Islamic Schools of the Southern Border Provinces, which formed the core of Nideh's power base, and was instrumental in negotiat-ing the current system of school subsidies. A parallel but less important association, the Islamic Private Schools Council, was headed by former senator Umar Tayib in Narathiwat. Both associations represented Cate-gory 15 (1) schools. In practice, Nideh's association was a "broad church" that included his own group of less than twenty schools, more than twenty schools belonging to Lutfi's Salafist Islamic schools network, and a much larger group with more traditionalist or hybrid orientations.[146] Schools in Category 15 (2) were represented by the Association of Private Islamic Schools 15 (2), headed by Babor Zakaria of Panare. Nideh's estranged cousin Nimukhtar Waba, who was elected as a Pattani senator in 2006,[147] headed his own association, the Association of Private Schools of Pattani Province; Lutfi's son was one of the vice presidents of Nimukhtar's association, as was Nideh's secretary, Abdulrahni Kahama.[148] Abdulrahni was also secretary of the Muslim Intellectuals Association, another part of Nideh's network. Prominent and ambitious private schools owners typically sought leading roles in Islamic school associations, as a stepping stone to wider power and influence. Creating a new association was a good way to ensure your inclu-sion in delegations to meet visiting ministers and Bangkok-based officials, and the associated opportunities to solicit funding for state-sponsored proj-ects. One academic predicted that "in the future there will be more crea-tors of new associations."[149] As a result, rather than combining forces in a single powerful association, pondoks and Islamic schools were becoming increasingly divided according to arbitrary and overlapping state-imposed categories, which were overlaid by competing personal loyalties.

In other words, the primary beneficiaries of the government's chang-ing policies toward Islamic education in the Southern border provinces from the 1980s onward were those babors who transformed themselves into the owners of successful private Islamic schools. Above all, benefits accrued to those who, like Nideh Waba and Umar Tayib, represented the interests of the Islamic education sector to the Thai state, transforming themselves into "*jao babor,*" or "babor barons."[150] From 2000 to 2006, both elected senators in Narathiwat came from this group (Umar Tayib and Fakhruddin Boto), while Nimukhtar Waba's successful Pattani Senate campaign in 2006 marked his definitive elevation to the baronial league. Nimukhtar attributed his electoral success largely to his school's extensive network of current and former students.[151] The presidents of the Islamic councils in all three provinces were school owners, as were the leading challengers in the bitterly fought 2005 Islamic Council elections. The Santiphap Party, created in June 2006 with the express intention of providing a parliamentary voice for Southern Muslims, selected a number of ustadz as candidates—including the personal secretaries of both Fakhruddin and Nimukhtar, and the son-in-law of the Pattani Islamic Council president.[152] The overall effect of this trend was to strengthen an elite class of educated Malay Muslim school owners, who were fluent in Thai, politically ambitious, and represented themselves to the state as the legitimate voice of the three provinces. Yet in reality, these babor barons were increasingly detached from grassroots opinion and were sometimes alienated even from the teachers in their own schools.

Ulama

In the Islamic context, decisions relating to important or controversial matters should be taken in consultation with respected scholars, or ulama. This applies with particular force to acts of violence, which should be properly approved and sanctioned by *fatwas* issued by religious experts. But this principle raised certain definitional and practical problems: Who constituted ulama? How were they to be appointed? A leaflet circulated in the name of the Alumni Association of Students in Thailand, Malaysia, and Indonesia put the matter quite starkly:

> Did the movements try to show that they have religious scholars (*mujtahid*) on their side? We can see that no one knowledgeable about religion dares to declare themselves as leaders. The only people we heard of are the people at the *ustadz* level, which is not even enough knowledge to judge anything. Besides, those *ustadz* still have to follow those who have more knowledge than they do. Who dares to issue a fatwa today saying that killing is not a sin, when Islam forbids unjust killing as Allah stated in the Koran, Surat al-Ma'ida, Ayat 119?[153]

Defining the ulama was extremely important in the three provinces. In the past, the militant movement was known to have its own well-respected in-house ulama who gave prior approval for violent actions.[154] While many disagreed with the workings of these militant ulama councils, this consultation mechanism allowed some Malay Muslim community leaders and intellectuals to tolerate, or even collude with, a certain level of political violence. Violence was notionally constrained and delimited by Islamic principles, which stressed that women, children, and the innocent should not become targets. After January 2004, numerous incidents took place which contradicted Islamic teachings, including the murder of women, children, and Buddhist monks.[155] The initial response of many elite Muslims was to insist that these incidents must have been carried out by the Thai state, or by other non-Muslim actors. This defensive reaction was predicated on the assumption that the militant movement could not have gained approval from their ulama for these actions.

A separatist leader interviewed in the media, known as Hassam, claimed that ulama had little role in the more recent activities of the fighters (*juwae*), other than providing inspirational and moral guidance: they did not direct attacks.[156] Juwae did receive low-level support from local Islamic teachers and imams in some places; in hostage incidents at Ban Lahan and Ban Ai Batu in Narathiwat, local religious figures provided holy water for the militants to drink, which was supposed to empower them. But these figures did not count as real ulama, with the religious authority to "authorize" acts of violence carried out against the Thai state. Their involvement was symbolic and magical rather than strictly theological.

One informant suggested that ulama in the Southern border provinces could be broadly divided into three groups.[157] The first group comprised nonseparatist ulama, who emphasized tolerance and reconciliation; this group included most prominent Islamic scholars, including leading Salafists. A second group comprised ulama of the kind who previously advised the militant groups, who harbored separatist sympathies, but nevertheless believed that political violence must conform to Islamic principles and would not countenance actions such as the killing of women, children, or monks. A third group comprised new, more radical ulama, who supported new forms of violent action, such as the killing of "hypocritical" (*munafik*)—Muslims who had allegedly betrayed their religion. In the Patani context, radical ulama were conservative traditionalists, not Salafists; calls for violence did not come from "Wahhabi" elements, and the quest for international links with Middle Eastern radicalism was essentially misplaced. Ulama in the first and second categories would argue that the radical third category were not "real" ulama. Malika Zeghal has coined the term "peripheral ulama," to apply to those who adopt dissident, nonmainstream positions;[158] in the Southern Thai context, sanctioning violence was a similarly "peripheral" stance and also a clandestine one. The informant suggested that radical ulama formed a tiny minority of the thousands of scholars in the three provinces. He feared that if these radicals ever gained the upper hand, moderate, category-one ulama might be murdered, in purges comparable with the 1965 Indonesian massacres.

Ismael Lutfi wrote that ulama were literally "knowledgeable people" in Arabic. According to the hadith, "indeed the ulama are the heirs of the Prophet": those who could deeply understand and access Islamic scriptures, with a calm mind and with respect for Allah.[159] Ulama were broadly defined as educated and learned persons, who were practicing in their daily lives according to their knowledge, and were widely accepted by people in the region.[160] In other words, three central elements were needed to gain the status of membership within the ulama: profound knowledge, exemplary moral and religious practice, and recognition from the community. By definition, it was impossible for any state or secular agency to award the title of "ulama," or to debar anyone from attaining this status. The status derived from free-floating notions of wisdom and sanctity, which were collectively understood within Muslim society. At the same time, no one could directly invoke his own status as ulama to legitimize a statement; the respect associated with this status had to be bestowed by the community. The principle that an ulama needed to be accepted by the community posed problems for the militant movement, since if the identities of the ulama sanctioning acts of violence could not be known (or at least assumed), their claims to be ulama were potentially bogus.

Prominent ulama were relatively easy to identify, notably Lutfi, Ismael Saponyan, and Ghazali haji Zakariah (the leader of the Yala-based Tablighi Jamaat). Other candidates were Ismail Ali, director of PSU's College of Islamic Studies, and Maroning Salaeming, a lecturer there. Maroning held a Saudi doctorate in Islamic jurisprudence: a crucial field of study for ulama, since experts in jurisprudence were well qualified to make pronouncements on what was, and what was not, permitted.[161] But there was some debate over whether civil servants or lecturers in public universities, such as Ismael Ali or Maroning, could be considered as true ulama, since ulama status implied a degree of moral independence from the state. In this respect the private Yala Islamic College was more prestigious in religious terms, since its staff were not employed by the Thai government.

It was very hard to put a figure on the total number of ulama in the three provinces. One informant argued that people in the region were reluctant to accept the term, feeling that in order to qualify as an ulama, an individual needed a really high level of knowledge.[162] Another suggested that true ulama were very senior—more than sixty years old—as well as extremely devout.[163] Of course, the fact that ulama were perceived as having sufficient knowledge to authorize acts of violence made the award of this status something of a burden. One academic argued that ulama were supposed to preserve their dignity and could not easily defend themselves if criticized.[164] If ulama were only those with sufficient Islamic knowledge to make original religious interpretations, no one in Patani qualified: arguably, even Lutfi was only elaborating the ideas of others and was himself not an internationally recognized Islamic thinker.[165] Discussing one highly esteemed ulama in Narathiwat, an academic explained that his Islamic knowledge was not very great:

> But actually he is not a particularly impressive Islamic scholar or teacher, he doesn't even say much. But in the three provinces, not saying much is a great way to be well respected and regarded. The less you say, the better. He got a lot of credit for speaking little, and was seen as very wise. He is a very virtuous person, who does not like to perform a public role. Speaking a lot is not good. If you say ten words, nine of them right and one wrong, people will focus on the one word that is wrong. It's best to say as little as possible.[166]

Using this broad definition of ulama, including all those who commanded popular respect as Islamic teachers, there were probably around fifty famous teachers in the three provinces, and hundreds more who were also highly regarded. A 2006 research paper by a team of Malay Muslims suggested that ulama could be classified into five levels; the great majority of those in the three provinces were in the fifth and lowest category, that of "general teachers."[167]

Because of the links between ulama and violence, the state took great interest in monitoring, controlling, and co-opting ulama. The accusation that the state was manipulating ulama appeared in one leaflet purportedly issued by the militants:

The Ten Commandments of Despicable Reconciliation

6. The kafir Siamese state are building up conflict that causes division among the ulama. They spent a large budget to create fake ulama in Islam such as the Chularatamontri,[168] "turning Wajib into Haram, and Haram into Wajib."[169]

By the same token, ulama themselves sought safety in numbers. There was an Ulama Association of Patani Darusalam, but this group became factionalized, had been widely criticized for serving as a tool of Wan Nor and his Wadah faction MPs, and by 2006 was largely moribund.[170] After Islamic scholars found themselves on the receiving end of considerable state attention following the upsurge of violence in 2004, they formed the Muslim Intellectuals Association, whose secretary, Adbulrahni Kahama, was a close associate of Nideh Waba. With around two thousand members, 90 percent of whom had graduated from abroad, the association comprised mainly Islamic scholars who formerly worked closely with the Southern Border Provinces Administrative Centre—abolished by Thaksin in 2002.[171] Following the dissolution of the center, the group split up, and many members found their way onto blacklists of ulama suspected of supporting the militants. Even Abdulrahni himself had his house searched in 2005, following a meeting between Islamic teachers and the some members of the National Reconciliation Commission, at which he had raised some issues concerning investigations by the security forces.

Joining the Association of Muslim Intellectuals was a means by which individual ulama could increase their bargaining power vis-à-vis the state; at the same time, Thai government agencies also appreciated having a formal organization with which to consult. Again, important beneficiaries of the association were those in leadership positions, who could invoke enhanced credentials for themselves. Like imams and babors, ulama were pressed and co-opted into structured, bureaucratic relationships with the Thai state.

Violence

Another anonymous leaflet provided a detailed list of the strategies used by the Thai state to subvert Islam and Malay Muslim society in the border region, centering on the corruption of leaders and manipulation of ulama:

Satan Deceived the Leaders

1. The Siamese kafir harbi government launched projects that limit the free thinking of Malay Muslims. We have to obey only the Kaprae Tanbe (people who are outside real Islam)
2. Officials appointed by the Siamese government impregnated Muslim women in several areas: Yuho, Yulapong, Nam Dam Nam Kam Bakong, To Ke Kaluwang in Tanyongmas district, Rangae, Narathiwat; Ban Bayat, Ban Rico, Chane, Narathiwat; and other districts. The offspring then becomes an outcast. They do this to destroy the Malay family line.
3. The Siamese government is destroying the cultures and unity of Malay Muslims.

4. The Siamese government tries to change the translation of the Koran and Hadis according to the desire of a person who is irresponsible ("Taksin Chinawatra").
5. The Siamese government is about to issue a law to persecute the religious leaders (ulama) that won't obey their commands
6. The Siamese government gives money to the religious leaders to be on their side. They order the leaders to alter the Islamic principles and to teach the modified doctrine. Chularajamontri is one of these.
7. The Siamese government leads Patani Malay youth away from the direction of Islam with music, gambling, and other methods, like the training which takes place in each district.
8. The Siamese government has changed around Islamic principles by using the name of our Prophet to pray for Buddhist Thais.
9. The Siamese government is changing the habits of the Patani Malay Muslims to worship money.[172]

Such accusations stung. Following the January 4, 2004, attack, relations between the Thai state and prominent Islamic leaders became extremely fraught. A meeting of Islamic leaders at CS Pattani Hotel on February 4, 2004, had criticized military behavior and methods in response to the weapons heist and resolved to withdraw cooperation with state agencies unless a list of conditions were met;[173] one of these conditions was appointing a new Fourth Region Army commander, and Pisan Wattanawongkiri's name was put forward.[174] Pisan's rise to the post of Fourth Region Army commander at the end of March 2004 followed a lobbying campaign supported by the presidents of the Islamic councils in the Southern border provinces. It is extremely ironic that both the Kru-Ze and Tak Bai incidents took place under Pisan's command; he received relatively little direct criticism from local leaders even after Tak Bai. But the show of "disloyalty" by these Islamic Council presidents in February 2004 was not readily forgotten and marked the beginnings of plots by Thaksin loyalists and some Thai state actors to oust the sitting Islamic Council presidents in the November 2005 elections.

Underlying much of the ambiguity about the role of the Islamic councils was the persistent demand of the Thai state for the councils to issue an explicit *fatwa* against violence—which they always rejected. A young Pattani Muslim woman hoped in a vox populi interview published on a local news website that the Islamic councils would persuade delinquent youths to change their minds and cooperate to build peace in the South.[175] But as the former president of Narathiwat Islamic Council explained:

The religious leaders are reluctant to side with any one agent. We can't support either state or militants. There's no guarantee. Will the government support me if I sided with them? I couldn't issue a *fatwa*, since I have no confidence of protection. I am always by myself. Nobody cares about this point. It's even more so with other people....There are some places that I can't even voice my opinions. There are some flyers issued by both Thai Buddhists and Muslims accusing me of taking sides with their opponents.[176]

Leaders of the Islamic councils were in a classic double-bind; if they acceded to state demands to denounce violence, they might be branded as lackeys of the government. Yet by refraining from criticizing the militants, they were suspected of sympathizing with them. One activist complained that in the past, provincial chairmen would pass down instructions from the Chularajamontri to individual imams, but now provincial councils either did not wish to or did not dare to assert their authority and were effectively colluding with the forces of darkness.[177]

Similar issues came to the fore during meetings of the National Reconciliation Commission, which included among its members the presidents of the three provincial Islamic councils and Yala Islamic College head Ismael Lutfi. Following an NRC meeting the day after the murder of a monk and two temple boys at Pattani's Wat Phromprasit in October 2005, the NRC gave a press conference condemning the attacks. Senior Muslim figures from the South all refused to take part in the conference, claiming they felt "uneasy."[178] They privately claimed afterward that if they joined in condemning the attack, this could have affected the outcome of the forthcoming Islamic Council elections—presumably because opponents could criticize them for taking sides with the Buddhist Thai state. When the NRC made an official visit to Wat Phromprasit on the morning of November 13, 2005, led by Anand, none of the senior local male Muslim members of the NRC joined the visit. All, however, showed up shortly afterward for a lunch at Yala Islamic College.[179] The reluctance of these Islamic leaders to distance themselves from the acts of violence committed at Wat Phromprasit was a painful reminder of the challenges facing any reconciliation process in the Southern provinces and was in sharp contrast with the sympathy many Buddhist NRC members had demonstrated for the plight of Muslims affected by the violence.

When Privy Council president Prem Tinsulanond had a private meeting with a small group of Islamic leaders in Pattani on August 14, 2006, Nideh Waba used the occasion to accuse the three chairmen of the three Islamic councils—who were also present—of knowing all about the violence. Nideh's boldness in making such claims reflected his proximity to the palace, and especially to Privy Councilor Palakorn Suwannarat. When Thaksin complained to the King in late 2004 that Nideh had publicly called for him to be replaced by a royally appointed prime minister, the King supposedly replied: "Never mind. Nideh Waba is one of us."[180]

Conclusion

Islam in Thailand's Southern border provinces underwent a series of changes from the 1970s onward. The resulting picture was complex, given the range and diversity of Islamic orientations in the region, and the varied nature of Islamic education, and generalizations are difficult to make. But cumulatively, these changes undermined the moral and spiritual authority of imams and babors, and weakened both mosques and pondoks as community institutions. Some of these changes emerged from within Malay Muslim society, notably a growing antagonism between traditionalists and the new school, which had been partly triggered by the return of large numbers of graduates from the Middle East and South Asia. The rise of modernism produced demands for new mosques catering to alternative schools of Islam, which contributed to the fragmentation of already vulnerable communities. New provisions for the direct election of imams allowed this fragmentation to be acted out at close quarters, producing deep divides between different social groups. In some villages, tensions between the old and new schools spilled over into physical violence. Yet when these doctrinal tensions gradually subsided after the early 1990s, new pressures took their place.

Arguments that the violence in the South resulted from a distortion of traditionalist Malay beliefs and practices by Salafist, "Middle Eastern" Islam were misguided: the violent struggle was closely linked to pondoks and ulama affiliated with the khana kao, and had little connection with the Salafist teachings of Ismael Lutfi and his supporters. At the same time, it would be simplistic to draw too clear a distinction between a "traditionalist" Islam aligned in places with Malay separatism, and a "modernist" Islam that was essentially universalist. The khana mai became gradually aware that to reject Malayness was to risk criticism and marginalization. In May 2006, PSU's College of Islamic Studies took the remarkable step of hosting a conference on Malay Studies; in his opening remarks, Director Ismail Ali acknowledged that ignorance about the Malay way of life could contribute to violence.[181] Imtiyaz Yusuf saw this emerging stance as based on "Wahhabi-Malay cultural understandings," arguing that there was an affinity between the Arab ethnocentrism which characterized Wahhabism, and the "Malay-Islamic" "insularity" he attributed to Lutfi.[182] Such an affinity was strongly rejected by critical voices, such as the Saudara student group at PSU, who sought to construct the Salafists as enemies of Malay identity.

Since the 1960s, the Thai state had been engaged in a systematic policy of encouraging babors to convert their pondoks into private Islamic schools, teaching both a religious and secular curriculum. The state was supported in this endeavor by a group of khana mai–inclined Islamic teachers, who now saw the pondok system as a pillar of traditionalist Islam and an obstacle to the spread of "new school" thinking and practices. For them, Islam allowed for no separation between different kinds of knowledge. A leading group of prominent school owners entered into a collaborative relationship with the Thai state, seeking to advance their own religious ideas, expand and develop their educational activities, and in the process to further their own leadership and political ambitions. Some of these babors went on to assume prominent public positions, such as leadership of provincial Islamic councils and membership of the national Senate. But in the process, this collaboration led to the erosion of their moral authority: men who had previously been regarded as otherworldly Islamic teachers came to be seen as political entrepreneurs, babor barons.

Increasingly, the babor barons and their associates were drawn into a complex set of arrangements brokered by the Thai state through agencies such as the Southern Border Provinces Administrative Centre. Initiated by Prime Minister Prem Tinsulanond and closely linked to the monarchy, the SBPAC crafted a form of social compact with the Malay Muslim elite of the Southern border provinces. Under the terms of this elite ethnic bargain, leading babors supported the Thai state's attempts to curb "separatist" political violence, in exchange for which they received due recognition and advancement. By the 1990s the bargain was providing rich pickings, in the form of a generous and dubious system of financial subsidies for private Islamic schools. The owners of these schools were now firmly entrenched as a dominant social elite in the Southern border provinces. Yet their activities had contributed to the alienation of many ordinary Malay Muslims, who were not direct beneficiaries of the new deal. The new baronial elite lacked moral and religious standing, and were often disliked by the ustadz in their own schools, who viewed them as untrustworthy and exploitative. Traditional babors were forced to look to the barons for political protection, but often did so with gritted teeth.

Meanwhile the Thai authorities continued to interfere with Islamic activities at all levels. The central Islamic Council of Thailand became a political football; around the turn of the millennium, the Chularajamontri was a nonogenarian ex-Democrat MP, while the secretary-general of the council was veteran Pattani politician and serving senator Den Tohmeena. The 1997 Islamic Organizations Administration Act politicized provincial Islamic councils, turning them into proxies for wider national and local power plays. The 2005 provincial Islamic Council elections saw a wide range of actors, ranging from Bangkok politicians to the military, engaging in attempts to manipulate the outcomes in the Southern border provinces. As the electorate for the Islamic councils, ordinary imams were caught up in these machinations. The trends toward increased co-optation of Islamic leaders were reinforced following the September 2006 military coup, which saw Ismael Lutfi named a member of the military-appointed National Legislative Assembly and Nideh Waba become the prime minister's advisor on Islamic matters.[183] Both men began spending much of their time in Bangkok.

With the erosion of religious authority that was accompanied by the transformation of babors into big businessmen, and the conversion of imams into glorified vote canvassers, society in the Malay Muslim provinces had lost its moral center. Ulama could no longer be readily identified, adjudicating right from wrong had become increasingly difficult, ordinary villagers were deeply alienated from local elites, and there was a profound crisis of leadership. By 2004, Patani was open territory for extremists, separatists, jihadists, and advocates of violence. And as the next chapter will explore, politics in the border provinces was just as murky and compromised as Islam.

2

POLITICS

Politics in the deep South from the 1980s onward were characterized by two main forms of transformation: the domestication of dissent and a parallel dissent from domestication. During the 1990s, conditions in the region were apparently "normalized" through the rise of representative politics, but just as Thailand's supposed "democratization" had shallow roots—as shown in the widely welcomed 2006 military coup—so the South's "normalization" proved a mere façade. Far from reducing conflict, greater political openness after the 1997 "people's constitution" actually coincided with a rise in violence.

Who was best able to represent the views and interests of Malay Muslims to the Thai state? And who was best placed to communicate government positions to Malay Muslims? The creation of legitimate mechanisms for popular representation is a crucial problem in political systems. Holders of elective office tend to regard themselves as authorized to act on behalf of voters without consulting them closely; yet democratic theory suggests that officeholders require continuing popular consent in order to perform representative roles.[1]

Thailand is a tricky case to classify: while representative politics appeared gradually to displace military, bureaucratic, and royally dominated rule from the 1980s onward, there was no smooth "democratic transition": military coups took place in 1991 and 2006. Soldiers, bureaucrats, and monarchists typically disparaged elected politicians as corrupt and self-serving. At the same time, elected politicians became stronger, more influential, and increasingly popular with voters. The 1990s saw a modest form of decentralization established at the subdistrict level. By 2001, Thailand had an unprecedentedly dominant political party—Thaksin Shinawatra's Thai

Rak Thai—which completely controlled the parliament for more than five years. Both the 1991 and 2006 military coups had an anachronistic character, raising expectations that soon proved hopelessly unrealistic; before long, the public was demanding a return to the flawed politics of representative elections. For some, representative democracy in Thailand has failed to transcend a spurious "electoralism" that allows the Bangkok elite to bully and exploit more marginal groups and regions,[2] but others suggest that representative democracy simply has yet to be properly established.[3] This begs a central question: Were politicians elected in Patani really serving as representatives of their communities? Or were they participating in the politics of tokenism?

Problems of representation are greatly exacerbated where the legitimacy of the state itself has been widely questioned and challenged. They are further accentuated when challenges to that state have grown violent, as in Thailand's Southern border provinces since 2004. This chapter examines some of those individuals and groups who appeared to represent Malay Muslims in Thai politics. It centers on a singular problem of legitimacy: if the Thai state is not considered fully legitimate in the Southern border provinces, those who mediate between the Malay Muslim population and the Thai state are likely eventually to suffer a loss of credibility and legitimacy. This was complicated by a basic Muslim unease concerning the proper exercise of worldly authority. While the Thai authorities would insist their power in the deep South was exercised legally, that power certainly suffered from a legitimacy deficit, and in some areas the population had arguably begun withdrawing its consent.[4] Under such conditions, Malay-Muslim politicians were paralyzed as representative go-betweens, ineffective both to their own communities and to the state.

In other words, entering this representative space was to begin a process of corrosion that leads to self-destruction. Individuals affected by this process ranged from the leading Malay-Muslim politicians of the region—such as Den Tohmeena, Wan Muhammad Nor Matha and the Wadah group—to local-level leaders, and even to well-intentioned Thai bureaucrats. In an attempt to head off processes of corrosion, voters have often selected those who appear singularly rust-proof: the scions of devout or noble families, men sanctified by their credentials as the owners of Islamic schools, or even those whose own past history with the Thai state suggested that they were incapable of selling out. This was illustrated by the landslide victory of Waemahadi Wae-dao in the April 2006 Narathiwat senate election; Wae had spent more than two years in jail on charges of plotting to bomb Western embassies in Bangkok. When the case against him was finally dropped for lack of evidence, he was lionized locally. Finally, Malay Muslims have provided substantial electoral support to Thai Buddhist candidates, such as Pattani 2006 Senate election winner Anusart "Pong" Suwanmongkol. Some of Anusart's supporters argued than a liberal Buddhist would be better placed to speak in Bangkok on behalf of Pattani, since he could not be accused of disloyalty. In other words, some Malay Muslim voters opted to forgo opportunities to represent themselves, in effect endorsing virtuous rule rather than representative rule.

Bureaucrats

For the Thai state, managing the population of the three provinces meant working largely through middlemen—for the most part, village and subdistrict headmen (*phuyaiban* and kamnan). More senior government officials, normally Buddhists from other parts of the country, had little direct contact with ordinary villagers, who spoke a different language and inhabited a very different religious and cultural realm. The negative attitudes and prejudices displayed by local government officials toward Muslims constituted a major political grievance in the Southern border provinces. The argument went like this: too many government officials were Buddhists from outside the area, who did not understand the local religion, culture, or language and exercised their power over locals in a condescending or even abusive manner. Charnvit Kasetsiri has written that the deep South became "the Siberia of Thailand," a repository for low-grade government officials.[5] One normally mild-mannered Narathiwat imam became so enraged over his treatment by an obnoxious land department official that he now understood why some people decided to shoot civil servants.[6] A community leader in Pattani explained that in his area most men sent their wives to the district office to deal with the officials; they were afraid of escalating the problems if they went themselves.[7] The National Reconciliation Commission (NRC) report noted that law enforcement officials from other parts of the country could exacerbate problems in the South.[8]

Bangkokians tended to view the South as one undifferentiated whole, but an important subtext to these tensions was a deep-rooted historical antagonism between the lower and upper South. Malay Muslims in the lower South deeply resented the way in which Bangkok had subcontracted the tasks of colonizing and ruling them to natives of other Southern provinces, primarily Songkhla, Patthalung, and Nakhon Si Thammarat. They hated the way in which Buddhists from Songkhla and above lorded it over them, occupying many of the top positions in the bureaucracy. In their eyes, second-rate upper southerners who could not make the grade in their own provinces were rewarded for this incompetence and mediocrity with plum jobs in Pattani, Yala, and Narathiwat. Malay Muslims disliked speaking the Southern Thai dialect and favored a central Thai accent; they preferred to deal directly with Bangkok rather than through the unreliable mediation of upper southerners. A common refrain was that government officials who came originally from the North or Northeast were much better accepted than upper southerners. The NRC report proposed the creation of a new body that, like the old Southern Border Provinces Administrative Centre (SBPAC), would be empowered to "Recommend the transfer of wayward officials out of the area"[9]; yet the NRC's conservative assumption here was that officials came from other parts of Thailand and could readily be transferred out of the area.[10]

Ironically, the upsurge of violence in the Southern border provinces created some space for a new breed of district officers. As permanent officials of the Interior Ministry, district officers were recruited and appointed on a national basis. Faced with serious difficulties in attracting capable people to the region, the ministry opened up posts in the area to applicants who had previously failed to make the grade for district officer.[11] In July 2005, twenty "volunteer" district officers were appointed to posts in the three provinces, the majority of the thirty-two districts in the area. Most had been stuck for many years at the lower level of *palat amphoe*,[12] often because they lacked the necessary political connections to gain promotion through the ministry's notoriously suspect internal examinations. Instead, they underwent a two-stage interview process; in the second stage they faced a panel of twenty assessors, including religious leaders from the area. This little-publicized innovation demonstrated a recognition by the Interior Ministry that district officers in the three provinces needed to be sincere, dedicated, and able to make accommodations with local conditions. Those who received these appointments were generally delighted to have achieved a long-awaited promotion; most were somewhat unconventional officials, often Ramkhamhaeng graduates from rather lowly backgrounds, and with little appetite for sucking up to their superiors.[13] As I noted after speaking to one such official: "He considers himself an outsider in the Ministry, does not cultivate connections with senior people, does not play golf, and believes in doing his job properly rather than trying to ingratiate himself. This accounts for his slow promotion."[14]

Those assigned to Pattani (under royalist Prem protégé Governor Panu Uthairat) were generally more comfortable than those working for Thaksin loyalist and hardliner Governor Pracha Terat in Narathiwat: Panu was big on "public work,"[15] involving lots of meetings and consultations, in contrast with Pracha's top-down, CEO approach.[16] The idea of the volunteer district officers was an example of classic royalist thinking, assigning "good people" to serve as the frontline of the Thai state in the Southern border provinces, a continuation of the prescriptions proposed by Rama VI. Such a policy might be termed "virtuous bureaucracy"; a form of colonial administration carried out by officials of high moral caliber. Such palliatives did not address the underlying structural problems of the area. During this period, there was more serious violence in Narathiwat than in Pattani, but there was little evidence that Panu's "more virtuous" leadership had much to do with the lower levels of violence in his province than in Pracha's: the causes lay elsewhere.

If some nonlocal Thai Buddhists were ill-qualified to serve as officials in the deep South, the logical corollary was to replace them with local Malay Muslims. Echoing a demand originally articulated by Haji Sulong, some Bangkok academics expressed interest in the creation of a "representative bureaucracy" to ameliorate tensions between Malay Muslims and the Thai state, a bureaucracy staffed largely by locals.[17] Yet this solution had its own problems. Resentment against Malay Muslim government officials was extremely strong in some communities. A common complaint was that those Malay Muslims who entered the bureaucracy quickly became more Thai than Thai Buddhists, speaking in a rude or patronizing fashion to villagers, refusing to speak to them in Pattani Malay, and seeking to curry favor with their bosses by adopting Thai modes of dress and behavior.[18] It was ironic that while some Thai Buddhist officials were trying hard to learn Malay, some officials of Malay descent had apparently forgotten their mother tongue.[19] Low-level officials were often particularly rude. One informant argued that Malay Muslims were too jealous and competitive and did not try to support the advancement of their own communities.[20] Youngsters employed on the 4,500 baht job creation scheme were accused of refusing to speak Malay to people from their own villages.[21] Malay Muslims who entered the bureaucracy could be ostracized by their own communities. One former official who retired to his old village found that no one would speak to him; for more than two years he went to the mosque each day and prayed alone, before other villagers finally began conversing with him.[22] Nor was such treatment confined to government officials—local managers at a leading Pattani supermarket had similar experiences; they could live in urban areas, but found it very hard to return to their home communities for festivals such as *hari rayo*.[23]

Malay Muslim communities in the three provinces tended to be suspicious of those who made successful careers in mainstream Thai society; they were seen as having sold out to a morally questionable state. Straddling two worlds was terribly difficult: to participate effectively in the Thai system was to risk alienation from Malay Muslim society. Haji Sulong's proposals had framed "representative bureaucracy" within the broader context of autonomy; he envisaged local officials as working for an elected regional government, not for Bangkok. But if a Malay Muslim who joined the Thai bureaucracy ceased to be representative as a matter of course, then the idea of a "representative bureaucracy" was doomed to fail. The only alternatives were to persist with "virtuous bureaucracy"—sending in good administrators to administer the colony of the lower South—or to carry out a radical reform of power structures.

Autonomy

Haji Sulong had proposed autonomy for the three provinces as long ago as March 1947, in a seven-part submission to a government committee. Sulong's proposals called for (1) one entity to govern the four provinces (including Satun), with a "local-born" governor empowered to appoint and dismiss officials; (2) the use of Malay as a language of instruction in primary schools; (3) local spending of taxes collected in the area; (4) 80 percent of government officials should be local Malays; (5) acknowledgment of Malay and Thai as official languages; (6) granting provincial Islamic committees the authority to issue regulations concerning Islamic affairs; (7) and separating the Islamic courts from the provincial courts.[24] These proposals, submitted to a Pridi Phanomyong–backed government that had expressed a willingness to consider autonomy,[25] outraged conservatives. Intolerance toward ideas of autonomy only grew over the next six decades, spurred by the gradual hegemonic rise during the Ninth Reign of royalist accounts of Thai history, as taught in schools and as popularly understood by the majority of Thais. These accounts stressed the unitary nature of the Siamese state, and the diplomatic genius of its primary architect, King Chulalongkorn. Successive constitutions stated that Thailand was one indivisible kingdom; the partition of the country into provinces was a matter of administrative oversight, which did not imply any recognition of local identities. While this assimilation policy had been relatively successful in other parts of Thailand, including Satun, Malay Muslims continued to believe that their own historic region of Patani—comprising the contemporary provinces of Pattani, Yala, and Narathiwat, along with some parts of Songkhla—was a legitimate entity, distinct from the rest of Thailand. Ultimately, his public call for autonomy led to Sulong's being branded a separatist, allegations that resulted in his arrest, trial, and later murder by the Thai authorities. In fact, Sulong's position was quite different from the separatist stance adopted by the former sultan of Pattani, Tengku Abdulqadir, and his son Tengku Mahmud Mahayiddin.[26] Because the Thai state was unable or unwilling to distinguish between calls for autonomy and demands for separatism, it actually pushed some Malay Muslims—such as Ameen Tohmeena, Sulong's son and Den's brother—in a separatist direction. Jim Ockey persuasively argues that Sulong's desire to promote autonomy drew him into Siamese politics on the losing side, the side of Pridi Phanomyong: "Ironically, it was his involvement in Thai politics, rather than any attempt to separate from it, that would lead to his untimely death."[27]

Most educated Malay-Muslim informants privately favored some form of autonomy.[28] But because any Malay Muslim who publicly demanded autonomy was likely to be viewed by the Thai state as a closet separatist, such arguments were mainly advanced in a coded form. At one academic workshop concerning options for decentralizing power in the area, the local chairman opened the proceedings by declaring that all the day's discussions would be framed by the constitutional stipulation that Thailand was a unitary kingdom.[29] A Bangkok-based lecturer then asked why more radical options could not be discussed in a closed-door academic forum, but no one replied. Our hosts were clearly anxious to head off any allegations that they were promoting—or even tolerating—disloyal or separatist ideas. A serious discussion of the principles and practicalities of autonomy, let alone a separate Patani state, simply could not be conducted in public, and precious few Malay Muslims would explore these topics very far with outsiders, even in private conversations. The oppressive ideology of the unitary kingdom was remarkably hegemonic throughout Thailand. Buddhist government officials regarded any decentralization nervously, fearing a thin-ended wedge, a prelude to separatism.[30] During another lengthy workshop, all the Malay Muslim participants expressed support for modest amendments to the existing system of local government. But over dinner that evening, one participant remarked that he fully expected some sort of special administrative zone in the deep South within a few years—and everyone round the table nodded in agreement.[31]

There was some early hope that the NRC would broach ideas of autonomy in its report, that Thai Buddhist NRC members might say things that Malay Muslims dared not utter: the desirability of giving local people genuine political control of an area that differed greatly from the rest of Thailand in terms of culture, language, and religion. But while a number of NRC members—primarily Bangkokians—sought to advance the idea of some form of substantive decentralization, it soon emerged that NRC chair Anand Panyarachun was not willing to pursue the idea. After a brief flirtation with the notion of a "Pattani metropolitan area" during the first few weeks of the NRC's existence, Anand effectively banned all discussion of such proposals.[32] Some speculated that Anand had been given a "red light" from the palace, an indication that the King was implacably opposed to any kind of decentralization; Anand himself insisted that no one supported autonomy, even the separatist groups.[33] Individual NRC members used other means to advance their arguments for decentralization: Gothom Ariya promoted his views by appearing on a televised discussion to talk about options for decentralization, including elected governors in the three provinces.[34] Gothom pointedly observed that Thailand had no traditional of local government, only national autocracy or local autocracy. In practice, the idea that avowedly loyal Buddhist NRC members could venture far into political territory where potentially disloyal Malay Muslims feared to tread was difficult to translate into reality. There was some evidence, however, that the virtual taboo on mentioning proposals for autonomy was gradually fading. Shortly after his appointment as interior minister in February 2008, outspoken former police officer Chalerm Yumbamrung proclaimed his interest in exploring autonomy for the South.[35] While Chalerm was quickly slapped down by Prime Minister Samak Sundaravej, he had broken new ground by openly saying the unsayable. In doing so, he may have been responding to an earlier call by influential social critic Prawase Wasi, who had suggested in November 2007 that autonomy for the South ought to be discussed freely.[36] Prawase insisted that to talk about autonomy was not to show a lack of love for the monarchy—a crucial consideration.

Many local politicians favored building on the creation of subdistrict administrative organizations (often referred to as TAOs, the T standing for *tambon*, the Thai word for "subdistrict") by further decentralizing power structures in the deep South. One Malay Muslim TAO *nayok* (or TAO chairman) argued that the existing bureaucratic structure should be dismantled and gubernatorial elections introduced:

> I support elections for the governor and *nayok* TAO. We can abolish *kamnan*, because we already have TAOs in place. We now have two systems running in parallel...the people sent down here by the government to solve the problems don't know anything about it. None of them ever ask for my advice. I cannot rely on those people.[37]

Informants who expressed these sorts of ideas often pointed out that Bangkok and Pattaya had their own distinctive governance arrangements, and that the constitution allowed for the election of provincial governors.[38] Bangkok Thais stood accused of hypocrisy, electing their own governors from 1985 onward, but withholding the same rights from people with a strong historical and cultural claim to oversee their own affairs. The failure of the NRC even to raise elected governors as an option for the three provinces testified to the difficulty of mainstreaming quite modest proposals for reorganizing governance in the area—and had the effect of legitimating violent struggle against an apparently intractable Thai state. A further difficulty concerned fears of a "contagion effect": would granting some form of decentralization in the South lead to parallel demands in the Northeast, the North, and other parts of Thailand?

Den

One veteran observer of the political scene in Southern Thailand has observed that "unless we understand Den, we will not understand the politics of Pattani."[39] Den Tohmeena,[40] the son of Haji Sulong Abdulkadir al Fattani, was Pattani's leading politician from the 1970s onward. Den's electoral support was built on a network of imams and was inextricably linked with the politics of the provincial Islamic Council. As a son of the legendary Islamic teacher and martyr Haji Sulong, Den was able to invoke religion as a means of political mobilization. Yet his own education was almost entirely secular; he spoke Thai perfectly, held a law degree from Thammasat University, and married a Buddhist. Den's family were major landowners in Pattani, and operated several bus concessions. Den was clean-shaven, generally wore the Western style of dress favored by Thai politicians and bureaucrats, and could represent himself in Bangkok as thoroughly Thai. But in Pattani he invoked his Malay-Muslim credentials, giving emotional speeches about the oppression of the border provinces at the hands of an uncaring and oppressive Thai state. Haji Sulong and his son Ahmad (acting as a translator) were taken in by the police on August 13, 1954, and then apparently murdered extrajudicially. Den was well-known for his public displays of emotion, frequently bursting into tears on stage (and occasionally on television) when talking about his late father, and his brothers Ahmad and Ameen. A two-term Pattani MP in the 1950s for government parties, Ameen ended his days in the Malaysian state of Kelantan after fleeing Thailand in 1980, facing charges of involvement in separatist violence and believing himself targeted for extrajudicial killing.

The Tohmeena clan's story of mutual fear, mistrust, and misunderstanding was a metaphor for the dark recent history of Thailand's Malay Muslim provinces.[41] But it was also a story that Den had crafted into a political legend, repeatedly recycled for electoral purposes. Den consistently argued that his family's awful history—which invested him with heroic credentials in the eyes of many rural Malay Muslims—with the Thai state made him uniquely qualified to represent the area politically.[42] More problematically, Den also argued that it was essential for the Tohmeenas to retain a seat in parliament, for their own protection. Den's view of the Pattani electorate was both emotional and instrumental, holding that voters had a moral responsibility to elect one of his family:

> When I go out campaigning, I always tell people I ask for just one [family member] to work in the parliament. If we don't have one, it's inconvenient. If we fail this time, that's it: we will wash our hands of politics if the Tohmeena *trakun* don't get a seat. . . . We lost the Senate election, if we also lose the parliamentary election, that's it. We won't send anyone else, we are moving to some other country. I've had it with Pattani people.[43]

Den started off in local politics, was first elected to parliament in 1976, and under various party banners won a Pattani seat in every subsequent election except that of July 1995.[44] Later, Den stepped down from the lower house to contest the "apolitical" elected Senate created under the 1997 constitution. He secured an extraordinary level of support in the 2000 Senate elections, winning more than 100,000 votes. This was testimony to his remarkable success in gaining backing from local imams and religious leaders, who formed his primary network of *hua khanaen* (vote canvassers) and constituted a central element in his *phuak* (personal clique).[45] Den had long deployed his credentials as the son of Pattani's most important modern Islamic leader to exert considerable influence over the provincial Islamic council.[46] Another central element in Den's political activity was his role as a mediator between the Thai state and ordinary Malay Muslims. Den's links with imams and the Islamic councils gave him direct political access to every community in Pattani, a formidable asset. Yet this support base was only useful in Muslim majority areas; the same Islamic and Malay nationalist credentials that served as electoral assets with Muslim communities made Den unpopular with many Buddhist voters, who were strongly represented in the Pattani municipal area. In Pattani town, Den's archrival Wairot Phiphitphakdi's image as a moderate Muslim of part-Chinese descent, with excellent ties to the Thai state, was well received by Buddhists. Den operated best under the pre-1995 constituency arrangements, which had used large, province-wide parliamentary districts; by moving to the Senate, he played to his broad-based strengths, avoiding the further narrowing of constituency boundaries after the political reforms of 1997. The division of the province into constituencies split Den's vote base (*than siang*).[47]

Den firmed up his own position through the passage of the 1997 Islamic Organizations Administration Act, which created elections for provincial Islamic councils. Den was able to exert strong influence over the selection of the Pattani Islamic Council through his ties to imams and was also able to assume a prominent national role as secretary-general of the Islamic Council of Thailand. Waedueramae Mamingchi, the president of the Pattani Islamic Council, owed his initial election in 1999 directly to Den's patronage.[48]

During his time as deputy interior minister, Den became involved in the 1993 school burning episode. A series of arson attacks were targeted on schools in the South, and scapegoats were arrested. Den and Pattani governor Palakorn Suwannarat engaged in a public slanging match over the arrests; Den claimed that Palakorn subsequently abused his authority as governor to ensure that he lost the July 1995 election.[49] Den was out of parliament for less than eighteen months, but this defeat was crucial for his political future and marked a turning point for Wadah, the political faction he had founded in 1986. As a non-MP, Den had no choice but to hand over the leadership of the faction to Wan Nor,[50] who swiftly abandoned the rotation principle, never relinquished control, and continued to hold a series of high offices for the next decade.[51] Den later lamented that Wan Nor had wanted to "fly alone," yet had not achieved much other than becoming wealthy.[52] Three overlapping interpretations are possible: Den was thwarted by a political accident; Den fell foul of a personal conflict with Palakorn; or Wan Nor's installation as Wadah leader was deliberately orchestrated by the Thai elite, for whom Wan Nor was a vastly more loyal and trustworthy figure. The result was the same: Wadah's Malay nationalist roots—not to mention the *ali ulama,* or council of Islamic scholars—were now far less prominent. Wadah ceased to be a vehicle for Den's ideas—or political ambitions—and instead became simply the basis of Wan Nor's phuak, so losing its potential significance as a source of political representation.[53]

Where did Den really stand? Or was his career simply a series of pragmatic situational adjustments? For the Thai security and political elite, Den was viewed as a threat, and Wadah was a means by which he sought to expand his power and influence. Yet on another level, Den showed every sign of craving support from the Thai establishment: the desire to become a Wan Nor figure. Den was so eager to domesticate his reputation for dissent that he sometimes protested his loyalty a little too much. After he began a controversial project to build a charitable Haji Sulong Hospital at Ban Di, on the main road to Yaring, Den invited Princess Sirindhorn to perform an opening ceremony on September 16, 1996. This attempt to demonstrate his loyalty backfired when funding for the construction apparently dried up;[54] following an anonymous letter of complaint, the governor of Pattani forwarded Den a letter from the palace, asking him to answer charges that he had improperly involved the princess in a project designed to boost his electoral image.[55] Den sent a typically meticulous fourteen-page reply to the Pattani governor, in which he pointed out various factual errors in the complaint and catalogued his repeated but unsuccessful attempts to secure funding to construct the hospital.[56] He never received a response. The tone and strategy adopted by Den in the letter illustrated a curious compound of deference and venom, combining detailed legalistic arguments with the pursuit of extended personal vendettas. Despite his remarkable successes in gaining a series of high offices, Den persisted in viewing himself as tormented, maligned, and misunderstood by the powers-that-be in Thailand.

Den had good reason to believe that he was seen negatively, as developments in 2004 illustrated. Following the January 4 weapons seizure by militants at a Narathiwat army camp, he was accused by the authorities of involvement in separatist violence. In a book he published later that year, Den complained: "I have never been let off the wheel of fate of being accused of involvement or complicity in the Southern unrest, both directly and indirectly."[57] The 2004 allegations were simply the latest manifestation: "This issue has caused me pain and suffering for a long time. For several decades, it's as though someone has been endlessly bent on my destruction, and someone had placed a skeleton in my closet."[58] At the press conference, Den shed public tears (which he recorded for posterity in a photograph published in the book), while his daughter Pechdau gave a lengthy statement affirming the loyalty of the Tohmeena clan:

> Don't you think that we love this land as much as everyone else does? We feel grateful for this land and we want Thai people to have reconciliation and unity to repay the graciousness of their Majesties the King and the Queen, who have been working towards the development of the southern region for many decades, along with all the members of the royal family who have shown their loving-kindness[59] towards the Southern people.[60]

She insisted that anyone who knew her father would realize that he was not capable of supporting violence, and concluded with an emotional request: "Don't let we Tohmeena family be the accused of society any longer—if there isn't any basis, stop the accusations. Please let us live our lives in peace and happiness like any other family."[61]

Despite Den's protestations of innocence, a belief that he was somehow involved in separatist violence remained pervasive among government officials in the South and was surprisingly widely shared within sections

Fig. 2.1 The Tohmeena family: (l to r) Pechdau, Den's son, Den, and (seated) Den's late wife Phatcharaporn (Charoon Thongnual)

of the Malay Muslim community. One local informant handed me a dossier about the causes of the violence, the first sentence of which read: "BRN Organization: the leader is Den Tohmeena, replacing his brother Ameen Tohmeena (deceased), who was the former president of Pattani Islamic Council."[62] A lengthy intelligence document produced in early 2004 similarly attributed some of the Southern violence to Den.[63] For the Thai state, Den's relationship with his one-time separatist brother was his Achilles' heel: Was it possible to believe that the two men had chosen totally different paths?[64] At the same time, Den had been placed in an impossible position. Working explicitly for autonomy (his father's goal) was not permitted in the Thai context: had Den advocated it openly, he would have been denounced as a separatist and perhaps compelled to follow his brother into exile. The Thai state forced Malay Muslim leaders into the artificial categories of "loyalist" and "separatist"; to pursue the cause of maximizing autonomy for the region, Den was forced to adopt the guise of loyalist. Later, Den started to speak of exiling himself from the province, not because he had fallen foul of the Thai state, but because his proximity to Bangkok had alienated him from his core voters ("we are moving to some other country. I've had it with Pattani people"). Whereas Ameen had been banished by the Thai authorities, Den feared banishment by his own former supporters.

During 2006, Den erected huge posters on the main roads out of Pattani, offering congratulations to the King on the occasion of his sixtieth anniversary on the throne. These gestures—which were not emulated by other Muslim politicians in the three provinces—were not the actions of a conventional Malay nationalist. Den also admitted that he would very much like the job of Chularajamontri, a position whose authority was rejected by many Malay Muslims as illegitimate.[65] The dominant reading of Den's stance—by his political opponents, and by many commentators and students of Pattani politics—was that he sought protection from the Thai state in order to advance an agenda based on ideas of Malay nationalism. Yet an equally plausible reading, conforming with his public position, was that Den sought primarily to parlay nationalist rhetoric into conventional political power within the Thai state. In this respect, Den, like many other Malay Muslims in Thailand, occupied the sort of hybridized position described by Morton Grodzins as the "traitriot," an individual who combines elements of the traitor and the patriot.[66] In fact, Den supported neither the political status quo in Thailand, nor a violent separatist movement. Rather, he hoped for the creation of an autonomous region in the Southern border provinces, in line with his father's 1947 proposals.[67] But because the Thai authorities were incapable of imagining autonomy other than as a disguise for separatism, Den was terminally branded as a separatist.

Den faced serious political problems when his Senate term ended in 2006. First, he had recently been ousted from his position as Islamic Council secretary-general. His replacement, former Thai Rak Thai Party minister Phichet Sathirachawala, used substantial financial resources to create a rival network of Islamic Council presidents;[68] with some well-targeted campaign contributions during the November 2005 provincial Islamic council elections, Phichet bought up much of Den's power base. While Waedueramae Mamingchi's team won nineteen out of thirty seats on the Pattani Islamic Council with support from Den, the president subsequently turned on his major backer. As the price of his support, Den had expected Waedueramae to appoint his nephew as Pattani's representative on the central Islamic Council, and to use his influence to back Den's daughter Pechdau in the April 2006 Pattani Senate election. But following his reselection, and boosted by a more diversified support base, Waedueramae sought to assert his independence. He broke with Den, had himself appointed to the central Islamic Council, and did nothing to help Pechdau—who was narrowly defeated in her Senate bid. In a matter of just a few months, Den's power had ebbed away. The Tohmeena clan (*trakun*) no longer held any major political position. Den was left a bitter man, no longer able to position himself as the link between Pattani's Malay Muslims and the central authorities. He chose to blame his defeats primarily on the influence of money politics:

> I feel disappointed with the people of Pattani when there's money involved. It's like I can trust no one any more these days, even my old acquaintances. They don't come to my house any more. They know that MPs or senators cannot do much to help them. People now got smarter. Some even have the nerve to approach the governor. It's totally different from the old days.[69]

Pechdau accepted that Den had no longer been able to rely on support even from groups he had personally created, such as the tadika organization in Pattani province:

> We had a meeting to find out why my father's *tadika* groups turned away from us....We have to find out why the same musical band that my dad used to play with was not the same when I took over the lead singer position. Some band members are old; some are still young. The audience has changed. Six years ago my father got about a hundred thousand votes. What's happening now? Why couldn't my father handle his own *tadika* group that he set up himself? We've reached the conclusion that within the six year period, my father got so busy dealing with the Central Islamic Council of Thailand that he didn't have time to have a meeting. We were not united.[70]

In his pursuit of national power and influence, Den had neglected his own grassroots political base, wrongly assuming that Pattani voters would never turn against his family. Den had fallen victim to his own political mythology: during his long absences in Bangkok, his power and standing in Pattani had significantly eroded, and neglect had loosened his ties to the voters. His attempts to straddle two worlds, operating as a senator and Islamic Council leader in Bangkok, while remaining a largely absent local hero in Pattani, had come unstuck. By allowing the Thai state to domesticate his reputation for dissent, Den triggered his own rejection by his erstwhile Pattani supporters.

Wadah

The Wadah group was originally created by Den Tohmeena in 1986 as a political faction, "a collaboration of a group of Muslim politicians, Muslim intellectuals and Islamic interest groups in order for them to have a way of communication and to build political negotiation power."[71] Wadah aspired to represent the interests of the Malay Muslim community of the Southern border provinces at the national level and succeeded in gaining at least five or six parliamentary seats in every election from 1986 to 2001.[72] Wadah's founders assumed that a Muslim political party had little future in Thailand; instead, they formed a political faction that could join ruling coalitions and so secure a quota of ministerial positions for its members.[73] Thai political parties typically comprised loose alliances of factions; faction bosses did not hesitate to lead their followers from party to party in search of greater recognition and benefits. Wadah would remain mobile, ready to embrace the party best-placed to serve its interests. Other core members included Wan Nor, Najmuddin Umar, Ariphen Utarasint, Muk Sulaiman, Paisal Yingsamarn, and Buranudin Useng, as well as Sudin Puyuttanont.[74] As Daungyewa Utarasint argues,[75] Wadah MPs were mainly lawyers and teachers from low- or middle-income families, rather than the businessmen who now dominated electoral politics in most other areas of Thailand. Indeed, they had much in common with previous generations of Thai MPs from the 1970s and much earlier. Wrong-footed by the premature election of 1986, Wadah initially joined the Democrat Party. Den went to elaborate lengths to consult local religious leaders about the process of candidate selection, staging meetings, and even making candidates pledge an oath to adhere to the principles of Islam if they were elected. Wadah had an informal ali ulama, a council of Islamic scholars; Den invoked their authority as a negotiating ploy in his dealings with the Democrats:

> If the Democrats don't agree to follow the way of the Wadah group at all, we have received a resolution from the *ali ulama* that we can withdraw from the party. This is a promise to God made in front of the *ali ulama*. If the *tok guru* and *to imam* see that the Democrat Party will cause damage to Islam and doesn't respond according to our needs, the representatives of the Democrat party in Pattani, Yala and Narathiwat are willing to resign. If we leave the party, that means we will resign as MPs. If it's the will of Allah, the three candidates of the Wadah group in Pattani and at least two candidates in Narathiwat and two in Yala are ready to resign, if we feel that the Democrat Party is one in which we should stay no longer.[76]

Den's approach was a mixture of Islamic rhetoric and legalism, arguing to the Democrat leadership that his support for their party and government was conditional upon religious oaths. The objective of these devices was twofold. First, for religious leaders and voters in the border provinces, this high-sounding rhetoric reinforced the view that Wadah was an Islamic organization dedicated to advancing Malay Muslim interests. Second, by invoking the authority of the ali ulama, Den hoped to strengthen his hand at the national level, by arguing that his conditions for supporting the Democrats were nonnegotiable. The basic demand of Wadah was for at least one ministerial or deputy ministerial position, which they could use to advance their own agendas. But the rule book of the Wadah group, which closely resembled that of a regular Thai political party—providing for branches at provincial, district, subdistrict, and village levels—made no reference at all to the ali ulama.[77] Apparently, the ulama could be invoked at will, but had no official power or standing.

Despite Den's elaborate bargaining ploys, Wadah was unable to secure a ministerial seat in the 1986 Democrat-led administration. Den was slated for the post of deputy interior minister, but when the final cabinet list appeared, his name was missing. According to some rumors, the security agencies had rejected Den as insufficiently loyal to the Thai state to occupy such a sensitive post. Den's rejection formed part of a wider internal crisis within the party, which led to the resignation of secretary-general Veera Musigapong. This episode marked a decisive break between Den, Wadah, and the Democrats; from then on, most leading Muslim politicians from the Southern border provinces believed that the Democrats could not be relied on to support their cause. After a brief sojourn in the small Prachachon Party (later absorbed into the Solidarity Party), Wadah joined Chavalit Yongchaiyudh's recently created New Aspiration Party (NAP), where they resided for another decade. Wadah members spoke with immense fondness of Chavalit, whom they saw as the only senior figure in Thai politics who was really capable of sympathizing with the plight of Malay Muslims.[78] Den finally became a deputy health minister in Chatichai Choonhavan's ill-fated and short-lived last cabinet;[79] after the 1991 coup, he was deputy interior minister under the NAP quota for two years: from September 1992, before stepping down on October 25, 1994 (as previously agreed) in favor of Wan Nor.[80]

The NAP years proved Wadah's heyday: after Thaksin became prime minister in 2001, Wadah was increasingly subordinated to the designs of a politician who proved deeply unpopular in the South. New Aspiration merged with Thai Rak Thai in 2002, and by default Wadah MPs became Thaksin MPs. Wadah's support for Thaksin was extremely fraught after January 2004, when Thai Rak Thai MPs struggled to defend the government over such controversial actions as the storming of the Kru-Ze mosque on April 28 and the Tak Bai incident of October 25. Wadah MPs were reduced to mouthing platitudes about their past achievements—including religion on Thai identity cards, permitting the wearing of the hijab at government educational institutions,[81] and setting up an Islamic bank.

Wadah was viewed with persistent suspicion in Bangkok. Ariphen Utarasint,[82] an eight-term Narathiwat MP, was a Thammasat law graduate and former professional lawyer who briefly served as deputy education minister in 1997. The leading politician in Narathiwat, Ariphen was not a Wan Nor protégé; he came from the old Den group[83] and served as the link between Wan Nor and Najmuddin.[84] Ariphen argued that the violence had made it impossible for representative politics to work: most of the violence was committed by the militants, but the villagers did not want to hear this:

> Now, when things happened in any village, rumor has it that the killing was done by the authorities. About 10 per cent of the time, it's really the officials [That leaves about 80 per cent to the work of *naeoruam*]. Illegal activities are just a small portion of the problem. But we can't really say that. They will accept us only if we say the authorities did it all. The villagers will automatically perceive us as the government's men. That's why I say it's hard to be in politics these days...the villagers, they are ready to jump to the conclusion that the authorities did it.[85]

To speak out openly about the problem of militant violence was impossible, since voters simply did not want to hear the truth from their political representatives. Under these circumstances, politicians could do or say very little: "Not only the Wadah group are like that, but some MPs from the opposition parties are acting the same way. Nobody really wants to take any role."[86] To be elected in the three provinces, Ariphen added, you now had to say negative things about the government. Ariphen's statements would have surprised those who saw him as implicated in the violence.[87] Along with Den and Najmuddin, Ariphen was accused of involvement in violence in March 2004 by Anupong Pantachayangkul, a former Toh Deng kamnan, who later insisted that he had made the false allegations under torture.[88]

One Narathiwat imam argued that Ariphen also lacked achievements and "could not do anything for himself"; he was also tainted by allegations of "benefit seeking."[89] Ariphen had also "lost credit" by defending his brother Romali ("Ber Li"),[90] who had fled Thailand for Malaysia after being accused of separatism; as a result, he was unpopular with Buddhists and state-oriented Muslims.[91] Ariphen was criticized by Buddhists for supposedly having advocated some form of autonomy for the border provinces in a research paper he had written, but the paper in question was actually rather anodyne.[92] The story of Ariphen and Romali had strong echoes of the Den-Ameen story: one brother working within the Thai system, the other supporting separatism. One veteran Pattani politician insisted that the old allegations about Romali had nothing to do with Ariphen, whose brother now had no influence in the militant movement.[93]

In the April 2, 2006, election, Ariphen narrowly failed to win a parliamentary seat after he gained around 19 percent of the popular vote. One leading Narathiwat politician attributed this failure to Ariphen's lack of groundwork and detachment from the voters.[94] Yet shortly afterward, his wife Halimoh won a Senate seat in Narathiwat, testifying to the residual strength of Ariphen's political networks. According to Ariphen, her success derived from his vote canvassers and support base.[95]

Najmuddin Umar[96] was closer to the grassroots than other Wadah MPs: proud of his "big-hearted rogue" style,[97] he kept an open house in violence-prone rural Tanyong Mas and was often asked to mediate between villagers and the authorities—for example, during the marine hostage incident at Tanyong Limo in 2005. Elected to parliament in March 1992 and in 2001, he was without a seat for most of the 1990s.[98] Najmuddin retained close ties with Den and was the most distant Wadah member from Wan Nor.

Both Ariphen and Najmuddin faced intense political competition from the Yawohasan clan, which controlled the Narathiwat Provincial Administrative Organization from 2004 and took Najumuddin's old parliamentary seat in 2005.[99] Political violence in Narathiwat was rampant. Najmuddin's rival Kuheng Yawohasan was shot at with an AK-47 during the 2005 elections. In 2006, senator Fakhruddin Boto, was shot and seriously injured, while former Provincial Administrative Organization president Nisoh Meuka was shot dead, also with an AK-47. Distinguishing between "militant" violence and violence driven by electoral contestation and turf wars was extremely difficult.

All Wadah group MPs who stood for constituency elections in February 2005 lost their seats, punished by the electorate for abandoning their interests. Veteran MP Muk Sulaiman[100] was a key member of the Wan Nor group within Wadah and had served as Wan Nor's political secretary. A nimble-tongued lawyer descended from a former sultan, he had been involved in politics since the 1975–76 forty-five-day protests, triggered by the extrajudicial killing of five Muslim youths.[101] There was little love lost between Muk and Den: in the 2004 PAO elections Muk had supported Set Alyofaree, who easily defeated Den's nephew Ameen, a development that marked the beginning of Den's political problems.[102] But 2004 was also a bad year for Muk. Muk argued that the only way to advance the interests of Malay Muslims was to join the government: "That's the only way I can fight for my people. During my twelve years in politics, I have accomplished a lot—better infrastructure, the Islamic bank, and the opportunity for Muslims to serve in state positions. This is just the beginning of our fight for our rightful opportunities."[103] Arguments that limited past successes validated a lasting Faustian pact with Thaksin failed to impress the voters. The more the Wadah group supported central government policy that ran counter to the wishes of local voters, the more retribution from the electorate.[104] In one widely discussed incident, Muk stood up to speak in a mosque—and everyone walked out.

> I won election all along until the Tak Bai incident. I failed because I was with Thai Rak Thai. People came up to me in tears saying that they wanted to vote for me but couldn't do that, knowing that I would have to support Thaksin. I tried to tell them that we really needed to be on the administrative side. It's useless to be in the opposing team. I can understand the hatred the people must feel. I personally was upset with him over the way he handled the violence. However, we have to look towards benefits in the future.[105]

Muk claimed that the government had been very unhappy with him after he criticized in a television interview its handling of the Somchai Neelaphaichit case, in which a prominent Muslim lawyer was kidnapped and murdered in Bangkok. After this episode, he had usually made such comments privately. In the 2005 general election, Muk produced two contrasting campaign posters: one featuring Jawi script,[106] showing him in Malay garb, and a Thai-style poster in which he wore Western dress. The two posters nicely illustrated Wadah's pragmatic political stance. In Muk's parting words to me: "We can't have the best, only the least worst."[107]

When Thaksin visited the South during 2005, Wadah ex-MPs rarely turned up to greet him in public.[108] Yet despite this distancing, Wadah remained hopelessly tainted; in the abortive and farcical April 2, 2006, general election, only former treason suspect Najmuddin Umar gained more than 20 percent of the popular vote: Wadah members could not win election to parliament, even if they faced no opposition candidates.[109] Even Ariphen accepted that there was considerable popular disillusionment with the performance of parliamentary politics in the wake of Wadah's incorporation into Thai Rak Thai: "[People] didn't know who to turn to anymore. Politicians need to be responsible for their duties, not just concerned about their posts."[110]

As a political experiment, Wadah largely failed. Starting with ambitious aims of providing a voice for Malay Muslims in national politics, the grouping gradually assumed the character of a typical Thai political faction, characterized by infighting, paralysis, and lack of substantial

Figs. 2.2–2.3 Former Pattani MP and Wadah member Muk Sulaiman displays both Malay Muslim and Thai credentials on contrasting posters for the February 2005 election. He lost his seat (Duncan McCargo)

achievements. After Wan Nor assumed control in 1995, the pursuit of power became an end in itself, rather than a means of serving Wadah's supposed constituency. Wadah had become Wan Nor's personal vehicle, the core of his extended phuak. During 2006, a group of Malay-Muslim politicians backed and led by former minister Phichet Sathirachaval, formed the new Santiphap Party. This avowedly Muslim party sought to displace Wadah, creating an alternative political faction; most prospective parliamentary candidates were closely connected with the Islamic school system. Alas, Santiphap had foundered by the time of the December 2007 elections.

Wan Nor

Wan Muhammad Nor Matha[111] had been brought into politics through the invitation of former prime minister Kukrit Pramoj, who had recruited him into the Social Action Party in the 1970s. Strikingly handsome, unmarried, and with a reserved, gentlemanly demeanor,[112] Wan Nor possessed immense personal charm which masked a determined and opportunistic player of the political game. Originally a lecturer at the Songkhla Teachers" College (now Rajabhat Songkhla), he quickly became a vice principal; he was very active and admired for his excellent personal characteristics.[113] He was not from a powerful political family, though his grandfather had been a Dato Yuttitham (Islamic judge) at a time when the position was not especially prestigious. He received backing from an uncle who served as a kamnan and traveled all over Yala's province-wide parliamentary constituency, building a political base, helping people out and campaigning. In the eyes of Yala voters, one of Wan Nor's strong points was his name: no other "Muhammad" had achieved high political office in Thailand. Other leading Muslims used neutral-sounding or Thai names likely to reduce prejudice against them, but Wan Nor had never compromised in the presentation of his identity.

In 1986, Wan Nor joined Den's Wadah group, eventually taking it over when Den was defeated in the July 1995 election. During his time as communications minister and then as house speaker (1995–96; 1996–2000), Wan Nor was able to firm up his personal dominance of Yala politics, developing a very strong network of political leaders under his control. While New Aspiration lost power following the Asian financial crisis in late 1997, Wan Nor managed to retain his post as president of parliament, which gave him a strong and continuing national political base, as well as immense *barami*.[114] Village and subdistrict headmen formed the core of Wan Nor's Yala network.[115] But in his determination to control Yala politics at all levels—including the Senate, the provincial council, and the Islamic Council—creating a powerful and extended phuak, Wan Nor sullied his early reputation for integrity. Some of these around him were rather less scrupulous, and Wan Nor's image as a very clean and decent politician was increasingly besmirched. He had long served as a channel for funds from the Middle East into local communities, supporting activities such as tadika. During the period from 1993 to 1997, Wan Nor and two fellow Yala MPs channeled funding worth almost 66 million baht (roughly $2.64 million at precrisis rates) to tadika in the province.[116] He also provided financial support for hajj activities, paying for selected local politicians and their spouses to visit Mecca.[117] But he relied increasingly on "influence"[118]—darker forms of power—and forged a close alliance with a core group of Wadah MPs: Ariphen Utarasint, Muk Sulaiman, Phaisan Yingsaman, and (via Ariphen) Najmuddin Umar.

Yala politics were dominated by Wan Nor: his principal ally was the powerful provincial administrative organization president, Aziz Benhawan, with whom he shared his vote base, along with veteran MP Phaisan Ying-saman.[119] Wan Nor's brother Mukhtar served as Yala's sole senator from 2000 to 2006. Phaisan acted as a loyal liaison and bagman, linking Wan Nor, local politicians, and the Islamic Council, through which Wan Nor sought to control imams.[120] Opposition to Wan Nor came mainly from the Democrat-aligned Dawut Sa, a charismatic Saudi-trained religious teacher who had spent nineteen years as one of Wan Nor's principal lieutenants before becoming disillusioned with him.[121] Dawut narrowly failed to defeat Aziz in the controversial 2004 PAO elections, but Democrat candidates ousted Phaisan and Buranuddin Useng in 2005.

Wan Nor's relations with all of these associates were highly unequal: "Wan Nor is the school principal, and the others are just ordinary teach-ers."[122] But after Wadah joined forces with Thai Rak Thai,[123] Wan Nor struggled to maintain his standing. Although he held the apparently power-ful offices of communications minister, interior minister, deputy prime minister, and agriculture minister during Thaksin's first term, he did not serve for more than eighteen months in any of these positions: Thaksin seemed deliberately to rotate his lieutenants so frequently that they could not develop much independence. While president of parliament, Wan Nor had commanded immense respect in Yala, but holding high ministerial office in the Thaksin government fractured his relationships with Malay Muslim voters at home. Thaksin proved extremely unpopular in the South as a whole, and especially in the Southern border provinces. His outspoken comments about "Southern bandits"[124] infuriated Malay Muslims, his politically mo-tivated disbanding of the SBPAC and Civil-Police-Military joint command (CPM 43) won him few friends, and his crass mishandling of the April 28 and Tak Bai incidents in 2004 made him a bête noire in the border region. Voters in the Southern border provinces had supported Wadah and the NAP, but then found that Wadah had sold out to Thaksin.

Wan Nor's achievement in holding high national political office almost continuously between 1995 and 2005[125]—virtually the only Thai politician to do so—was remarkable in any terms, let alone for a Malay Muslim, and illustrated his considerable bargaining power with Bangkok. Yet the longer he exercised power, the more questions emerged about Wan Nor's personal wealth and his penchant for ostentatious display. This was epito-mized by the elaborate residence he constructed for himself on the out-skirts of Yala town, a cross between a teak palace and a Disney castle. Some other Wadah MPs had built fine houses,[126] but Wan Nor's enormous mansion, one of several properties he owned, beggared description. As one former senator put it, the grand houses of Wadah politicians were one of the group's main achievements.[127] Wan Nor's newfound wealth became the subject of investigative and speculative reports in the Thai language press, and in 2004 the politician filed a libel suit against the business newspaper *Prachachat Thurakit*, over stories alleging that he had concealed millions of baht in assets by listing them in the names of his close aides.[128] As one informant observed, according to the Prophet Muhamad, your house was something you might be asked about after your death: Wan Nor was likely to face a fair few questions about his Yala mansion.[129]

Some of Wan Nor's old associates, such as Dawut Sa, watched with growing unease as the mild-mannered *ajan* was slowly seduced by the lure of power and money.[130] For them, Wan Nor gradually betrayed those who had helped him achieve electoral office, changing from an outspoken critic

Fig. 2.4 One wing of bachelor ex-minister Wan Muhammad Nor Matha's immense mansion on the outskirts of Yala town (Duncan McCargo)

of money politics to a masterful dispenser of political patronage and favors of all kinds.[131] His earlier dissent was thoroughly domesticated by his immersion in electoral politics. A more generous reading was that Wan Nor simply found himself enmeshed in bureaucratic power structures that he could not effectively manage or control, especially when he became interior minister. Some of his supporters urged him not to take the post, believing that accepting it was asking for trouble.[132] According to one sympathetic informant, when Wan Nor took the job he was blocked by the mafias within the ministry and lacked access to accurate information from well-informed people on the ground.[133] For Wan Nor's sympathizers, his cooperation with Thaksin had placed him in an impossible position; for Wan Nor's detractors, he had brought these difficulties on himself through arrogance, overweening ambition, and simple greed. Exactly why Wan Nor persisted in his self-destructive alliance with Thaksin is difficult to explain, but over time the bonds between the two men became harder and harder to sever.

It is striking that the upsurge of political violence in the border provinces broadly coincided with Wan Nor's elevation to the position of interior minister in late 2002. After Wan Nor assumed this post, disappearances became commonplace in the deep South, and Thaksin's notorious "war on drugs"—a policy of systematic extrajudicial killings—was soon under way. Wan Nor himself said of drug dealers: "They will be put behind bars or even vanish without a trace. Who cares? They are destroying our country."[134] Some informants saw the renewed violence partly as a concerted attempt to create trouble on Wan Nor's watch, so undermining his standing.[135] Wadah had become part of the problem, not part of the solution. In one underground leaflet apparently from a Buddhist group disgusted with the performance of both government officials and local politicians, Wadah politicians were portrayed as senior figures in a corrupt and dysfunctional political order, inextricably allied with Thaksin: "It's the fate of the Yala people to have corrupted administrators—Den, Muk, Din, Ariphen and Manor. Those damned Thaksin and all the army commanders! Can you promise us that no more Thais will be killed? I'll wait for you to announce that on TV."[136]

Den and Wan Nor were two contrasting examples of Malay Muslim political careerists. Den's political life was based on his "rebellious" family credentials, credentials that made him supremely electable in Pattani but deeply mistrusted in Bangkok. He spent his entire career trying to square this impossible circle, seeking to make himself fit for the great offices of full minister or Chularajamontri—yet these high honors were to elude him, despite his incessant efforts. Den's failure was made explicit when he was accused of separatist activities in March 2004. By the time of the 2006

Senate elections, Den was losing control of his local base, having spent far too much time in the Thai capital's corridors of power. Wan Nor, by contrast, was the golden boy of the Siamese elite, the "good Muslim," who was willing to accommodate and domesticate himself completely to the requirements of Bangkok.[137] As such, he was able to reap great financial rewards and to hold the exalted offices of Parliament president and interior minister, pinnacles of which Den could but dream. Yet Wan Nor's subservience to Bangkok soon led to his downfall; his long, increasingly distasteful liaison with Thaksin Shinawatra, during which he fronted the brutal repression of his own people, eroded his credibility and triggered the dissent that undermined his electoral base. The two most successful Malay-Muslim politicians Thailand had ever known were both ruined by their inability successfully to negotiate their relations with Bangkok.

TAOs

One major political innovation of the 1990s was the creation of elected subdistrict organizations all over Thailand. These tambon administrative organizations (TAOs) allowed the Thai state to engage in a low-level form of decentralization, yet one that did not challenge the overarching authority of unelected provincial governors, career bureaucrats from the Ministry of Interior.[138] The creation of TAOs was championed primarily by the Democrat Party, at a time when many local officials (including headmen and kamnan) had close ties to the rival New Aspiration Party; "decentralization" was partly about subverting existing patronage mechanisms and creating new networks of local canvassers. Many TAOs had close personal ties to the cliques of provincial administrative organizations and MPs. Despite their limited budgets and powers, TAOs offered new political space for Malay Muslims in the Southern border provinces. The great majority of TAO members and chairmen (nayok) were local Muslims. Nayok commonly argued that as the TAO became better established and had more scope to dispense budgets, villagers took more interest in the TAO and were more likely to seek assistance from the nayok.[139] To some extent, TAOs displaced more traditional modes of leadership in the area: both the standing of religious leaders and the customary supremacy of kamnan and village headmen. At the very least, the introduction of TAOs introduced an additional dimension to political life in the region, enhancing electoral contestation and competition for resources. In parallel, the creation of TAOs raised more questions about the nature of political legitimacy: did elected local leaders (usually Muslim) have greater legitimacy than appointed officials such as district officers (almost always Buddhist)? Did TAOs offer some sort of model for the further expansion of decentralization?

As with parliamentary representation, local representation was a problematic issue. In an extreme reading of the problem, a TAO head explained that for devout Malay Muslim villagers, whoever controls a budget cannot be trusted; whoever derives benefits cannot be trusted; and whoever is elected cannot be trusted.[140] TAOs were widely viewed by local people as corrupt organizations that needed to prove themselves,[141] while nayok were often viewed negatively.[142] After gaining office, some nayok took up drinking, neglected to pray regularly, and socialized with district officers and other Buddhist officials at nonhalal restaurants.[143] Most TAOs had removed the logos from their official pickup trucks; ostensibly, this was for security reasons, but in practice concealing their identities was useful if they went out drinking and parked in entertainment areas.[144] Politicians did not command respect in their own right, but only on the basis of the positions they held and the favors they could dispense: a politician who lost an election became a nobody. If people spoke at a seminar, the speakers who were able to refer to the Koran and demonstrate religious knowledge would command the most attention and respect.[145] For many Muslims, the only legitimate authority was spiritual,[146] and all worldly authority was inherently corrupt; there was an inherent tension between religious values and the realities of Thai societal organization. Accordingly, the decentralization of power and associated expansion of political space was a mixed blessing for Malay Muslim communities. Some informants even suggested that introducing more elections was part of a plot by the Thai state to destabilize their communities and to set Muslims at one another's throats, emulating the British imperial policy of "divide and rule."[147] Notionally, TAOs were responsible for economic development,[148] while kamnan dealt with matters of security—yet in practice, the distinction was not always hard and fast.[149]

The situation for TAOs became more difficult after January 2004, especially in Narathiwat, where Governor Pracha Terat treated nayok with open contempt and stated publicly that TAOs were full of militants and militant sympathizers.[150] By contrast, nayok insisted that the militant movement barred members from participating in electoral politics, viewing this as a form of collaboration. To enter local politics was a risky business, inviting the mistrust of both the state and the militants. TAOs in areas with high levels of militancy struggled to operate effectively. Many TAO offices were the targets of arson attacks: one nayok kept the TAO fire truck parked on his drive at home, because it was unsafe to leave it at the office.[151] Another TAO relocated its offices to a local school for safety. One nayok hired suspected militant youths to guard the TAO office at night. Villagers in one area rejected TAO funds to complete a nursery center, saying they did not want to take money from the Thai state. In such communities, collecting local taxes was practically impossible: one nayok explained that he could only collect 70,000 baht of the 400,000 baht local tax bill, and much of what he collected came from Buddhist businesses and households.

In the deep South, questions relating to competence and corruption were inextricable from larger matters concerning loyalty to the Thai state: a corrupt TAO was implicitly a disloyal TAO; a nayok who questioned instructions was not just independent minded, but a closet separatist; a bullying district officer was not just a bad official, but an example of Thai state oppression. Despite the fact that they were not actually civil servants, elected TAO members were regularly targeted by militants; at the same time, they were viewed with suspicion by the security forces, who paid regular and often unwelcome visits to the homes and offices of TAO nayok.

As elsewhere in Thailand, TAO elections were deeply vitiated by money politics. One nayok estimated that around 1.5 million baht was needed to secure election to the post: many people spent similar amounts and yet still lost.[152] Some nayok won election "unopposed"; in fact they normally did have opponents, whom they had intimidated or bought off in some way. One nayok had made his former rival his deputy. But in many other areas postelection bitterness and bickering divided communities and deepened existing tensions.

Discussions with TAO members often raised questions about the limited powers of the organizations. Some nayok wanted the power to close down entertainment places (such as karaoke lounges) within their subdistricts.[153] In fact, however, TAOs did have the power to issue local bylaws and were perfectly entitled to take a tough line on matters such as building controls.[154] Over one workshop lunch, it soon became clear to me that most nayok did not want to enact or enforce bylaws, which would make them unpopular and could potentially jeopardize their reelection.[155] Only a handful of TAOs in the three provinces had exercised their right to set bylaws. While they were happy to criticize state agencies for their failure to regulate "undesirable" activities, most TAO nayok did not actively seek to enhance their own authority to address such issues. A common observation was that Malay-Muslim villagers were usually silent in official meetings, but would complain furiously in the teashops;[156] in similar fashion, TAO nayok would use seminar discussions to berate the Thai state, yet often showed little interest in using their own powers to effect changes in their localities.

One study has suggested that Malay Muslims had higher levels of political participation and more positive views of decentralization than people in other parts of Thailand.[157] In theory, TAO members had greater legitimacy than Thai government officials, or than headman and kamnan who, though elected, were directly answerable to the Interior Ministry. Yet in practice their involvement with electoral politics had the ironic effect of delegitimizing many TAO members in the eyes of their communities. Although most TAO nayok in the border provinces were Muslim, they were often viewed as having sold out to the Thai state. This made it difficult for TAOs to offer a prototype for any more substantive form of decentralization in the region; innovative and impressive TAOs did exist in places, but most had been captured by political or financial interests.

Conclusion

This chapter has explored the manifold contradictions surrounding the politics of representation—both by bureaucrats and elected representatives—in the Southern border provinces of Pattani, Yala, and Narathiwat. It began with the assumption that the power and authority of the Thai state in those provinces is not fully legitimate. Many Malay Muslims, openly or privately, believe that Bangkok has no right to govern their provinces in the same highly centralized fashion as it governs the rest of Thailand. This leads minimally to some version of the following positions, which are widely supported by Malay Muslims:[158] local politicians such as nayok TAOs should be drawn mainly from the ranks of Malay Muslims and should implement policies appropriate to the distinctive character of the area; national politicians elected from the three provinces should be local Malay Muslims who are able fully to represent the concerns of the population; Malay Muslims should have some formal or informal quota of ministerial posts, or high-level representation; Malay Muslims should have their own political grouping or party, which forms the basis for negotiation with Bangkok; the participation of Malay-Muslim politicians in national-level politics should always be conditional on securing certain policy concessions from the state; Malay-Muslim politicians should never allow themselves to become incorporated into the ruling apparatus of the Thai state, but should always remain on the side of the people who elected them.

These conditions amounted to a formula for "representative politics on Thai terms," a politics of minority representation, according to which Malay Muslims would enjoy certain political space and privileges in return for accepting the framework of the Thai state. During the 1990s, several of these conditions were met, and representative politics on Thai terms appeared for a time to be working. During the Thaksin period, however, the Wadah group abandoned its supporters, leading many Malay Muslims to question the sincerity of both local elites and the Thai state. This breakdown of trust fuelled more radical demands for substantive decentralization—such as the election of provincial governors—for some form of autonomy, or even to demands for the creation of an independent Patani state. These demands implied a shift away from seeing Malay Muslims as a minority within Thailand and toward recognizing them as a majority community within their own region. In other words, the politics of minority representation would be replaced by a politics of majority representation.

Leaders seeking to present themselves as representatives of the Malay Muslim community could draw on seven alternative sources of moral legitimacy, or some combination of these (examples in brackets), which offered alternative paths to political power:

1. Noble descent from former *jao muang* (Wairot Phiphitphakdi)
2. Family suffering and struggle (Den Tohmeena)
3. Personal morality and integrity (Wan Nor)
4. Personal suffering and struggle (Dr. Wae)
5. Dedication to local interests and community service (Ariphen, Najmuddin)
6. Religious standing (Fakhruddin Boto)
7. Disinterested sincere Buddhist (Anusart Suwanmongkol)

None of these alternative paths was a sustainable one, however; the moral and personal assets that could launch a political career were inherently perishable. Sooner rather than later, successful politicians had to parlay these assets into a strong set of alliances and support networks: trakun (clan) needed the backing of hua khanaen (canvassers) and an extended set of phuak (personal cliques), whose continuing support could only be secured by deploying patronage and resources, including the buying of votes. In this sense, Malay-Muslim politicians in the deep South resembled politicians elsewhere in Thailand. The difference was that Malay Muslims had to keep up a higher standard of appearances than their counterparts in the rest of the country; if the discrepancy between their notional moral legitimacy and their actual political behavior grew too large, they risked rejection at the polls.

The opposite risk loomed equally large: many politicians were linked to the ongoing violence, at least in intelligence reports, and in the collective imaginations of security officials, and so were mistrusted by the state. Den and Ariphen had bothersome brothers,[159] Najmuddin was actually charged with treason, Dr Wae capitalized on his status as an ex-suspect to win a Senate seat, and the Santiphap Party recruited one of his fellow suspects as a candidate. Meanwhile leading Narathiwat politicians Kuheng, Fakhruddin, and Nisoh were all shot, Nisoh fatally, in incidents where the overlap between local politics and militant activity could not be clearly distinguished.

From at least the 1980s onward, the Thai state brokered a social compact with the Malay Muslim elite, mediated largely by Prem and the SBPAC. By the 1990s, the New Aspiration Party had taken over from the Democrat Party the role of the leading Bangkok-based broker in this social contract; the deal reached its apex during Wan Nor's tenure as president of parliament. The social contract embraced the Phiphitphakdi trakun, whose royal claims were subsumed by the Thai monarchy; but the Tohmeena trakun was deemed essentially unreliable. Den Tohmeena was politically marginalized after 1995, when Wan Nor assumed the leadership of the Wadah group. Den sought alternative spheres of influence in the Senate and the Central Islamic Council, but the prize of a major ministry was never to be granted him. At the turn of the millennium, Wan Nor had looked victorious and Den appeared to have been vanquished. Yet eight years later, both men were greatly diminished. Thaksin exploited Wan Nor as interior minister to front his hard-line security regime until March 2004, and so destroyed his political credibility. In the wake of Kru-Ze and Tak Bai, Wan Nor and Wadah were seen as Thaksin's tame political captives. Meanwhile Den lost his once-formidable grip on the imams of Pattani, along with control of the provincial Islamic Council, and so failed to pass on his Senate seat to his daughter Pechdau in April 2006. The two titans of Malay Muslim politics had both been felled, double-crossed by their allies and undermined by their own overconfidence and excessive ambitions.

The story of Malay Muslim political representation has been presented as an example of an increasingly tolerant and progressive Thai state (especially after the promulgation of the 1997 constitution) opening up new levels of opportunity for politicians from the region.[160] But this was an overgeneralized and misguided reading. What really happened was that one specific alliance, that between Chavalit and Wan Nor, created a window of opportunity for the Wadah group. Once Wan Nor had crawled through that window, he had lowered himself in the eyes of Malay Muslim voters: his political demise was already foreshadowed. By contrast, the Democrats had never given a single ministerial position to any Malay Muslim, however briefly. Whereas the upper South was the electoral heartland of the Democrat Party, the Democrats were much weaker in the three border provinces, dominated by Wadah from 1986 to 2005. The Democrats had strong support among Buddhist communities, especially in municipal areas—where politics much more closely resembled that of the upper

South—but tended to be mistrusted by Malay Muslims, who believed that the Democrats had never really sympathized with their plight. This perspective partly arose from Malay-Muslim suspicion of Upper southerners. Only the post–January 2004 political violence had allowed the Democrats to oust Wadah in the 2005 elections; the farcical 2006 elections proved a further humiliation for Thai Rak Thai, while Pattani Senate candidate Anusart was able to mobilize a Buddhist-Democrat bloc vote to secure victory in April 2006. Surin Pitsuwan served as minister of foreign affairs under the Democrats: but although a respected Muslim academic specialist on Patani, Surin hailed from Nakhon Si Thammarat.[161] The idea that Surin could claim to represent "their" South infuriated many Malay Muslims. As Den wrote in 1998: "Do you see yet or not, our Democrat MP friends from the four border provinces? The standpoint of the Democrats and NAP is as different as the sky and the earth. But how are you going to answer your brethren in the four Southern provinces, or to Muslims all over the country?"[162] The defeat of Wadah in the February 2005 election allowed a new group of Democrats to enter parliament, but most were undistinguished, and none made any great impact.[163]

By 2006, the politics of despair were in the ascendant in the Thailand's Southern border provinces. Past dissenters such as Den Tohmeena had been thoroughly domesticated by the Thai state. The Wadah group was in a sorry condition, most of its members unable to gain the requisite 20 percent of the vote in an April election where they faced no serious opponents. This was a real indictment for a political grouping with deep and longstanding ties to the Malay-Muslim community. In the Senate elections that same month, Pattani voters backed a wealthy Buddhist businessman as their favored candidate, testifying to the salience of money and the vicious infighting of the Malay Muslim elite. In neighboring Narathiwat, former Jemaah Islamiyah suspect Dr. Waemahadi Wae-dao won more than 100,000 sympathy votes. The NRC, which had raised some early hopes that the unmentionable issue of decentralization (code for some form of autonomy) might be articulated, failed to deliver. The focus of the NRC's report was on matters of justice, which the commission neatly detached from core questions of governance. The decline of Wadah and the Tohmeenas demonstrated that the Thai state had proved unable or unwilling to nurture a representative Malay Muslim elite that could broker peace and prosperity in the Southern border region. The only "new" alternative on offer was a Muslim party that dared not speak its name, fronted by a discredited former Thai Rak Thai minister from Bangkok: Could such a party really speak to the center on behalf of dissenting Malay Muslims? Furthermore, the state was unwilling to think seriously about any substantive proposals for decentralization, although public statements by some leading figures testified to a gradual thawing of attitudes on the subject.

When the Thaksin government was overthrown by a military coup on September 19, 2006, the new administration—an extension of network monarchy—appeared to envisage a revived, 1980s style social compact, brokered by a re-created SBPAC and based on negotiations with the perpetrators of the violence. The staging of the coup illustrated the impatience of Thailand's monarchy and military with messy and intractable processes of representative politics. Under such circumstances, some radicalized Malay Muslims saw violence as a more viable way of advancing their agendas than engaging with processes of political representation managed by the Thai state for illiberal purposes. Despite the naming of several prominent Malay Muslims to the coup group's appointed parliament, the National Legislative Assembly, the situation in the South continued to deteriorate.

Wan Nor was one of 111 executive members of Thai Rak Thai who were banned from holding political office for five years when the party was dissolved by the courts in May 2007. By the time the ban expired in 2012, he would be approaching seventy. With Wan Nor out of the fight, Den Tohmeena returned to head the Wadah faction in the December 23, 2007, post-coup general election. Standing for the People's Power Party—a re-packaged version of Thai Rak Thai—in Pattani's District One, Den lost to two Democrat candidates. His failure to win election even in a two-member constituency was a further blow to the Tohmeena clan's political dreams. Najmuddin Umar, ever the local hero, was able to secure a constituency seat in Narathiwat District Two; while Wan Nor's brother Sukarno came third in Yala's sole constituency. Ariphen Utarasint narrowly picked up the PPP's sole party list seat in the South. Wadah was reduced to just three seats in parliament. Even with Thaksin out of the country, Wadah could not regain anything like its former dominance. Dr. Waemahadi Waeda-oh and Nimuktar Waba, 2006 senate seat winners in Narathiwat and Yala, both topped the polls in their constituencies in the 2007 parliamentary elections, standing under the Puea Pandin banner. Malay-Muslim voters in 2007 demonstrated deeply conflicting loyalties: of the twelve constituency seats in the three provinces, five went to the Democrats, three to Puea Pandin, two to Chart Thai and two to PPP. The idea that the deep South could speak with one voice to Bangkok looked more implausible than ever. Once again, developments at the national level had divided the Malay-Muslim electorate. While the failures of representative politics in the deep South were not a direct cause of the upsurge in violence, they had helped create an open political space where such violence could thrive.

3

SECURITY

To what extent was the Southern Thai conflict provoked, shaped, or exacerbated by the operations of the state authorities and security forces? The appropriate use of security forces in an internal conflict is closely related to questions of state legitimacy: nation-states claim a monopoly on the use of force, but where a state resorts to invoking force against its own population, it risks eroding its legitimacy. Militant groups dedicated to delegitimating a state have a vested interest in provoking state violence, since unwarranted aggression by the security forces follows the scripts of militant propaganda. Yet when states become afraid of acting firmly and decisively, militants are able to exploit their weaknesses and expose them to various forms of humiliation. Faced with an opportunistic, unpredictable, and manipulative militant movement like that in the Thai South, the lumbering apparatuses of state security forces can easily be mesmerized and paralyzed.

The failings of the Thai security forces in the South were initially related to a reluctance to "name the problem,"[1] a persistent belief that the enemy they faced was not in fact a politically motivated militant movement, but something else. During the Thaksin period, the "something else" was variously understood. Alternatives included simple banditry, a conflict over benefits such as the spoils of smuggling or the drugs trade, or the malevolent machinations of local and national politicians (typically Wadah or the Democrats). Following the September 2006 military coup, the Surayud Chulaonont government settled on a different reading: the problem in the South was really about justice. Like the Thaksin government, the new administration was very focused on apprehending perpetrators and "masterminds" of the violence; but unlike Thaksin, Surayud and Sonthi

Boonyaratkalin tended to believe that if the security forces behaved decently, the violence would diminish. This approach might be termed "virtuous security" and had been gradually embraced by the military top brass since the Tak Bai incident of October 2004. Yet despite the supposed centrality of justice in addressing the conflict, the criminal justice system was not delivering: by late 2007, after more than six thousand violent incidents and nearly three thousand deaths, only a handful of people had been convicted of security offenses in the South, almost all of them minor. This chapter will examine the performance of the justice system and security forces in this light.

Justice

Issues of justice were central to the conflict in the South. The National Reconciliation Commission report identified "injustice at the hands of state officials and shortcomings in the judicial process" as primary grievances of Malay Muslims[2] and suggested that the violence could be substantially ameliorated by addressing justice questions. Similarly, Amnesty International entitled a 2006 report on the conflict "If You Want Peace, Work for Justice."[3] In practice, the catch-all term *justice* frequently conflated a range of diverse and overlapping concerns: economic equality, equality of educational and employment opportunities, social justice, the operation of the police and security forces, and workings of the courts. The focus here will be on the criminal justice system, and specifically on matters of process: how those suspected of committing security-related offences are identified, arrested, questioned, prosecuted, tried, and imprisoned. In the context of the Southern border provinces, "criminal justice" had a broader reach than elsewhere in Thailand, since under martial law and emergency decree provisions, the military participated in processes normally the domain of the police and the court system. Areas of concern included how evidence and leads against suspects were identified; how arrests were made and interrogations conducted; how decisions were made concerning prosecutions; how prisoners were kept while awaiting trial or being tried; and how trials themselves were conducted. Critics argued that Malay Muslims lacked confidence in many aspects of the criminal justice system; this lack of confidence alienated them from the Thai state, undermined state legitimacy, and contributed to the deepening of political tensions, conflicts, and violence. Defenders of the criminal justice system pointed out that very few suspects had been apprehended and even fewer had been convicted; under these circumstances, it was hard for critics of the system to identity substantive miscarriages of justice.

A recurrent problem in high-profile criminal cases across Thailand was the persistence of political interference: in the aftermath of a serious crime, the prime minister or other prominent politicians regularly demanded that arrests be made urgently, sometimes within specific numbers of days. The police faced immense pressure to come up with "achievements,"[4] on which rested the credibility and promotion prospects of senior officers. One conspicuous example was the insistence of senior police officers on prosecuting and detaining 58 Tak Bai protestors, despite the lack of compelling evidence against them.[5] The core police "achievement" was always a highly publicized arrest, normally involving a press conference at which suspects would be paraded along with weapons or other crime-related paraphernalia, often making televised confessions of a kind that would be illegal in most Western criminal justice systems. Convictions were of marginal importance—by the time a case actually reached a trial verdict, the officers who had stage-managed the original arrest and postarrest performances had already moved on to higher positions.[6] Arrest had become a kind of dramatic art form, only marginally related to the pursuit of justice. In the highly charged conditions of the South, staged arrests were an attempt by the authorities to demonstrate their successes in pursuing those responsible for the violence and were warmly received in Bangkok; yet these performances also served as a provocation to Malay Muslim communities, who saw their young men presented to the entire nation as guilty, long before any trials had begun. Lawyers and suspects reported that arrests were often carried out in underhand ways; in a typical story, one prisoner in Pattani jail explained that he had received a letter asking him to visit the District Office to sort out a problem with his identity card, only to be arrested when he showed up,[7] while a female prisoner claimed that she had been arrested simply in lieu of her absent husband.[8] Although complaints about the harsh manner of arrests were widespread—a typical prisoner recounted how he had been arrested by a group of around fifteen soldiers and police officers at 5:00 A.M.[9]—in most cases arresting officers removed their shoes before entering the houses of suspects.[10] Whereas in most Thai communities villagers supported the arrest of troublemakers by police, in Malay-Muslim communities local people typically distrusted and resented arrests:[11] fear of being scapegoated caused villagers to rally around (sometimes literally) those taken in by the authorities.[12] Some lawyers and community leaders argued that village headmen, imams, or Islamic Council members ought to be informed when arrests were made, so that the arresting officers could be accompanied by respected neutral figures;[13] in practice, however, some community leaders were reluctant to become involved in arrests, and security agencies were equally reluctant to involve them. Arrests and confessions often became a form of theater. During 2005 and 2006, the authorities distributed DVDs of confessions by recently arrested suspects in the Wat Phromprasit and other cases;[14] in one, Narathiwat governor Pracha Terat personally interrogated three bomb-making suspects in front of a large audience of imams to emphasize the importance of proper Islamic teaching,[15] while on November 26, 2005, Prime Minister Thaksin Shinawatra himself was shown interviewing suspects on live television and lecturing them on the meaning of the Koran.[16]

The 2005 Emergency Decree lowered the standard of evidence required for making arrests in areas where the decree was in force; while the criminal law required grounds for suspicion based on evidence before a warrant was issued, the emergency decree required only grounds for suspicion. Warrants had to be signed by a judge, even for administrative detention under the Emergency Decree,[17] and they were on a duty rota 24 hours a day for this purpose. An estimated 80 or 90 percent of Emergency Decree warrant requests were signed immediately by judges; in a small proportion of cases, the police were asked to come back with a better explanation for their request. In 2005, a bomb was planted outside the house of the Yala chief justice; local sources claimed that the bomb was placed there after he had refused to sign an arrest warrant.[18] Judges apparently had mixed feelings about the Emergency Decree provisions, fearing that prolonged use of such procedures could undermine public confidence in the criminal justice system and could even play into the hands of the militant movement. A further concern among judges was the length of time suspects could be held in administrative detention without being charged: thirty days.[19]

From mid-2005 until September 2006, the military, police, and Interior Ministry pursued a "surrender policy": suspected militants or those at risk of developing militant sympathies were asked to turn themselves in. Those who surrendered often underwent "peace training" in army camps or at the Yala Police Academy, for periods ranging from a few days to a month. Participation in such activities was in principle voluntary; participants "reported themselves" to the authorities, usually after receiving invitation letters, or verbal requests passed on by village headmen or other local officials. In practice, however, the distinction between "reporting oneself" and being arrested was largely moot in the eyes of Malay-Muslim villagers.[20] Some of those who reported themselves under the surrender policy were also arrested prior or subsequent to their "surrender," including many former Tak Bai protestors.

While the messy process of arrests was one shortcoming of the justice system, a second set of problems lay in the way prisoners were questioned. In principle, prisoners were entitled to legal counsel, but in practice many of those arrested—especially administrative detainees held under the emergency decree—had little or no contact with lawyers during the period immediately following their arrest.[21] Two prisoners held in Narathiwat jail on security charges claimed that they had been hit by soldiers during interrogation in a Pattani army base; they were threatened with being shot if they did not confess.[22] After nearly sixteen months in jail, they had seen their lawyer only once and did not know his name. A suspect detained at Yala Police Academy for a month was kept in solitary confinement throughout this period, during which time his legs were always chained.[23] He was interrogated continuously for five days—only pausing for meals and prayers—by five or six questioners who threatened to lock him up for the next fifty years if he refused to confess. Another prisoner admitted that he had signed numerous documents after his interrogation: he did not read them, nor were they read to him, and he had no idea if any of them were confessions.[24] He never saw a lawyer during this time. The police often asked suspects to sign away their rights to have a lawyer with them during questioning, and many did so.[25] Senior police officers recognized the weaknesses of the confession system, a tool on which the Thai police had become overreliant, yet weaning them away from confessions and towards evidence-based casework was a struggle.[26] As one official explained, if a suspect had confessed, there was no reason not to prosecute—yet confession evidence alone was not sufficient to secure a conviction.[27]

Broadly speaking, prison conditions in the Thai South were reasonable: prisoners generally had access to plenty of fresh air, and Muslims were at liberty to pray. Visiting regimes were often generous; indeed, some prisoners reported that their families brought them meals on a daily basis.[28] The governor of Narathiwat jail was a strong advocate of a liberal regime. Although prisoners were kept in large rooms housing up to hundred, he preferred a degree of overcrowding to transferring prisoners to facilities in other provinces, since this would involve detaching prisoners from the support provided by their families.[29] His was the first jail in Thailand to open a teashop, and he had experimented with a suggestion box that allowed prisoners to communicate anonymously directly with him about problems in the prison. Major concerns about jails in the South involved the excessive use of leg shackling and the reluctance of the courts to grant bail in low-level security cases—a policy that baffled even prosecutors.

Lawyers involved in defending security cases in the Southern border provinces were generally well-disposed toward the judiciary but were highly critical of the police and largely unimpressed by the performance of prosecutors. In theory, prosecutors were responsible for screening the cases brought to them by the police, selecting for prosecution only those cases with sufficient evidence to secure a conviction. In practice, prosecutors and the police worked very closely together and tended to bring most cases to court. As one prosecutor put it, he had to believe 100 percent in the police, otherwise he could not do his job.[30] This was especially the case during the Thaksin period, when the police were very powerful. One lawyer claimed that prosecutors frequently faced pressure from the police to bring charges, and the police would not hesitate to lobby the bosses of noncompliant prosecutors.[31] Some senior police officers even tried to lobby the judges themselves. Yet prosecutors felt under pressure from both sides; prosecutors who feared retribution from militants sometimes asked the defense lawyer to explain to defendants that they were only doing their duty and were not prosecuting them out of any personal animus. As a basic working principle, prosecutors felt that courts should make decisions about the quality of the evidence and were reluctant not to bring cases to court. However, prosecutors were extremely overburdened with cases, and faced a relentless round of court appearances.[32] During one trial I observed in Pattani, the prosecutor asked permission to leave the court room early, missing the chance to cross-examine a witness, saying that he needed to appear in another case.[33] The same prosecutor seemed poorly prepared and a well-prepared defense lawyer effortlessly ran rings around one of the prosecution witnesses.

Unlike in some other judicial systems, Thai prosecutors had no investigative powers and were entirely reliant on the documents provided by the police: documents that were often sketchy and inadequate, having been prepared by inexperienced junior officers with little or no input from their bosses.[34] A prosecutor showed me the file for one nationally prominent security case, which had been countersigned by fifteen different police officers from the rank of general downward. He believed that only the lowest ranking officer, number fifteen on the list, actually had any detailed knowledge of the case; this officer was the only one to attend the court proceedings.[35] Prosecutors only met defendants and witnesses in the courtroom itself. Many of the challenges facing prosecutors were far from unique to the South, but pressures of work there were exacerbated by the reluctance of well-qualified people to work in the area. Prosecutors were recruited nationally through an entrance examination system and then given assignments around the country that reflected their preferences and performance. If a hundred new prosecutors were appointed in a given year, those who were ranked 98, 99 or 100 in the entrance examination would be ordered down to Pattani, Yala, or Narathiwat. In other words, the most capable prosecutors were never sent to this part of the country, where so many complex and demanding cases were being tried. Many of those working in the border provinces were trainees, or had less than three years' experience. Most of the burden for dealing with complex security cases therefore fell on a small number of very overworked prosecutors, some of whom handled as many as two hundred criminal cases in a single year. Some critics of the judicial system saw prosecutors as the weakest links in the judicial chain, singularly failing in their duty to weed out flimsy cases brought by the police; others argued that prosecutors were simply the captives of vested interests and were subject to extensive political influence; prosecutors themselves insisted they were doing the best possible job under very difficult circumstances.

Like prosecutors, judges were reluctant to accept assignments in the Southern border provinces—a reluctance doubtless increased by the unsolved assassination of one Pattani judge in 2004. At the time of fieldwork, all judges in the border provinces were Buddhists, many in their twenties or early thirties, and were often rather inexperienced to be trying serious security cases.[36] In Thailand, the judiciary is effectively a free-standing profession; prospective judges work as lawyers for a token period, before taking an entrance examination and becoming judges at a very early age. Unlike other Thai officials, judges do not have to accept the assignments they are given, so long as they can find another judge to trade places with them. Unpopular postings such as the Southern border provinces are often traded with junior colleagues and frequently rotated. Strict contempt of court laws mean that criticism of judges and trial procedures is virtually unknown in Thailand, and longstanding shortcomings in the Thai judicial system have gone unchallenged for decades. The most conspicuous of these is the absence of any verbatim transcripts of trial proceedings—the only summary of proceedings is dictated by judges themselves—a provision which curtails the scope for appeals.[37]

For security cases in the South, however, judicial procedures have not proved a significant source of injustice. Paradoxically, for all the talk of injustice, and of the need to monitor trials very closely, the great majority of security case trials in the South ended with the defendants being acquitted, or, more commonly, in the charges being dropped by the order of the courts. Lawyers defending Malay Muslim suspects generally looked to the courts as a source of hope, believing that most judges were well-disposed toward the defendants.[38] One lawyer argued that the distrust felt by many Malay Muslims toward the Thai state did not extend to judges themselves, who were generally believed to be very fair.[39] The February 2008 conviction of five of the eleven original suspects for the Wat Phromprasit murders, involving the killing of an elderly Buddhist monk and two temple boys by a gang of youths in October 2005, marked the first time a major security case had been brought to a successful conclusion.

For many Buddhists and government officials in the South, by contrast, the real source of injustice was not the heavy-handed role of the Thai authorities, but the failure of those authorities to secure any substantial convictions. One official suggested that less than 20 people had actually been convicted of any security-related offences in the three provinces since January 2004, almost all on very minor charges.[40] Practically every serious case had collapsed. Famous debacles included the trial of Narathiwat medical doctor and social activist "Mo Wae," Waemahadi Wae-dao, and three associates who were accused on planning bomb attacks on Bangkok embassies. After charges against him were dropped in 2005, Dr. Wae ran successfully in the April 2006 Narathiwat Senate elections; his landslide win was a virtual referendum on Malay Muslim views of Thai justice. In another well-known case, treason charges against former Thai Rak Thai MP Najmuddin Umar were dropped in December 2005.[41] While Najmuddin and Dr. Wae made national headlines, lower-profile security cases were fizzling out unnoticed every month. One reason for the collapse of security cases was the differing standards of proof required at the various stages of the judicial process. To make an arrest under the Emergency Decree, the police needed nothing more than simple suspicion. To bring charges, the police were generally satisfied with confession evidence, ideally supported by some witness testimony, and were happy to press charges even when they harbored real doubts about the suspect's guilt. One justice official explained that the police worked on the principle that if there was a 40 percent chance that a suspect was guilty, they would simply bring him in and charge him.[42] Prosecutors were supposed to be convinced that there was at least a 50 percent chance the charges would stick; but the courts would reject cases if judges had any significant doubts about their solidity.

Some lawyers working in the South argued that a cultural shift had taken place among judges over the previous five years or so.[43] Previously, judges had tended to take prosecution evidence, confessions, and witness statements largely on trust, and showed a pronounced tendency to convict defendants. More recently, judges were showing much greater skepticism toward the cases presented by the prosecution. Cases relying solely on eyewitnesses were more likely to be dismissed than before.[44] In part, this change reflected greater public concerns about the performance of the police in Thailand, which had been generated partly by the high-profile work of the flamboyant forensic scientist Khunying Pornthip Rojanasunand.[45] There was a growing awareness in Thailand that police investigations did not meet international standards of evidence, fuelled by bungled high-profile cases such as the headline-grabbing Sherry Ann Duncan murder trials.[46] A standard police practice was to bolster weak criminal cases by hiring fake witnesses to support their allegations,[47] but a good defense lawyer could confuse most such witnesses and destroy their credibility.[48] The trickiest trials were those in which the police produced "professional" witnesses (sometimes former police officers) who were familiar with court procedures and had been well coached on the details of the case.[49] One lawyer explained how the police had been unable to secure convictions in one high profile case, where the only evidence was a combination of confessions and a single witness, an off-duty police officer.[50] As the lawyer elaborated:

> In the new judicial system after 2004 when the violence emerged, if the confession to the police is dubious, judges have the right to exclude the confession in the verdict especially when the case lacks reliable evidence. Previously the Court of First Instance would sentence based upon evidence from policemen, taking the view that defendants could take the case to the Appeal Court and Supreme Court if they were unhappy. The judicial system has changed after the violence, partly from the attitude of judges, and partly from outside demands.[51]

Yet judges did not accept this argument that there had been a "cultural shift" in the way the courts viewed evidence.[52] Rather, the police and prosecutors had lowered their own standards of performance, in a desperate but misguided attempt to secure convictions. One lawyer suggested that local police officers came under intolerable pressure from above to produce results.[53] Most problems related to witnesses: local people might initially agree to testify for the prosecution, but would later come under strong pressure from their own communities to alter or withdraw their testimony.[54] A second problem was "lack of clarity" from police witnesses, their failure to provide unambiguous evidence that would stand up in court. But many police officers, prosecutors, and defense lawyers believed that they detected a cultural shift, a growing reluctance to convict on the part of the courts. In the past, confession evidence alone could secure a conviction, but this was no longer the case. Under Thai law, the prosecution was entitled to appeal against an acquittal, but this right was rarely exercised, perhaps since prosecutors were well aware that their cases were too weak to convince a higher court. Yet even some defense lawyers involved in security cases in the South admitted that they doubted the innocence of certain clients. In some of the cases dropped through lack of evidence, their lawyers believed defendants were actually guilty as charged.[55]

There were very few well-qualified criminal defense lawyers in the South-ern border provinces, and some local Buddhist lawyers were reluctant to assume the defense of controversial cases.[56] One Buddhist lawyer who suc-cessfully defended a well-known security case expressed his reservations about the outcome:

> Actually, I was afraid of handling this case and I don't want to be famous from the case. I am a local person and have to stay in this area. I have tried to tell everyone the verdict from the court is not simply the result of my work but results from the lack of evidence, so the court dismissed the case.[57]

In an attempt to ensure that those charged with security offences in the South received effective legal representation, a group of local lawyers had organized a law center based initially at the campus of Prince of Songkhla University, Pattani, with pump-priming funds from the NRC.[58] The center had links to the Law Society—a national body with branches in every prov-ince in Thailand—to the Muslim Lawyers' Association, and to the National Reconciliation Commission. It was also closely associated with the Interna-tional Commission of Jurists, and with a newly formed NGO, the Working Group on Justice for Peace. Buddhist lawyers who had previously been reluctant to take on security cases—some of whom had quite conservative orientations—actually became mainstays of the center's activities. During its first year of operation, the law center handled some seventy-eight legal cases relating to the Southern violence.[59]

Although justice was a major theme of Malay Muslim complaints about the Thai state, the South of Thailand was not characterized by major mis-carriages of justice. Indeed, virtually no one accused of involvement in po-litical violence had actually been convicted of a crime. Rather, the criminal justice system had become a form of structural harassment, characterized by bungled or downright deceitful police work, abuses of interrogation procedures, a failure by prosecutors properly to vet police cases, a reluc-tance of judges to grant bail in security cases,[60] and the apparent pursuit of certain cases—such as that of the 58 Tak Bai protestors—as a form of political vendetta. The NRC report called for the formulation of "a unified and consistent criminal justice policy and justice process,"[61] and contained some detailed suggestions on achieving this. High profile judicial failures such as the Dr. Wae case undermined confidence in the criminal justice sys-tem on both sides of the Buddhist-Muslim community divide. In the end, the police and prosecutors were generally trumped by skeptical judges who found their cases unconvincing and threw them out. On one level, this gap between the police and courts reflected a wider divide between a hard-line

"Thaksin" security policy and a more compassionate "royalist" approach to justice. But the continuing mismatch between these two approaches left many Malay Muslims confused and hurt, without in any way addressing the need to apprehend the real instigators of violence. In the end, calls for greater "justice" in the south were primarily a euphemism for the abuses perpetrated by the security forces and the bad attitudes of many government officials. A senior general closely involved in security policy in the South argued that the government's preoccupation with a law-and-order approach to resolving the conflict was misguided.[62] The Southern border region was not at peace, and judicial mechanisms designed to operate in peacetime were inadequate there. In other words, the Southern conflict placed impossible strains on the criminal justice system, which was being set the impossible task of covering for the shortcomings of the security forces.

Army

The January 2004 escalation of the already-growing violence in the South was initially directed at the military, symbolized by the daring raid on an army camp staged by a large group of militants. Thaksin's response was to criticize the incompetence of the military, famously declaring that soldiers who could not defend themselves deserved to die;[63] but he quickly proclaimed martial law in the region and assigned the army the central role in quelling violence. The Royal Thai Army, however, is a uniformed bureaucracy that does not fight wars. Unlike other powerful militaries in Southeast Asia—notably the Burmese and Indonesian armies—it never waged an independence struggle and has never repelled invaders in modern times.[64] The core pursuits of the Thai military are playing politics and engaging in business activities (including illegal activities, such as smuggling); when the occasion arises, commanders are not averse to killing a few dozen unarmed civilians.[65] The only major military success the army can claim was against the Communist Party of Thailand (CPT) in the early 1980s, but the defeat was achieved largely through a "political offensive" based on an amnesty policy. Thousands of communist insurgents slipped quietly and voluntarily out of the jungles; they were not overwhelmed by superior armed forces. Questions have long been raised about the competence and battle-readiness of Thai forces. The reemergence of a substantial internal security threat to the Thai state by 2004 therefore posed a troubling and largely unwelcome challenge to the military. The Thai military had no strong grasp of counterinsurgency techniques or strategy, subjects which were not really taught at the Chulachomklao Military Academy.

A standard army line on the conflict was that the situation in the South had been provoked partly by the incompetence of other Thai government agencies: elements of the police, certain district officers and even some provincial governors had been engaged in systematic "incident creation" for their own benefit.[66] According to this reading, the army was the only really sincere and well-intentioned government agency and was engaged in a moral mission to unravel the misdoings of inept and ill-intentioned elements of the Thai state. The standing of the army in relation to the royal household was sometimes invoked; many of the troops sent down to the South from late 2004 onwards were members of royal guard regiments. In practice, the King's and Queen's guard regiments were very numerous, and they did not all constitute elite troops. Nevertheless, Buddhist villagers in Narathiwat expressed some satisfaction that royal guards had been sent to their area, in place of ordinary "Thaksin" troops, and expected the new troops to be much more effective.[67] As a former police officer, Thaksin was also associated with the police, while the army was seen as more loyal to the palace. The application of royal wisdom—summarized in the maxim "Understand, access, develop"—to the Southern conflict was emphasized especially by the army.[68] The persistent conflation of royalist moralism with issues of security strategy and basic military competence testified to the muddled thinking of army officers and their attempts to reduce complex social and political problems to black and white alternatives. A researcher at the Thailand Development Research Institute, Nattanan Wichit-aksorn, wrote in *Matichon* that the inefficiency of Thai security forces, with their excessive attachment to using and displaying force, was a major factor behind the escalation in the violence.[69]

During 2006 around twenty thousand soldiers were deployed in the three provinces, many of them embedded in local communities.[70] One core component of the military force was the elite "Santisuk" forces, numbering around a thousand men, and concentrating on psychological and unconventional warfare. The Santisuk forces sought to train loyal militias of village defense volunteers, organized in two parallel programs: the largely Buddhist Or Ror Bor, patronized by the Queen, and the Chor Ror Bor, containing both Buddhists and Muslims, and overseen by the Interior Ministry. The Santisuk forces had three elements: special combat units working on intelligence and village defense groups, units working on psychological operations, and commando units from the special forces (Red Berets) in Lopburi.[71] A second, much larger core component of the military was the Srisunthon forces, numbering around 14,800 men, who were primarily focused on providing security for local people, and carrying out routine intelligence work to identify suspected militants. The Srisunthon forces comprised troops from the regular army, marines, and border police; rangers, including a reserve corps of 3000 troops; and a locally recruited militia commanded by professional soldiers.[72] In February 2005, the cabinet approved the creation of a major new permanent force for the South, based in Joh-Ai-Rong, Narathiwat (symbolically, at the same camp where the January 4, 2004, incident took place), later designated Infantry Division Fifteen.[73] The new division was to have thirteen thousand troops by 2009; the target was for between 30 and 40 percent of the staff recruited to be Muslims from the Southern border provinces.

For the most part, the Srisunthon forces were billeted at government schools or Buddhist temples—using surplus accommodation resulting from falling student enrolments and declining numbers of ordinations. Core duties for such soldiers often involved guarding the temples, protecting monks, and escorting teachers to and from schools. Soldiers received some basic training in Malay history and culture, Islam, and the Malay language.[74] Other duties involved patrolling Muslim communities, talking to villagers and community leaders, and gathering information. Although based in their communities, many soldiers had little interaction with local Buddhists; disciplinary regimes varied from one district to another, but officially soldiers were discouraged from fraternizing with members of their

Fig. 3.1 Thai soldiers on patrol in Narathiwat (Anon.)

host communities, and especially from drinking or gambling with them, and from dating local women. One notice prepared by the Southern Peace-Building Command in Yala listed ten rules for soldiers:

10 Rules

1. Don't act like the bosses of the people, behave politely and respectfully.

2. Don't bother the villagers—it you want to eat something, pay for it.

3. Don't act improperly toward the children or wives of villagers.

4. It's forbidden to drink alcohol while on duty.

5. Don't abuse your power, violate the law, or exceed your authority.

6. Don't use coarse language, look down on people, or hold them in contempt.

7. Don't neglect to help out or give support to people.

8. Don't neglect morality.

9. Don't violate peoples' customs, religious beliefs, or things they respect.

10. Don't act on the basis of ethnicity—you must always respect the sacredness of humanity.[75]

Conscripts suffered from discipline problems. The abbot of one Pattani temple that sometimes housed two or three hundred soldiers at a time complained that some of them behaved badly, that heavy drinking among them was rising, and that they often brought women to stay overnight at the temple.[76] Commanders frequently had to punish the troops for their rowdiness, and relations between monks and soldiers were poor. The abbot was doubtful that the presence of the soldiers made the community any safer and personally refused a military escort when traveling around the area—a stance emulated by many other local abbots. Soldiers complained to him that their routine patrols were futile, and they had no chance to use their combat training—many were Special Forces troops from Lopburi—since they were forbidden to fire their weapons. A Buddhist informant in Narathiwat explained that she often took soldiers on duty in her area coffee and snacks: they were mostly underpaid conscripts from poor backgrounds, who were neglected even by their commanders.[77] One major explained the difficulties of working in a "red zone":

> During the first three months, I was very stressed and couldn't sleep. We also were discouraged when visiting villagers and found that we were not welcomed. When we *wai*-ed them,[78] they ignored us and didn't speak to us. However, we comforted ourselves that next time they would gradually be friendlier if we keep expressing our sincerity.

> After 4–5 months, they became nicer and invited us to have meals at their houses. Some villagers complained that the police couldn't take care of them. I told them that we wanted to help but how could we do if the villagers didn't inform us anything.[79]

The lives of these conscripts were dull and restrictive, yet overshadowed by constant physical danger. Around 60 percent of soldiers in the South were conscripts serving two-year stints in the military; many of them were rather immature. The Tak Bai investigation report specifically criticized the use of conscripts and rangers in dispersing the demonstration.[80] Rungrawee Chalermsripinyorat argued that rangers and conscripts were responsible for most of the human rights violations committed by the military in the South and suggested that these troops should not be used in the region.[81]

Yet increasing numbers of rangers were deployed in the South—more than seventy-five hundred by October 2007.[82] Rangers had more flexible command structures and operating procedures than regular troops, and in theory were more appropriate to fighting nonconventional wars. At the same time, they were widely feared and mistrusted; in March 2007, for example, they allegedly shot two young Muslim men from a checkpoint in Ta Seh, Yala, one fatally, and then carried out an aggressive raid on a nearby pondok, firing numerous shots. Given the historical allergy of the Royal Thai Army to engaging in actual combat, the military had a long-standing tradition of buck-passing and delegating. Wherever possible, dangerous frontline duties were subcontracted to other groups or agencies. In the South, this increasingly meant relying on rangers and other forms of "voluntary" militias. Hence despite the dreadful image of *thahan phran*, the government announced a new policy of recruiting additional rangers in 2006; these locally recruited troops, often former conscripts, could be hired at a lower cost than professional soldiers and would work on a more long-term basis, since they came from the area. While creating Infantry Division Fifteen implied military professionalization, the parallel "rangerization" of the South was a potentially dangerous and counterproductive strategy, given the negative image of the rangers in the area. Anonymous leaflets contained specific criticisms of the ranger policy:

> One other thing for Muslim brothers and sisters to be aware of!! is that the Siamese kafir government has a dirty policy to get us Malay people to kill those of the same religion, nationality, and race. They want to hire Malay Muslims to work as volunteers and rangers. Each village can send in two people. These people will become a shield for the kafir government and victims of the Patani Mujahidin warriors. They have set the salary at only 7,000 baht per month.[83]

One study by a military academic suggested significant differences in tactics and performance between troops from different parts of Thailand.[84] She found that while all military units assigned to the area adopted the same mission of "winning over the villages,"[85] units from the Southern Fourth Army tended to rely primarily on establishing strong personal relations with communities, drawing on their familiarity with local cultures and norms, and tended to have very good working relations with the police and civilian authorities.[86] Troops from the central region stressed their standing as "royal soldiers," promoting the slogan "understand, access, develop": "discipline is the most important rule for these military units in order to protect the royal reputation."[87] Troops from the Northeast tended to draw on experiences from fighting communism in their approach to creating mass support, but were markedly less successful; the study notes, "Only women's groups and community leaders tend to cooperate with soldiers from Isan, whilst the men and youth groups refused to cooperate with them."[88] Some military analysts viewed these claims with skepticism, however.

To some extent, the success of military units was related to the strength of militant organizations in the areas to which they were assigned. In an attempt to classify such areas, every village in the three provinces was graded using a color-coding system. Thaksin caused an uproar in February 2005 when he suggested using the same system to allocate public funds (in other words, that militant strongholds would be deprived of state resources), but the zoning policy was primarily a classification exercise for security purposes, rather than an instrument of economic development or deprivation. Introduced by former Fourth Army commander General Sirichai Tanyasiri, and based on the old anti-CPT strategic planning system, red areas were those with clear levels of militant activity, green zones were peaceful, and in yellow zones the level of militancy was not fully determined.[89] In a fifty-seven-page white book submitted to Thaksin early in 2005, Sirichai proposed the following approach:

1. Analyze (X-ray) and check the target area carefully to classify which area is in favor of supporting the movement, such as giving hiding places. Also, the head of the village, religious leaders, religious centers, schools, transportation and roads will have to be checked as well.

2. Analyze (X-ray) and check local people carefully such as their movements, who is new to the area, when did people arrive and for what purpose.

3. Use the information from the X-ray process (people and environment) to classify who stands on the government side and who the enemy is. Then, plan a strategy to win the people in the village from the information and classification.[90]

In other words, Sirichai advocated a politically focused, intelligence-based approach to addressing the conflict; there was broad consensus about the desirability of such methods from Tak Bai onward. As Prem had declared in his major speech on the South on February 28, 2005: "To solve the problem in the south is like we are at war. We need to know who the enemy is, where they are, and what their strategies are. Then we also have to estimate their power, weapons, and aims."[91]

The sexual behavior of soldiers was the focus of many rumors and considerable tension. Some prominent leaders consistently argued that Buddhist soldiers were becoming sexually involved with Muslim women, a serious moral, cultural, and religious violation. In a March 2005 joint session of parliament, then Narathiwat senator Fakhruddin Boto claimed that soldiers in the three provinces had recently made more than a hundred Muslim women pregnant.[92] Abdul Rahman Abdul Shamad, chairman of Narathiwat Islamic Council, acknowledged that such stories were often speculation, but cautioned: "Local girls and women are crazy about men in army and police uniforms, but the men hate such kinds of uniforms so if the military does not resolve the problem the tense situation will escalate even more."[93] Thai military officers claimed they had no evidence of any such cases, other than the well-known instance of an Isan soldier who had converted to Islam to marry a local woman and had later been shot by insurgents.[94]

Two young Malay Muslim women did tell me that soldiers tried to "chat up" local women in their village.[95] Whether such affairs were really widespread was unclear, but the theme was a potent one for propaganda purposes, and invoked regularly in anonymous leaflets. One leaflet featured a savage cartoon:[96] three Muslim women working on a government job-creation scheme were walking towards a temple, where watching soldiers from Isan were mentally undressing them and anticipating that they would soon have sex. The father of one of the women was telling a friend that he had asked his daughter's cousin to give him a dowry of 100,000 baht to marry her, but was willing to sell her to the soldiers for 4500 baht (the monthly salary of the job scheme). One of the women was saying "Money is God." The title of another leaflet was unambiguous:

Mass interaction or mass sexual intercourse?[97]

We can see from the behavior of the soldiers in the area; they killed innocent Muslims, they raped our women and children, and they caused us pain and humiliation that is hard to erase....

The government has received a policy from Police Lt-Col Dr Thaksin Shinawatra for soldiers from all military camps to take Muslim women to be their wives, and leave them when their missions are completed. Now, they have achieved 80 percent of their plan.

In Raman district, soldiers impregnated local women. Some of them are in high-ranking positions. The governor and district officer actually know about this, but there's nothing they can do because the power is in the hands of the army. They treated us like baby chicks in their fists.[98]

For all these reasons, do the soldiers deserve to live? They should be punished and pay for the crimes they have committed.

Claims that rangers had raped a woman in Patae, Yaha, on May 22, 2007, were a major grievance underlying five days of student-led mass demonstrations at Pattani mosque from May 31 onward.

In a project personally backed by the Queen, soldiers from other regions of Thailand were encouraged to ordain as monks in the deep South. In 2005, seventy-five soldiers were ordained at one Pattani temple alone.[99] This policy proved controversial, linking the monkhood with the military and so exposing monks to greater risk of attack. After he assumed office in October 2005, Muslim army commander Sonthi Boonyaratkalin sought where possible to shift soldiers out of Buddhist temples and base them in more neutral locations, often in smaller units.

The junior officers heading military units based in the South had often volunteered for these commands, either out of a genuine desire to help the situation—many were quite idealistic—or simply out of a wish to improve their own promotion prospects.[100] Some officers insisted that after several months of working in a given area they were fully aware of the identities of the militants. Most militant activity was targeted and specific; soldiers who were skilled in building up personal relationships with local informants would be able to secure a good flow of useful information, though much of it was unreliable. Estimates of the reliability varied widely. Their strategy was to keep an eye on the militants they had identified, go and meet them regularly, and monitor them constantly so that they could not commit any violence. In some cases, the militants would decide to move out of the area, because their cover had been blown.[101] My fieldnotes describe how, visiting the office of a local politician in Narathiwat, I experienced the military's special attention at firsthand:

Then the soldiers arrive—a whole group of around a dozen of them with red caps suggesting they are Special Forces. The officers go to talk to the politician and I chat for a while to the men, who are eating lunch outside. Then the officers come out and talk to me—claim they are here because of the chor ror bor, local security program, which they oversee. A young one is very friendly, a captain who looks about 16. He is accompanied by a lieutenant, a silent

character who writes down everything in a notebook, terribly serious. Another officer is very friendly but does not give me his name or contact details.
They take several photographs of me, and want to know exactly where I am
from, how I know the politician, how I got here, and so forth...I feel a bit as
though I am being interrogated.

Politician takes me for lunch. He is clearly a bit agitated by the visit of the
soldiers, who apparently had been looking for him previously (he's just back
from a seminar in the Northeast). He is annoyed by the way they asked him
a lot of questions—including questions about who I was and how he knew
me. Luckily we both gave the same answers. He says the way they take pictures and write everything down is rather irritating. They told him they were
coming to introduce the new unit head, but I get the feeling it's an excuse to
keep an eye on him, especially since he is supposed to be on the blacklist, and
because the village security schemes have apparently been penetrated by the
movement in some places.[102]

The politician was open about the fact that his name appeared on a "blacklist" of militant suspects; as a consequence, he was subjected to visits of this
kind regularly. Senior army officers in the South argued that lots of elected
politicians were members of the movement and could not be trusted,[103] a
view contradicted by other informants who insisted that the militants did
not support their members standing for office.[104] Whatever the truth of the
matter, local politicians, headmen, and religious leaders were easy targets
for the military to monitor closely. Issued with digital cameras and required
to produce daily reports of their activities, military units were expected to
engage in what amounted to low-level harassment of community leaders.
On another visit to a village in Narathiwat, a group of soldiers more or
less surrounded me, prevented me from speaking openly to any locals, and
took literally hundreds of photographs while escorting me around military-
sponsored development projects.[105] At one meeting sponsored by the NRC
at Prince of Songkhla University, Pattani, a military photographer took
pictures of every single person in the audience, presumably for later identification.[106] Military officers routinely asked staff compiling attendance lists
at seminars on issues relating to the Southern conflict to give them copies,
and in some cases they simply stole the lists from under the noses of the
organizers. Far from winning over "hearts and minds," such lavish but
unwelcome attentions seemed more likely to encourage Malay Muslims
to harbor negative perceptions of the Thai state and all its works.

The deficiencies of military discipline in the South were plainly visible in
such routine activities as patrolling and the operation of checkpoints. Standard procedures for stopping and searching vehicles require coordinated
teamwork, in which some military personnel "cover" and secure the checkpoint zone from a range of angles, while others carry out systematic random

checks.[107] However, in the South of Thailand soldiers manning checkpoints normally performed their duties in a very casual manner, often all looking in the same direction. Had militants used sniper tactics, these troops would have been vulnerable to heavy losses.[108] Troops being deployed to the region did not go through intensive training using realistic facilities.[109] Checkpoints were maintained in the same places for months on end, immediately alongside improvised army camps; instead, they should have been rotated every few hours. Bunkers were flimsy and incapable of withstanding high-velocity rounds.[110] Soldiers and police were not equipped with weapons that could fire plastic bullets or baton rounds, leaving them with "nothing in between shouting and shooting to confront a situation."[111] The security forces initially conducted few foot patrols,[112] thereby surrendering advantage to the militants, and often traveled in single vehicles without proper cover or backup.[113] The army lacked suitable light-armored vehicles; exasperated with unwieldy, fuel-guzzling GMC trucks, soldiers resorted to using motorcycles and ordinary pickup trucks that left them highly vulnerable to attack. The apparent inability of Thai troops correctly to follow standard military procedures on checkpoints and patrolling used in conflicts worldwide—and on which their lives depended—raises serious questions about their capacity for carrying out more sophisticated security operations, let alone engaging in full-blown armed conflict.

Military officers also found the tactics of the militants difficult to deal with; one mid-ranking officer lamented that troops were not as well prepared as their adversaries, who had more information and were just as smart.[114] He argued that the January 4, 2004, incident had showed the weakness of the state and the inability of soldiers to defend themselves. With as few as fifty men, the militants had been able to damage the image of Thailand internationally, gaining more support for the movement in what amounted to a form of investment.[115] The seizure won them weapons with which to attack the state, but also considerable symbolic power. While Thai troops in the South had reasonable levels of manpower, they often lacked the material resources they needed—sometimes including fuel for their vehicles.[116] The Thai military requested an additional 2,785 million baht from the central state coffers in mid-2005, mainly to purchase weapons and helicopters for use in the South.[117] Local units did not have the discretion to adopt a tough line, so their authority was very limited; indeed, the overall power of the state was being successfully rolled back by the militant movement. Soldiers found themselves on the defensive within their own country. The mid-level Thai officer believed the use of women and children by the movement—both as victims and perpetrators—showed their lack of morality, and indeed their lack of masculinity: they did not fight like *luk phu chai* (real men), but as *na tua mia* (sons of bitches, behaving like women) who liked to *rop yu tai krapong* (fight from under women's skirts).[118] The Thai officer asserted that no one else in the world fought in this way: it was unbelievable that they claimed they were fighting for God. He revealed a strong hankering for a "straight fight" with the militants—one which the better armed and equipped Thai forces could win—rather than a vicious and amoral battle of the wits.[119] Military officers trained for conventional warfare—yet inexperienced in any kind of real fighting—had great difficulty grasping the nature of the decentered and disorderly Southern conflict. Worryingly, this informant was convinced that the conflict in the South was basically about corruption and benefits, and did not derive from any ideology or principles. The Thai military were somewhere between mediocre and incompetent at the best of times, but the situation in the South was for them the worst of times.

The limited competence of the Thai security forces, coupled with the troublesome and unfamiliar tactics of the militants, made for a very difficult situation. Yet this difficult scenario had been further complicated by the mishandling of some major incidents: the siege of Kru-Ze on April 28, 2004, and the transportation of Tak Bai protestors on October 25, 2004. In the case of Kru-Ze, an armed attack was launched on a mosque that was the most sacred religious site for Malay Muslims: grenades were thrown into the mosque itself.[120] Yet the militants inside the mosque, though they had only five rifles (two of them M-16s) twice fired an M-79 grenade launcher at the surrounding troops, so using the mosque for hostile purposes.[121] The rights and wrongs of the assault were extensively debated both locally and nationally, and an inquiry into the handling of events was quite critical of the army's actions. However, none of the military officers I interviewed had any doubt that the assault was justified; they argued that commanders were simply carrying out their duty when they attacked a group of men who had already killed members of the security forces and were refusing to surrender. As one major stated "We are trained to decide, otherwise we could not lead our units": the use of military force involved taking tough decisions.[122] Another colonel explained that, as a soldier, he would not have waited even half an hour to storm Kru-Ze. "If I agreed not to storm Kru-Ze, I'd be agreeing to give up our Thai land."[123]

This was the view of Panlop Pinmani, the retired general who had ordered the assault, in defiance of instructions from Deputy Prime Minister Chavalit Yongchaiyudh. Even some international observers and local human rights activists agreed that once a religious site has been exploited in a violent conflict, it loses its immunity from attack.[124] Yet the question posed in the title of Panlop's book, "Was I Wrong to Storm Kru-Ze?" needs considerable unpacking.[125] Panlop could certainly argue that the prior actions of those taking refuge in Kru-Ze justified a strong military response; yet provoking an attack on the mosque was precisely the objective of the militants. This was not a randomly chosen place of refuge, but one deliberately selected for its historical, emotional, spiritual, and political resonance. By storming the mosque, Panlop had actually followed a script written by his adversaries; his attack was an act of vengeance and retaliation for the humiliation of January 4. Storming Kru-Ze was a short-term solution that showed the capacity of Thai troops to act tough, but in the process of acting tough, they seriously alienated the Malay-Muslim community they were supposed to be winning over. As one officer lamented, the military were very weak in terms of public relations and "outreach work"; the Kru-Ze incident handed a huge propaganda victory to the enemies of the Thai state.[126] Such was the message of one anonymous leaflet:

> From the Kru-Ze incident (distorted by the government, unresolved emotionally for the Muslims), how many lives were lost at the hands of the government? 108 deaths, so they claimed. This also left hundreds of children in a fatherless situation.
>
> After all this, did the government condemn their own actions? Or did they ever explain about the truth to the world? Did they ever realize that killing innocent people is against Buddhist principles? Is killing Malay Muslims something that they deliberately planned? Can it be called an act that concerned only their own interests?[127]

As another leaflet more succinctly put it: "Who else burnt down the Kru-Ze mosque, if not the kafir Thai government?"[128]

Kru-Ze also raised fundamental questions about the chain of command: Who made crucial operational decisions? As a politically appointed head of the Internal Security Operations Command (ISOC), Panlop was not authorized to command any troops; though a former general, he had retired almost a decade before the incident. Panlop had reportedly been instructed by Chavalit Yongchaiyudh, the deputy prime minister responsible for overseeing security in the South, not to attack the mosque under any circumstances. Did Panlop make the decision alone, or was the storming order actually given by Thaksin, or some other senior figure in the Thai government?[129] Even the rather tame government fact-finding commission set up to investigate the Kru-Ze incident raised several critical points, finding that the security forces lacked sufficient training to bring the siege successfully to a peaceful conclusion and made excessive use of heavy weapons following a decision to attack that was taken "in good faith."[130] This report was not made public until the government allowed the NRC to release it on April 24, 2005.[131]

One former security official claimed that as many as twenty of the thirty-two men who died inside the mosque were innocent victims, dawah teachers who had been caught up in events and were effectively hostages.[132] Some of the dead had apparently been beaten and shot repeatedly;[133] photographs showing the condition of the bodies have never been released. By storming the mosque and killing those inside indiscriminately, the security forces passed up on the opportunity to arrest the militants and find out more about their real motives and intentions.[134] After the attacks, the military made initial repairs to the mosque—thereby further outraging some locals. One vendor declared that: "It is not decent for these soldiers, who are not Muslims, to repair our holy sacred mosque. There is no respect for our holy ground and religion....What can be worse?"[135]

If Kru-Ze proved a severe blow to the standing of the military in the South (though applauded by many Buddhists in the rest of Thailand), Tak Bai saw the reputation of the Thai Army reach an all-time low. The gratuitous deaths of seventy-eight protestors at the hands of the army were

Fig. 3.2 Arrests at Tak Bai, October 25, 2004 (Charoon Thongnual)

inexcusable: the victims had been put into the back of trucks, face down with their hands tied behind their backs,[136] stacked there as many as five high, and spent several hours on the road to the Inkhayut army base in Pattani.[137] Most trucks contained between sixty and eighty men; one contained ninety men, twenty-three of whom died.[138] Most of those killed had apparently been suffocated, though relatives and community leaders insisted that many of the corpses contained bullet holes.[139] A junior army officer in the vicinity—though not at the scene itself—was shocked by the level of shooting: "I asked myself why they shot like crazy—I heard rifle shots all over the place."[140] While the authorities claimed only six people were killed at the demonstration, witnesses insisted there were up to twenty fatalities before the trucks were loaded. Postmortems found that fourteen of those who died had injuries inflicted by blunt objects.[141] One man I interviewed confirmed that he had been shot in the back during the protest, and was thrown into a truck while unconscious, only coming round in hospital many hours later.[142] As Chermsak Pinthong wrote: "Close to death, those towards the bottom of the heap were suffocating. Screaming for help, they were instead trampled on by some of the soldiers, hit with the rifle butts and told: '[I] will teach you Hell exists.'"[143] When I asked a young man severely crippled during Tak Bai how he felt now when he saw the soldiers or policemen, he just laughed slightly and gave a faint smile.[144] Yet the impact of the incident on the Malay Muslim community, whether verbalized or not, could hardly be overstated. As one leaflet put it:

> *Black Thaksin, the source of the bloodshed*
>
> —Where has the first GMC[145] full of dead people after the mob dispersal gone?
> —Raise your hand if you know the whereabouts of the kubo[146] of those who have been killed and disappeared.
> —All 85 people that died in custody after the mob dispersal and being transported to the Inkhayut camp were treated like animals. They were piled up on the trucks like logs from rubber trees, which showed a serious lack of humanity. How could the transportation take six hours? What really happened concerning those 85 deaths?[147]

The military themselves were divided over Tak Bai: some soldiers, especially veterans of the border provinces who held Muslims in low regard, privately believed that the demonstrators were bandits, who fully deserved the harsh treatment they received. Others, like the idealistic younger officers who had volunteered for duty in the area, were appalled by the incompetence of the arrests. One claimed that the troops who loaded the trucks were mostly marines, who had not been well-trained for the task, and cared little for the welfare of their charges:

> Although there are classes about procedures for mass arrests in the cadet school, low ranking soldiers don't attend the cadet school, and their training focuses mainly on jungle battle. Those soldiers rarely deal with people and they were commanded to do something at which they are not expert. If commandos had been sent to deal with this incident, the result might have been different.[148]

In fact, the Tak Bai report states that the trucks were loaded by a combination of rangers, border patrol police, and marines.[149] Tak Bai discredited the military in the eyes of Malay Muslims and undermined community relations: for the next six months, villagers and especially children in some areas of Narathiwat would literally run away at the sight of army units.[150] Muslim army officers did their best to rebuild trust, visiting mosques every Friday to convince religious leaders of their sincerity.[151] The politicization of the Tak Bai incident in the February 2005 election campaign—when the Democrat Party distributed video CDs of the crackdown to discredit the Thaksin government—kept the issue alive: many who were not directly affected by the events then saw images of what took place. The military simply waited for memories to fade, while reviewing tactics to try and ensure that similar debacles did not recur.

As with Kru-Ze, the government set up an investigative committee to look into the Tak Bai incident. Then Fourth Army commander Pisan Wattanawongkiri was transferred out of the region, but was promoted to full general in 2005. Attributing blame was complicated by other factors. Though exonerated by the investigation committee, Thaksin had insisted at the time that he assumed personal command of the crisis: "Thaksin said he had personally supervised Monday's anti-riot operation from 11:00 A.M. 'I commend the anti-riot forces for adhering to my instructions,' he said."[152] Thaksin flew down to Narathiwat on the evening of October 25, and senior security officials including Pisan left the scene of the demonstration at 7.00 P.M. to receive the prime minister. Pisan testified that he went to an audience with the Queen which lasted until 4:00 A.M.; he claims to have received no information about the transportation of the prisoners, or their deaths, until 7:45 A.M. on October 26.[153] Pisan's account was contradicted by the deputy head of the royal guard; he insisted that Pisan arrived at the palace at 0:30 A.M. and left at 1:30 A.M., by which time military officers were already aware that many of the demonstrators had perished. Either way, the army commander who was responsible for Tak Bai spent crucial hours during which seventy-eight men died waiting on his superiors and out of contact with his troops: as the investigative report makes clear, he and other senior officers were guilty of dereliction of duty.[154] At the same time, the investigation reached the conclusion that the Tak Bai deaths were ultimately "unintentional." Senator Chermsak Pinthong, who conducted his own independent inquiry into the incident, argued instead that "the officers may even have intended to kill the detainees."[155] Tak Bai illustrated the extent to which royal, political, and military authority became acutely blurred during critical security situations. As with Kru-Ze, command structures were unclear. While the military typically sought to blame the police and other agencies for the security problems in the South, the army was directly responsible for the two most bloody and controversial episodes in the conflict.

In the wake of Tak Bai, the military reviewed its tactics. Hard-line approaches had proved counterproductive; in subsequent crises such as the Tanyong Limo siege of September 20–21, 2005, the army used kid gloves. Rather than risk inflaming the thousands of protestors blockading a village where two marines had been taken captive following the unexplained fatal shooting of two villagers in a teashop, the military abandoned the hostages to their fate: the marines were swiftly bludgeoned to death. Similar military tactics were used in comparable hostage and blockade-type protests around the three provinces. Recognizing the difficulties of fighting an invisible enemy, local units concentrated on intelligence gathering, using development projects to try and forge better community relations. In Tanyong Limo, for example, right after the hostage episode the army constructed fishponds in the gardens of most households, stocking them with fast-growing tilapia.[156] In Narathiwat's Ban Pari, formerly seen as a "red zone" militant stronghold, the military worked with villagers on a variety of "sufficiency economy" projects, including producing dried mushrooms and herbal products such as shampoo.[157] A noncommissioned officer admitted that the mushroom project was a failure, since the cost of producing them exceeded the market price; such projects were often more politically than commercially oriented. A local politician explained that these military "vocational training" and income-generation projects were not taken seriously by the villagers, who already had their own occupations.[158] To win the trust of villagers, all soldiers had to do was behave well, he argued.

Yet any goodwill generated by well-intentioned development projects could easily be wiped out by disciplinary lapses. At around 9:45 P.M. on the night of February 19, 2006, a group of soldiers drove into Tanyong Limo village 7 in a couple of Humvees and fired a large number of shots at six houses. One of the military vehicles appears to have run off the road. Fortunately, no one was injured.[159] While local commanders claimed they had been fired on by militants they had been pursuing, villagers insisted that the soldiers had been drinking and had entered the community to terrorize locals in an act of intimidation and revenge. Army commander Sonthi was so puzzled by the incident that he made a little-publicized inspection visit to the village on March 9, 2006.[160] The episode only came to light because of a chance visit by NRC members the following day; it was impossible to know how many similar uninvestigated incidents were taking place.

Allegations that the security forces were engaged in an informal policy of extrajudicial killing were commonly made by human rights activists but proving such claims was extremely difficult. The most comprehensive discussion appears in a 2007 report by Human Rights Watch, which catalogued twenty-one unexplained "disappearances" of men, relating to the South.[161] The majority of the victims had been suspected of involvement of militant attacks, and some had been seen with security officials shortly before they vanished.[162] In most of these cases, the Thai government had implicitly recognized official complicity in these disappearances by paying token compensation to the families of victims.[163] According to Rungrawee, well-informed locals, including journalists on the ground, believed that a certain proportion of drive-by shootings were actually carried out by men with military connections, normally rangers or reservists who received bounties for their clandestine assassinations.[164] While more common up to 2004, such killings apparently declined from 2005 onward because military commanders did not want to risk being implicated. Not a matter of policy, where incidents did occur, they were typically carried out not as revenge attacks, and often subcontracted to villagers.[165] Most army officers consistently denied that extrajudicial killings took place, but some incidents were difficult to explain in other terms. One very troubling incident took place at Bo-ngor on November 16, 2005, when an entire Muslim family of nine was shot dead, apparently at point-blank range.[166] More shots were directed at houses on the opposite side of the road, and a Claymore mine was then set off nearby, causing further damage and injuries.[167] Claymore mines are sophisticated military weapons and have never been accessed by militant groups in the South. Privately, a senior security official admitted that the incident had all the hallmarks of a revenge attack by the authorities.[168] A certain proportion of killings in the South were clearly the result of extrajudicial actions by elements of the security forces. Such killings fuelled Malay Muslim fear and mistrust of the authorities, and provided excellent copy for militant propaganda, as one leaflet illustrated with a catalogue of alleged incidents:

> From the Tak Bai incident until today, soldiers, policemen, and administrative officers and intelligence agents have shot and killed many innocent

Malays and ustadz. However, the state pays no attention to these horrific actions of these soldiers and policemen at all. They always blame the militants for whatever happens.

As Muslim citizens, we've had it with the evil behavior of state officials, such as:

- Soldiers shot dead innocent Malay villagers in Pattani.
- Police in Amphoe Waeng shot a tadika ustadz.
- Soldiers and informants from Bang-ngo Kue Dae school camp shot randomly at Muslim children in Riko, Sungai Padi.
- Police and soldiers fired indiscriminately at and threw bombs into a village in Sungai Padi, which injured many villagers and children, and destroyed houses.
- Soldiers and intelligence agents have killed an ustadz in Tambon Pawa, Sungai Padi.
- Soldiers at Ban Toh Deng, Sungai Padi, shot randomly at people in their area.
- Soldiers staged an ambush attack against Sukirin villagers, who were rubber tapping in Sungai Kolok.
- And many more...[169]

While the military did make significant progress in terms of community relations in the aftermath of Tak Bai—and showed evidence that it had learned important lessons from the terrible abuses of 2004—the armed forces remained largely on the defensive in the South, unable to fight effectively against a far more flexible and adaptable militant movement. At the core of the government's response to the Southern violence was an army from which little could realistically be expected, but a great deal was demanded.

Police

"Fantastic!" remarked one of my informants, recounting a violent incident in which a policeman had been killed.[170] Such sentiments, rarely expressed to Buddhists or outsiders, were quite widespread in the Malay Muslim community: while the military were generally viewed (with the exception of rangers) as relatively benign, or at least tolerable, the police were a focus for popular resentment against the Thai state. To some extent, these feelings mirrored the perceptions of wider Thai society. A nationwide survey conducted in 2000 found that the police were viewed as the most dishonest element of Thailand's public sector, while the armed forces were one of the honest institutions.[171] But in the Malay-Muslim South, concerns about the dishonesty of the police were compounded by other negative images: the police were routinely and casually accused of abusing power, exploiting local people, and holding local culture and religion in low regard.

They had clearly been responsible for the shockingly crass murder of Haji Sulong and his son in 1954. From 2001 to 2006, for the first time ever, a former police officer served as Thailand's prime minister: this development boosted the confidence of the police, who had been in a subordinate political position since the eclipse of police general Phao Sriyananda by Field Marshal Sarit Thanarat in the 1950s. Police-military rivalries, a recurrent theme in many conflict zones, especially in the developing world, were a potent issue in Thailand.[172] When he abolished the Southern Border Provinces Administrative Command in 2002, police lieutenant colonel Thaksin Shinawatra put the police in charge of security in the now supposedly "normalized" deep South. As part of their attempt to gain the upper hand over the Fourth Army, the police took the opportunity to assassinate or "disappear" at least twenty military informers, mainly former separatists who had surrendered to the authorities in the 1980s.[173] This provocative move undoubtedly helped reignite political violence in 2004 and helped focus resentment on the police. The police were also apparently to blame for the unsolved "disappearance" of Muslim human rights lawyer Somchai Neelaphaichit. Seven of the eleven locations attacked on April 28, 2004, were police stations and posts, and the police became constant targets of shootings and bombs. Tensions between the police and army were a serious issue, especially during 2004. Asked about these tensions, one senior police officer explained wistfully "We attend different academies."

Ordinary policemen worked under immense pressure.[174] Soldiers had support systems: they were housed in relatively secure camps, their food was prepared by army caterers, and they had regular hours of patrolling and periods of rest. Their families were normally far away, in safe parts of the country. After serving a tour of duty, soldiers could expect to be rotated to other areas. Low-ranking policemen, by contrast, were normally local to the area and had nowhere else to go. As one senior police general put it, "The army have it easy, the police are stuck here."[175] The police had to operate as ordinary members of the community, taking care of family and other obligations alongside their work. Working hours were long, and even when off-duty they were in constant personal danger. One Narathiwat barber with a lot of police customers explained that many officers were now afraid to come to his shop, preferring to have their hair cut inside the nearby barracks.[176] On the day I had my hair cut in his shop, two policemen were there together, in plain clothes, and apparently "covering" one another during their respective haircuts. Nor could the police readily take trips to other parts of the country; they were entitled to only ten days off annually and could not travel without permission from their superiors, who often wanted them on constant standby. Senior officers—like their army counterparts—were notionally entitled to ten days' leave a month, but most did not take their full allowance, and some took virtually no days off. Police work was highly bureaucratized and form filled. A policeman's lot in the South was not a happy one, and many of those drawn to such a life were tough guy, *naklaeng* types rather than idealists. Nevertheless, the police had its fair share of very dedicated officers, some of whom had volunteered to serve in the South and were extremely anxious to make a difference.

When a group of civil society activists raised a series of issues—ranging from arrest procedures to extrajudicial killings—concerning the performance of the police at a Pattani seminar in April 2006, the provincial police commander expressed shock at the negative light in which the police were viewed.[177] One prominent Malay Muslim participant argued that a core problem—the tendency of villagers to protect criminal suspects—arose directly from the lack of trust in which the police were held. A senior police officer argued that this lack of trust derived from excessive political pressures on them to make rapid arrests, an approach that was counterproductive. Rather than quick results, the police needed to conduct higher quality investigations, ideally using forensic evidence.[178]

Yet just when the police most needed to develop their investigative skills and capabilities, they also began a strategy of militarizing themselves, emulating the equipment and tactics of the army. Between July 2005 and January 2006, the police trained twenty-two batches of men (totaling thirty-six hundred) in "counterinsurgency" combat duties, creating one or two twelve-man "small fighting teams" on constant standby at every district police station.[179] Old-style police patrols by one or two officers were largely abandoned, especially in high-risk areas; after mid-2005, the police normally went around in groups of at least six, sometimes in joint operations with the army.[180] Visually almost indistinguishable from soldiers, police commandos carried automatic weapons, wore full camouflage gear, and moved around in pickup trucks.[181] Rather than adopting a "softer," more civilian image than the military in order to play a mediating role in the conflict, the police were busy arming themselves to the teeth. Police stations were fortified with sandbags and barbed wire, taking on the appearance of bunkers. Though arguably necessary to provide protection—the Kapho and Than To police stations, for example, had previously come under fire from M-79 grenade launchers—such measures had the effect of further alienating the police from the communities they served.[182] One teacher in a Narathiwat village reported that he had not seen a policeman in his community for many years; the police preferred to stick to major roads and were reluctant to patrol in less accessible areas.[183]

Police major-general Korkiat Wongvorachart, the commander of Pattani provincial police, argued that the activities of NGOs and other organizations created obstacles to the resolution of problems in the South, since they promoted misleading information and undermined the trust of the community in the police.[184] Many rank-and-file policemen were deeply wary of NGOs and nervous about discussions of issues such as human rights, believing that a tougher law-and-order approach would yield better results than one based on understanding and reconciliation.[185]

A prominent Malay Muslim speaker at one seminar lamented that the military had changed their manner and demeanor greatly since January 2004, presenting a much more friendly and helpful image to the community—yet the police continued to look as stern and remote as ever.[186] Korkiat insisted that the image of the police was improving, and that the militants had tried to exploit differences with between the police and the army to their own advantage—something the two forces were now working hard to counter. As one prominent Malay Muslim argued, "The three Southern provinces are like a fighting ring for soldiers and policemen."[187] At a training session for new junior police officers being assigned to the three provinces, one of the speakers came from the army, and the trainees were implored to work closely with their military counterparts.[188] Yet in practice many villagers did not draw much of a distinction between the army and the police. While they tended to dislike the police slightly more because of their petty corruption—demanding bribes for offences such as riding motorcycles without helmets—both agencies were just part of "the government," tarred with the same brush.[189] However, villagers for whom arrest warrants were issued, or who were invited to participate in "peace-building" programs, strongly preferred to hand themselves over to the army. In the wake of the April 28 incidents, Thaksin went on television and invited anyone who had been involved in the violence to surrender, assuring them they would not be treated harshly. Three youths from the same village who had taken part in the attacks turned themselves into the army and were soon released after a period of questioning; but another youth who was taken to Yala police station by his father—who knew a local Malay-Muslim police officer—ended up being charged with serious offences.[190] Conditions at the special detention center for security suspects built within the Yala Police Academy were much less comfortable than those provided at the Inkhayut army camp, which also offered a more liberal visiting regime.

In theory, localizing the police force by bringing in more Malay Muslims was a logical way forward; in practice, however, local Muslims who entered the police often came under strong pressure to conform. As one academic argued, a quota scheme that allowed Malay Muslims to enter the national police academy was often counterproductive: "The objective of sending this person to study in that school was to solve the [Southern] problem, but sometimes they forgot....These people who are from here and graduated from that school think that they know everything, they don't want to discuss or talk with villagers or leaders."[191] Any Muslim who began drinking would lose respect in the local community—yet drinking was more or less obligatory for police officers. In practice, Buddhist police officers from Bangkok, the North or Northeast (though rarely those from the Upper South, especially Songkhla, Phatthalung, or Nakhon Si Thammarat) could often establish a better rapport with Malay Muslim villagers than members of their own community who had been socialized into the institutional culture of the Thai police.[192] As in other components of the Thai bureaucracy, this culture involved looking down on, patronizing, and mistreating local people. Only a handful of Malay Muslims reached senior positions in the police—perhaps 5 percent of those ranked colonel and above—and they were obliged to embrace the organizational culture of the Thai police force. One former senior police officer explained that after undertaking the hajj, his life changed: "I quit smoking and drinking and was concerned more about the people. I refused to take part in mainstream police culture and started to return to my own real way of life."[193] Yet as a senior police officer, asserting his Malay Muslim identity too strongly created problems; once he began to move in this direction, his further promotion was blocked and he was eventually transferred out of the three provinces, accused of "whistle-blowing" concerning extrajudicial killings. After Thaksin took power, Bangkok-based officers close to the premier ordered the use of these draconian methods in a misguided attempt to "mop up" the supposedly small number of remaining separatists. This senior officer found himself conflict with high-ranking police commanders when he began questioning policies such as "shaking down" and torturing suspects in security cases—as well as the informal policy of extrajudicial killings. This policy went hand in hand with the illegal killings used as part of Thaksin's 2003 "war on drugs." Abuses of power such as extrajudicial killings placed senior Malay-Muslim police officers in an impossible position, forced to choose between their careers and their communities. Although difficult to prove, credible allegations about continuing abuses of power by a small number of rogue police officers persisted.[194] A senior police officer interviewed by a PSU lecturer admitted that in the past, he had supported extrajudicial killings: "If they are really bandits, I would not act peacefully towards them; towards those who shoot police officers, I would not respond peacefully. Before we used to lure bandits for extrajudicial killing. But now we don't, because it is state policy for the police not to act provocatively."[195] The informant noted that while senior police officers understood the idea of nonviolence, the same could not be said of frontline policemen.[196] Frontline policemen tacitly admitted that extrajudicial killings could happen: if a community leader such as an ustadz or kamnan was well known to be supporting the militants and was warned to desist but persisted in working against the state, at a certain point police officers might decide they had "had enough"—but this would never be a matter of policy, nor would there be any official order.[197]

The performance of the police in the three provinces improved after the appointment of Adul Saengsingkaew as the chief of Police Region 9 (covering Pattani, Yala, and Narathiwat) in May 2005.[198] Recognizing that the police were themselves a significant part of the security problem in the region, Adul sought to raise the quality of operations in district stations, moving out some "deadwood" senior officers who had been banished to the South as a punishment for inefficiency or worse. Perhaps one third of the senior officers based in districts were volunteers; many others, assigned there on four-year terms, were desperately requesting transfers out of the area at the end of their assignments.[199] Overall, numbers of police officers in the border provinces were well below par.[200] Shortfalls in police numbers were offset by a special program to recruit 1,170 police lance-corporals, who were given a year's training on local customs and conditions, and required to serve at least five years in the border area.[201]

District and provincial operations were supported by a major region-wide operations team stationed within the Yala Police Academy. This unit, known as the Forward Operation Center of the Royal Thai Police Office, was part of the central Thai police organization, rather than under local jurisdiction. Around 80 percent of the center's officers were volunteers, who had been transferred from other parts of the country to boost the capacity of local forces. Most Forward Operation Center officers lived inside the academy's extensive secure compound and enjoyed much better working conditions than those assigned to districts. Senior officers from the Forward Operation Center closely monitored the work of district police stations, and the center provided logistical and investigative backup for important cases. Unlike his predecessors, Adul headed both the Police Region 9 and the Forward Operation Center, giving him much greater powers of coordination and control. Adul introduced training programs in interrogation techniques:[202] he also planned to develop a research center, and new courses in political awareness.[203] But the all-important Forward Operations Center remained an ad hoc body, with no permanent standing in the structure of the police, and so was potentially vulnerable to future political pressures or policy changes. The structure of police operations remained excessively complicated, with large numbers of overlapping units; meanwhile the quality of cooperation between the police and other security forces hinged largely on individual personal relationships, and there was no joint task force to pool information and frame security responses on a day-to-day basis.

Overall, the police constituted a substantial security problem in the deep South. The force was so widely disliked and mistrusted that the best efforts of dedicated individual officers, or of reformist commanders such as Adul, could be readily undermined by the actions and attitudes of the men on patrol. At root, the organizational culture of the Thai police—including their petty corruption, heavy drinking, and willingness to resort to human rights abuses—was simply incompatible with the values and beliefs of Malay Muslims.

Militias

As well as the regular military and the police, a range of volunteers and militias operated in the South. As time went on, the security forces grew increasingly eager to subcontract frontline duties to paramilitaries such as the army rangers and a bewildering array of voluntary defense groups. Many of the best trained and equipped regular troops remained in Bangkok, or in the North and Northeast, where they performed mainly political functions. Control of troops around the capital was essential in order to prevent—or carry out—a coup d'etat. Following the September 19, 2006, coup, troops stationed in the old Thaksin strongholds of the North and Northeast were tasked with monitoring resistance to the junta.

Officials of the Ministry of Interior had a shared responsibility for security issues. In practice, lines of command were somewhat blurred; under Thaksin's "CEO governor" policy, individual provincial governors were supposed to enjoy considerable autonomy in decision making. But in the context of the three provinces, this autonomy was undermined by the overarching authority of the Southern Border Provinces Peace Building Command,[204] which brought together responsibility for security affairs under the Fourth Army commander. A bastion of conservative thinking, the Interior Ministry normally expected governors and district officers to take the lead in suppressing trouble—especially demonstrations testifying to substantial popular dissent—in the areas under the jurisdiction. District officers or governors who failed to comply might find themselves almost immediately transferred to lesser or inactive posts. Hence the first instinct of Interior Ministry officials was to disperse demonstrations by any means at their disposal, to avoid incurring Bangkok's displeasure; in the South, this often meant readily agreeing to protesters' demands. The Interior Ministry's preoccupation with ensuring orderliness and good behavior,[205] however, was not always appropriate in conflict situations; this mentality, echoed among the military and police, contributed to hasty decisions to "clear" the problem in episodes such as the Kru-Ze siege and the Tak Bai arrests.

Interior Ministry officials were in a somewhat paradoxical situation: charged with maintaining order, they had no troops or police under their direct command. In practice, they exerted power primarily through a combination of fear and respect; villagers in most parts of Thailand tended to defer to their authority, at least on the surface. In the deep South, however, where the legitimacy of the Thai state was much less robust, officials could put little trust in local deference. In theory, each district officer oversaw a coordinating body that was responsible for liaising with the army and police on security issues; every district office housed a "war room" from which incidents were supposed to be managed. In practice, the police and especially the army were reluctant to take instructions from district officers, and these "war rooms" never functioned properly.[206] The security of district officers—and offices—was provided partly by the military, and partly by paramilitary "volunteers" (known as "Or Sor") hired directly by the ministry, some of whom were former conscripts.[207] They received a month's military training and were generally armed with M-16s. These mainly Muslim paramilitaries were relatively well paid: a basic salary of seven thousand baht monthly, plus thirty-five hundred baht danger money and a per diem for daily expenses. Because they were seen as potential informers, Or Sor were often targeted by the movement and ostracized in their own communities.[208] But even those they protected had doubts about their loyalty; one official previously posted in the South discovered that a volunteer who had protected her later openly joined the militant movement.[209]

The Interior Ministry supported initiatives to improve security in the South; the most well-known was the Chor Ror Bor,[210] or community security volunteer program. Operating in every village in the three provinces, the program provided a budget of twenty thousand baht per month to village headmen, for local people to maintain their own security rosters. Many villages displayed impressive-looking lists of 30 or 40 program members, several of whom were allocated watch duties each night. By October 2005, there were more than 47,400 Chor Ror Bor in the three provinces.[211] In theory, the Chor Ror Bor were supposed to operate checkpoints on major routes into the village and to notify the military and police of any suspicious activity. While such programs functioned well in certain areas—especially in Buddhist majority villages—in many Muslim areas villagers were extremely reluctant to carry out roles that put them into immediate personal danger and also aligned them with state policies. Leaflets specifically warned villagers not to participate in the program:

> Therefore, whoever cooperates, supports, or works for these institutions or is employed as a running dog by the kafir Siamese government in the various agencies which have been created such as Chor Ror Bor, community police, 4,500 baht employees, volunteers and rangers are, intentionally or unintentionally, declaring war on the Patani Mujahidin.[212]

Casualties inflicted on members of Chor Ror Bor and other militias illustrated the inability of the Thai state to protect its village-level adjutants. As one local politician put it, they used to be protected by their patrons, but now their patrons were too busy taking care of themselves.[213] On various occasions, weapons were seized from Chor Ror Bor volunteers by militants.[214] Indeed, just such an incident—in which six volunteers were arrested after having handed over their weapons, possibly under duress— provided the trigger for the Tak Bai protests. Chor Ror Bor were often the targets of attacks and were not well trained or equipped to respond. In a notorious incident on April 9, 2007, Buddhist defense volunteers opened fire on a convoy of Muslim funeral-goers in Ban Pakdi, Bannang Sata, Yala, killing four youths and injuring six others.[215]

Driving into a Pattani village very late one Saturday night, I found no sign of any Chor Ror Bor on duty; my local Muslim companion explained that in most villages, the supposed volunteers simply split the money amongst themselves and "slept soundly."[216] In other cases, the village headmen pocketed all or most of the funds. Pattani governor Panu Uthairat explained that headmen had complete discretion to use the funds as they felt fit, but if there was an incident in any village and it emerged that the Chor Ror Bor had not been on duty at the time, the allocation would be cut to fifteen thousand baht; in the event of a second incident, it would be further cut to ten thousand baht.[217] He expressed concern that the media often identified victims of the violence as Chor Ror Bor members, which he believed exposed them to greater danger and made people reluctant to cooperate with the scheme. Panu's response was to ask the media not to report victims' affiliations with the program, but the targeting of volunteers was well known locally. While impressive on paper, in many areas the implementation of the Chor Ror Bor scheme bordered on farce. Ironically, the militant movement created its own versions of Chor Ror Bor, recruiting locals to watch out for the movements of troops and police. Nearly half of the participants in a series of peace-building camps in Songkhla admitted that they had been involved in such activities. Some claimed that they initially thought they were Chor Ror Bor, only later realizing that they were working for the movement;[218] others simply worked for the movement in the guise of serving as Chor Ror Bor.[219]

A parallel program to Chor Ror Bor was Or Ror Bor,[220] which operated in Buddhist communities and came under the patronage of the Queen.[221] A deputy royal aide-de-camp, General Naphol Boontap, played a key role in establishing this program and training the volunteers, who were generally better equipped and organized that Chor Ror Bor and more highly motivated. Or Ror Bor was also much better funded: the forty-six volunteers in one Pattani scheme received a hundred baht for every shift they worked, and eight people were on duty each night, operating in two shifts. Around thirty of them had their own guns, and twenty had been trained to shoot by rangers. Or Ror Bor trained around twenty-five hundred villagers by October 2004.[222] Whereas Chor Ror Bor was rather vague in focus, Or Ror Bor was implicitly organized to defend Buddhists from Muslim assailants, and security teams were often based in temples. Volunteers worked alongside soldiers and police officers, and constituted a de facto paramilitary force.

Yet another volunteer scheme was the community police, Tor Ror Chor,[223] which operated under the auspices of the regular police force.[224] This scheme was based at the tambon level; every tambon had two regular, armed police officers who served as head and deputy head of the program, and then four volunteers per village, some of whom were hired under the forty-five-hundred baht scheme. While Chor Ror Bor were normally stationary, the community police volunteers were supposed to engage in active patrolling of the subdistrict, and to report any problems or suspicious activity to the police.

The Interior Ministry also played a leading role in the 4500-baht scheme, a job creation program that was partly designed to win over young people to the side of the Thai state.[225] Many of those hired for the second phase of the program were given military training—ironically, often alongside "peace trainees" suspected of harboring militant sympathies—and were expected to play leading roles in village security activities.[226] The forty-five-hundred baht scheme was highly controversial and regularly criticized in anonymous leaflets apparently produced by the movement.

Another Interior Ministry project was the "peace village" scheme: *muban santisuk*. I first became aware of this when I spotted a sticker outside a Narathiwat shophouse, which declared that the household supported peace.[227] The residents could not explain what the sticker meant, but told me a community leader had put it up. Interior Ministry officials managed a process whereby communities were encouraged to declare themselves "peace villages" and proclaim their opposition to militancy. Pattani governor Panu, one of the principal advocates of the scheme, clearly saw the policy as part of a psychological warfare operation: "It's to get the villagers to feel they should cooperate.... It creates a feeling, creates cooperation, brings unity."[228] By May 2006, 407 villages in Pattani—almost two-thirds—had declared themselves peace villages. Panu explained that under the principles of the scheme:

1. No villagers belong to the militants.
2. The village has security procedures to report on irregular activities.
3. Chor Ror Bor are responsible for certain number of households.
4. Villagers will take care of themselves.

In practice, the initiative for declaring a village *muban sanitsuk* came largely from local government officials—including staff from the subdistrict offices—who visited the community to encourage local people to support the aims of the project.[229] While the actual declarations were made by the villagers, they did so under pressure from officials. One Pattani official who was directly involved in implementing the policy admitted that it made little sense, but explained that it had to be carried out because it has been ordered by the governor.[230] While a few local politicians were extremely supportive of the program,[231] which came with a special budget, some residents were apprehensive that making "peace declarations" could actually precipitate greater violence in their areas.[232] Just before one planned peace proclamation in Krong Pinang in May 2006, an attack was staged on the district office in an apparently deliberate preemptive rebuke. Such fears were shared by some senior military officers, who argued that the peace village scheme could provoke increased levels of militant activity.[233] For the military, *muban santisuk* was an example of the dangerous naivety of the Interior Ministry; disagreements over the program illustrated the tensions between civilian and uniformed officials about the management of security issues.

Not all schemes to defend communities in the region were directly endorsed by the Thai state. Some Buddhist groups began conducting their own military-style training, arguing that they could not rely on the security forces and needed to be ready to defend their own lives and property. A shooting instructor explained to me that the purpose of weapons training was not to use guns for day-to-day protection, but as a preparation for possible all-out civil war.[234] One unofficial and secretive group, known as Ruam Thai, was created by senior Yala police officer Phitak Iadkaew.

Phitak organized two-day training programs for more than six thousand volunteers, virtually all of them Buddhist.[235] Phitak was almost transferred out of Yala in June 2007, when allegations surfaced that some Ruam Thai members were involved in vigilante-style attacks on Muslims. He was only reprieved when local Buddhists staged a demonstration to protest against moves to transfer him. Other Buddhist militias not affiliated with Ruam Thai were established in Narathiwat and Saba Yoi, while in some places— including Kolomudo village in Saba Yoi—Muslims created their own village defense schemes which were not part of the official Chor Ror Bor program. Overall, these trends toward the subcontracting of security services to official and unofficial militias augured ill. Poorly trained and ill-disciplined militia groups could exacerbate an already tense situation, especially if they were tempted to move beyond a purely defensive role and undertake vigilante-style activities.

In November 2006, the Southern Border Provinces Administrative Centre (SBPAC) was reestablished; the first director was Pranai Suwannarat, younger brother of former director and current privy councilor Palakorn Suwannarat. The resurrection of the SBPAC marked an attempt to restore conditions in the South to the pre-Thaksin status quo ante, by trying to re-create an earlier social compact in which the civilian Interior Ministry, rather than the military, would play the leading role. But, at least initially, the new SBPAC seemed a shadow of its former self: the agency struggled to recruit staff of sufficient numbers and caliber, and lacked the popular touch of its predecessor.[236] The legislation that reestablished the SBPAC emphasized the powers of Interior Ministry officials, rather than community involvement.[237] The SBPAC's flagship project, a "justice maintenance section" to oversee the investigation and transfers of problem officials, got off to a slow start and was of doubtful effectiveness.[238] In the changed political and security conditions post-2004, the SBPAC's rebranded notions of virtuous bureaucracy seemed increasingly anachronistic.

Surrenders

Around August 2005, the Thai authorities began a policy of identifying suspected militants and those whom they believed were "at risk" of developing militant sympathies. Those in the "risk group" category would be invited to attend peace building camps, in order to be instilled with a more positive view of the Thai state. Most of these camps were held at army bases outside the three provinces; during the early phase of the program, most trainees were sent to an artillery base just outside Songkhla town, for seven days of intensive training. Later on, the length of training was increased to a month, and virtually all participants were sent to other parts of Thailand. The "surrender policy" reflected moralistic Thai notions that Malay Muslim residents of the three provinces could be divided into "good" and bad" people, those who sympathized with the militants and those who supported the Thai state. The aim of the surrender program was to convert the bad into the good.

Unfortunately, the surrender program suffered from at least three fundamental problems. First, most Malay Muslims in the Southern border provinces were neither "good" nor "bad" in the senses constructed by Thai bureaucratic thinking; they were struggling to negotiate their identities and manage their lives, and were above all anxious to avoid being targeted either by the authorities or by the militants. Second, the Thai state failed to develop any effective means to identifying militant suspects or sympathizers. While the authorities claimed that "blacklists" were compiled only on the basis of confirmed intelligence from the military, the police, and the Interior Ministry, in practice none of these agencies had sufficiently reliable information about village-level militant activity. The supposedly triangulated lists were actually almost worthless, and many of those ordered to report for training insisted that they had not been involved in any militant activity.[239] Some were there simply because they had personal conflicts with local informants.[240]

This led to a third problem: at times, the surrender policy actually played into the hands of the militants, since some of those obliged to surrender were extremely unhappy about the program, and were in turn radicalized into opponents of the Thai state. Those who returned from the surrender camps were explicitly regarded by the authorities as the "eyes and ears" of the government, by the militants as potential government spies, and by other members of their communities as either militants or state informers. Selection for the surrender program undermined the standing of individuals in the community—especially those in leadership positions, including imam and even village headmen. Eventually, military commanders became disillusioned with the surrender program, but not before it has done significant damage to community relations. One military officer insisted that surveys showed more than 50 percent of ex-trainees cooperated with the authorities after attending peace-building courses: even if true, this figure begged the question of what happened to the attitudes of the remainder.[241]

As one senior security official explained:

> The army has the idea that getting people to surrender is an achievement, a way of winning the battle. Trying to make the public believe that they are getting something accomplished. But these surrenderees are not really surrendering,

the whole thing is fake. It's all about pleasing the minister, and making news.[242] Some of those who surrendered were paid 1,000 baht each to turn themselves in by police officers or military people.[243]

In a bizarre twist, the Thai Ministry of Defense actually made the number of surrenderees one of its key performance indicators for 2006: the more people surrendered, the better, irrespective of whether they really harbored militant tendencies or sympathies.[244] Provincial governors in Yala and Narathiwat competed with one another to boost the numbers of surrenders, while Pattani governor Panu was rather more lukewarm toward the program.[245] Units involved in the program had a structural incentive to exaggerate numbers in order to boost their budgets. The surrenders were actually a form of dramatic performance, involving highly publicized ceremonies that were short on substance. I attended a large ceremony at Narathiwat's Imperial Hotel on August 27, 2006, at which more than 296 former "surrenderees" made a pledge of allegiance to the Thai state. Informants explained to me that the participants had actually been rounded up on a quota basis by village headmen, and paid 200 baht a time to attend; many of them had never actually participated in the surrender programs at all.[246] Eventually even army commanders expressed doubts about the surrender policy, and it was quietly scaled down. Fourth Army commander Ongkorn Thongprasom had conceded that the policy was disastrous and counterproductive in an interview with a foreign journalist in May 2006.[247] Immediately prior to the coup, one senior general overseeing security policy in the South played down the policy, describing it as a "Chidchai initiative"[248] entirely contingent on commitment from the government.[249] Yet although the postcoup government shifted policy on the South, the damage from the ill-conceived surrender program was already done.

Intelligence

Underpinning security work in any conflict zone is intelligence: detailed information about the enemy. The Thai security forces had very limited intelligence, much of it was of low quality, and they consistently failed to share it. This was a national-level problem in Thailand: distrust between the police, the various branches of the military, and the civilian intelligence agencies was a major obstacle to the pooling of information. Thailand's international partners were deeply disappointed at the lack of return on their investments in strengthening the country's defense and law enforcement capacity. A counterinsurgency and organized crime operations center based at the Supreme Command in Bangkok had been staffed and equipped, but in practice was not functioning.[250] Military professionalism was extremely low, despite the fact that many senior officers had received some overseas training, usually in the United States or Australia: the Thai Army still brought in U.S. trainers even for basic skills such as shooting. The Thai authorities repeatedly asked foreign governments for help in procuring more equipment, but their capacity to utilize existing equipment was widely questioned. The Israelis were believed to have supplied the Thais with very sophisticated telephone surveillance technology for use in the South, but Thai operatives lacked either the patience or the Malay language skills to reap any benefit from this investment. The Thais were also using unmanned aerial surveillance vehicles (UAVs), with no obvious direct boost to security effectiveness.[251]

Nine different agencies were involved in intelligence gathering, and there was no systematic process for analyzing the data they generated.[252] Information received by senior officials in Bangkok was heavily filtered and screened, to suit the interests of a small number of well-placed individuals and cliques. Because there were so many different intelligence agencies, no one knew who to believe. While intelligence coordination problems are common in many countries, in Thaksin's Thailand they were compounded by his highly personalistic management style. Thaksin had typically turned to a small number of people he trusted—police and military officers with whom he had strong personal connections—rather than any systematic intelligence process. He placed some of his own people in the National Security Council and drew on some military and National Intelligence Agency data, as well as information from the Special Branch. He was also alleged to have made use of eavesdropping technology operated by a team of around fifty Shin Corp employees—in effect, his own private surveillance agency.[253]

The core problem of Thai intelligence in the South was a lack of high-quality human intelligence from inside the militant movement.[254] The intelligence agencies had recruited some former low-level militants, who had been released from their loyalty oaths using a specially devised procedure, but lacked sources in the upper echelons of the movement. Very little intelligence was specific enough directly to inform military operations.[255] In theory, intelligence was pulled together by the National Security Council, but in practice this body had become largely moribund by Thaksin's second term. The prime minister distrusted the minority "peace oriented" NSC clique (which included Phichai Rattapol and Jiraporn Bunnag) responsible for drafting the 1999–2003 security policy on the South, whom he saw as allied with the Democrats and Surayud.[256] The NSC remained stuck in communist-era thinking and offered little by way of new interpretations or solutions concerning the rapidly changing Southern conflict. In any case, rather than encouraging the pooling or analysis of intelligence data, Thaksin insisted that all the various agencies report their findings directly to him—resulting in a confusing and incoherent picture of developments. Such confusions were evident in a leaked intelligence document apparently prepared for Thaksin early in 2004, which rehashed a bizarre collection of conspiracy theories and made no attempt to assess the relative credibility of its various sources.[257]

Repeated demands from senior officials—such as army commander Sonthi Boonyaratkalin—for hard data about the structure and membership of the militant movement yielded few results.[258] Military intelligence officers persisted in reciting well-worn mantras about a "people's war," encircling the cities, and the need for insurgent fish to live in the water of sympathetic communities.[259] There was an urgent need for a fully integrated joint task force, bringing together the various intelligence and security agencies, with daily meetings and sharing of information.[260] In the absence of concrete measures to coordinate intelligence, the security offensive in the South remained unfocused and incurably inept.

Conclusion

If 2004 was the year of sensational security failures—the massive blunders of Kru-Ze and Tak Bai—the period that followed was characterized by low-level ineptitude. The lesson of Tak Bai was that large crowds of protestors had to be dispersed peacefully, even if—as at Tanyong Limo—the price for this strategy was the sacrifice of hostages. Yet such sacrifices did not come cheaply: they undermined the credibility of the Thai forces, weakened their morale, invited the opprobrium of both Thaksin and the Queen, and played very badly with the majority Buddhist public. There was a fine line between averting unnecessary confrontation and betraying the lack of any stomach for a fight. Examples of such security failures were legion.

At the Narathiwat village Kuching Rupa on May 19, 2006, two female Buddhist teachers were taken hostage in a room at the village nursery, where they were beaten with sticks; one teacher, Khru Juling Panganmoon, lapsed into a coma and eventually died. The village headman had informed the district officer—his immediate superior—at around noon.[261] In theory, this should have been enough to trigger a full-scale security response, but the district officer failed to pass on the news, asking the headman and kamnan to deal with the situation themselves. Partly because confused reports suggested that around eight hundred villagers had surrounded the area, army officers were scared to act without orders. The roads into the village had been blocked by large logs, in an obviously preplanned operation. At around 2:00 P.M. Fourth Army commander Ongkorn Thongprasom learned about the incident, not from his own men, but from some reporters. Police commandos were then informed and immediately set off by helicopter.[262] But meanwhile the headman and one of his assistants, hearing the teachers' cries for help, had battered down the door, and the assailants had fled. At this point there were no soldiers or police in sight, and no sound of any helicopters.[263] None of the procedures for a coordinated security response functioned: local security commanders were terrified to take responsibility for their actions. This was partly a result of the militant "successes" at Tak Bai, and partly a product of the dysfunctional nature of the security apparatus.[264] In fact, troops and police could have reached the village by helicopter in little more than half an hour; the assailants, described by the headman as a group of teenagers, were apparently unarmed, and could easily have been apprehended. The Kru Juling case evoked a great outpouring of national grief, tinged with growing overtones of Buddhist chauvinism, yet the entire episode might so easily have turned out very differently.

In the fishing village of Rusamilae, less than a mile from the campus of Prince of Songkhla University on the edge of Pattani town, an army camp lay empty. Following a bomb on August 2, 2006, that killed a soldier, the Thai military development unit housed there abandoned their improvised base, erected by sappers building a school nearby. As I argued soon afterward: "The gates now stand wide open, and the silence of the camp speaks volumes about a nation that has lost its way, and a state that cannot exercise its authority fully, even inside its own territory."[265] Instead of reinforcing the base and demonstrating to the militants that they would not concede defeat, the symbolic response of the unit concerned was to flee—a response that gave succor to the enemies of the Thai state. Such responses raised serious questions about whether the Thai forces had the necessary grit to defend their territory. In November 2006, protestors successfully forced the Border Patrol Police to withdraw from a temporary base in Ban Bacho, Yala; similar tactics were later employed in other parts of the province. Most demonstrations followed a similar pattern: large numbers of villagers appeared quite suddenly to surround a village, a police station, or other government office; women were at the forefront of the protests, usually covering their faces (using a noncustomary "Muslim" practice for opportunistic purposes); men remained in the background, and no obvious leaders showed themselves (clearly a deliberate attempt to avoid creating targets for arrest).

The success of these "nonviolent" tactics could be seen very clearly in the case of two men arrested for suspected involvement in a militant attack in Kapho, Pattani, in November 2006. When the police made two successive arrests in connection with a fatal shooting incident, mass protests were sparked and the authorities eventually agreed to bail out the men, both of whom promptly disappeared.[266] By forcing the authorities to agree to the bail terms, demonstrators had effectively subverted the judicial process and left the Thai state powerless properly to investigate or punish very serious crimes. To make matters worse, two local village headmen had been forced to bail out one of the suspects and were left owing large sums of money when their charge absconded. What might appear superficially to be a successful example of peaceful conflict resolution actually undermined local leadership structures and left a community immensely vulnerable to future violent attacks. The Thai authorities were taking "easy" options that actually created serious long term problems.

There were few obvious ways out of the security impasse. Some analysts called for an Iraq-style surge, a doubling of troop numbers to create a "security grid" in the South, arguing that such moves could dramatically reduce levels of violence.[267] But especially given the poor performance of the Thai security forces to date, there seemed no reason at all to believe that such measures could work. National Security Council deputy secretary-general Jiraporn Bunnag proposed that more marines be deployed in the South, reflecting a view that marines were more effective and less abusive than soldiers.[268] However, the deployment of more naval personnel in the region was jealously opposed by the army.[269] The idea of replacing soldiers with marines reflected conservative, royalist notions of "virtuous security," again suggesting that the moral and behavioral qualities of the security forces were an important factor in the escalating conflict. This emphasis on the need for state officials to demonstrate their morality and exercise justice again showed a misunderstanding of the underlying causes of the violence. When General Anupong Paochinda took over as army commander in October 2007, he announced a policy of assigning Army regions normally based in other parts of Thailand to take the lead in the troubled Southern border provinces: the First Army was to work in Narathiwat, the Second Army in Pattani, the Third Army in Yala, and the Fourth Army in Songkhla. Such changes, while potentially an improvement on the status quo, fell well short of what was really needed: a substantive reorganization of the Royal Thai Army to reflect the country's actual security needs. While during the second half of 2007 there was some evidence that security forces were becoming more effective, 2008 opened with a fresh round of brutal militant attacks. Since 2004, violence had been cyclical, receding for a time before returning in new waves of blood-letting.[270] The military was always eager to highlight apparent downturns, but the real picture was less positive. Just as levels of violence yo-yoed, so the security forces oscillated between hard-line tactics and reconciliation approaches; to some extent, Anupong swung back toward the kind of securitization strategies favored by Thaksin's commanders.

The security policies of the Thai state in the South were a lamentable catalogue of criminal blunders, negligence, incompetence, lack of coordination, and sheer misdirection. Thaksin's claim that soldiers there "deserved to die" was a shameful outburst: many individual security personnel were incredibly dedicated and committed, carrying out dangerous daily routines with little reward. At the same time, the Thai state arguably "deserved to lose" the war for the South, given its woeful performance in so many crucial incidents and altercations. Thailand could not hope to normalize the security situation simply through dialog; militants were only likely to engage in serious negotiations when they understood that an armed struggle was unwinnable. During the years following January 2004, the militant movement consistently gained the upper hand in the Southern border provinces, placing the Thai security forces firmly on the defensive as they secured a succession of propaganda victories. The militant movement now requires some closer scrutiny.

4

MILITANTS

The nature of the militant movement behind most of the violence in Thailand's deep South remains a matter of dispute. Important questions include: How are militants recruited? What is the structure of the movement? How far is the movement subject to central command and control? How far is this an "Islamic" movement? What do the militants want? How closely is the movement related to former "separatist" groups such as BRN?[1]

Some analysts see the militant movement as a reconfigured version of earlier separatist organizations, probably led by a shadowy group known as BRN-Coordinate.[2] Others view the militants as a largely ad hoc network organization, with little formal leadership. These two readings can also be seen as opposite ends of a continuum, with the truth lying somewhere in between: the militant movement evidently combines both organized and ad hoc elements. Interpreting the Patani conflict involves staking out a defensible position at some point along this continuum. I am arguing that the militant movement cannot be readily equated with BRN-C but is best seen as a "liminal lattice," a loose network rather than a structured hierarchy.

The attacks of April 28, 2004, in which 105 "militants,"[3] one civilian, and five members of the security forces died, are by far the best documented element of the post–January 2004 violence, and many features of these attacks have parallels in other incidents and developments. These attacks provided a moment of clarity: the Thai state was really facing an organized militant movement. Prior to that, even some members of the security services had believed that incidents such as the January 4 weapons seizure had been staged by the army.[4] At the same time, no similar pattern of attacks has been staged before or since: April 28 was both an outstanding and a deeply unrepresentative example of militant violence in the Thai South.

This chapter will take those events as a major case study, before reviewing militant activity after April 2004 and offering some tentative conclusions about the nature of the movement. The question of how far the militants are linked with BRN-C is illustrated by the April 28 attacks, which were conducted by an organized group of men: some of its leaders expressed an affinity with BRN, yet the main leader Ustadz Soh apparently did not. Did the "two wings" of the April 28 attackers offer a model for the apparent dualism of the wider militant movement, combining "old separatists" and rootless, new-style members?

April 28

Early in the morning of April 28, groups of militants attacked twelve targets—mainly security bases and checkpoints—in Pattani, Yala, and Songkhla provinces. One hundred and eleven people died in the fighting, virtually all of them on the militant side; 32 were killed in the set piece of the day, the storming of the historic Kru-Ze mosque in Pattani. Youths who survived participation in the April 28, 2004, attacks gave a variety of explanations. Some were recruited directly by Ustadz Soh, the apparent mastermind of the attacks. Ustadz Soh had held swearing ceremonies with groups of young recruits a month or two before the incident; some of them also took part in training sessions, which involved only physical exercise, rather than combat or the use of weapons. Ustadz Soh or his associates gave some of the participants holy water to drink on the night of April 27. This "holy water" apparently boosted their confidence, because they believed that it would make them invulnerable to bullets.[5] Ustadz Soh seems not to have given his fighters anything to read; none of those I interviewed had seen the *Berjihad di Patani.*[6] One participant argued that some of those who joined in were not really devout Muslims; another explained how he and the leader of one incident used to go into Pattani town to pick up girls.[7] One, a teenager at the time, was at a loss to explain why he took part in the incident: "I can't really explain why I participated in the incident. I always stayed at home, never went anywhere else; I had never even been into Yala town before. I graduated from high school (M6) and never attended religious school. I'm not very religious."[8] Another participant stated:

> On that day, I didn't have any intention to kill. I was woken up by my friends and went along with them on a motorcycle. The only weapons we had were knives. I didn't think we could fight with anyone with those. They fired their guns and six of us were dead. I didn't really think it through before

being taken off by my friends. I heard from others that some participants were tricked into going to a "wedding." But they got shot as soon as they arrived at the scene. They didn't have any bad intention to kill anyone. They were deceived.[9]

These retrospective accounts of how young men naïvely blundered into joining attacks on security checkpoints are somewhat self-serving, shifting all blame for the April 28 attacks either to those who died, or to Ustadz Soh himself, who vanished without trace. But the men themselves were disarmingly ordinary and lacking in guile; the gist of their stories was entirely believable.

Ustadz Soh

One April 28 participant who had previously been a student at Ustadz Soh's school, Pondok Babor Ming,[10] asserted that Ustadz Soh had been like a father to him, often providing meals at his house, and giving him twenty or thirty baht each time he visited. Ustadz Soh had taught him some Arabic spells to protect himself from bullets, which he said would also make him invisible.[11] Ustadz Soh did not actually teach at the pondok but was a sort of administrator there.[12] In 2003, prior to working at the pondok, Ustadz Soh had taught tadika for six months at Ban Som in Pattani (one of the main centers for the planning of the Mae Lan and Kru-Ze attacks).[13] He regularly spoke at the Ban Kuwa village mosque after Friday evening prayers, and his audience always listened very attentively.[14] He used both his wife's village and the pondok as recruitment centers for the attacks. Ustadz Soh had a good understanding of psychology and was highly persuasive: in regular meetings with small groups of youths, he would typically talk about the history of Patani for around twenty minutes, stressing the need to recover Patani from Thailand and leaving listeners very aroused and inspired. He would then talk about the magic spells and their efficacy for around half an hour. Ustadz Soh also took some of them on visits to Kru-Ze and Ban Dato to learn about the history of Patani and to recount to them the events of the Dusun-yur "rebellion." Fixated with Kru-Ze, he misleadingly claimed that the mosque (which was actually an unfinished structure) had been severely damaged by the Thai state and showed them pictures of a planned restoration of the mosque after Patani's independence.

One informant reported that Ustadz Soh tried to convince him to join the movement by talking about ideas of jihad, saying that it was time to fight a jihad, and those who died fighting would go straight to heaven.[15] Ustadz Soh taught youths in the area near his school to pray, but also filled them with resentment about the Thai state, telling them about the cruelty and abuses committed by state officials—especially the police and military—and encouraged them to hate these officers.[16] Another informant described how Ustadz Soh was able to recount the history of Islam and of Patani, peppering his explanation with Koranic references to create a convincing case for supporting separatism.[17] As one informant put it, "most of the teenagers believed in Ustadz Soh, because he appeared very respectable. He groomed himself very modestly. He convinced us not to get close to the officials."[18] Another attacker recounted: "The villagers didn't really like police. The army is better because they get along well with the people. They told me to go to [attack] the police station and I thought it's the right place to go."[19] An informant explained how Ustadz Soh trained one group of twelve men intensively during the two or three months prior to the attacks. In nightly meetings inside the village mosque, he taught them to hate police and soldiers,[20] partly on the grounds that they mistreated Muslim women,[21] and also because the government was undermining Islam. Ustadz Soh talked about the cause of separatism and the great history of Patani.[22] He also quoted from the Koran to illustrate that killing was not a sin, as in the case of the American invasion of Iraq: just as Iraqi people were entitled to kill Americans, so Patani people must fight the Siamese.[23] Ustadz Soh used a variety of different themes in his rhetoric, ranging from history to jihad, apparently depending on his audience—yet the key to his success appears to have been his persuasive tongue, rather than any particularly emotive issue. A number of informants commented on his exceptional gift of the gab.

Another core leader in the April 28 movement, Yuso Mama, was said to have told audiences at regular monthly meetings after Friday prayers that after Patani gained independence, people would have a much better life, free from mistreatment or arrest by the police.[24] The informant believed that Yuso would become an important figure in the new Patani state. Ustadz Soh told some members of the group that when Patani gained independence, he would become the prime minister.[25] Another informant said he was really confident a separate state would be achieved after April 28, so persuasive was Ustadz Soh.[26]

Preparations

An informant who was recruited two weeks before the attacks,[27] by a close friend who asked him to join the movement to get the Patani state back, at first refused but later agreed out of a sense of obligation to his friend.[28] His friend never told him what they were going to do, but after recruiting him took his ID card, only returning it two days later. This implies that the details of recruits were formally logged and recorded in some way by the movement.

Some participants in the April 28 events had been part of local cells for an extended period; one had been recruited back in mid-2003.[29] His group had held monthly meetings at which they were asked to pay thirty baht a month in dues; members were urged to grow tapioca and kitchen vegetables, as well as to stock in staples such as rice, salt, sugar and *budu,*[30] which would be needed for self-reliance when the coming war started.[31] Another informant had been instructed to prepare stocks of food for the movement to fight the coming war, including raising ducks, chickens, and fish.[32] One informant knew in advance of the plans to stage the April 28 attacks; a friend had told him that if he did not return within a few days, he would be dead.[33] Ustadz Soh instructed another informant privately that if they seized the weapons from the Than To army post, they were to burn down the post afterward.[34] But he apparently gave them no instructions as to what they should do with the weapons.

Magic

Belief in magic is widespread in the Malay world, and the use of magic by militants in the Thai South must be taken seriously—however implausible it may sound to Western observers. Most of the April 28 participants had been issued with magic spells in Arabic, which they had generally acquired during visits to Kelantan, from "Ayoh" (also known as Ismael Jaffar, Ismael Yameena, or "Poh Su"), a Malaysian expert in the dark arts. Ayoh was described by various informants as between fifty and sixty years old, around 165 cm (five feet five inches) tall, clean shaven, and speaking with a Kelantanese accent. He lived in a detached one-story wooden house in Ban Baseh Buteh, Tanohmaeroh, with a wife (Mama) aged around fifty, a son and daughter in their twenties,[35] and two men, believed to be his assistants. One of these men, known as Ber Mae, was Ayoh's star student. He came from Waeng in Narathiwat and was able to administer spells himself in Ayoh's absence; the other was a Malaysian aged around forty, known as Datoh.[36] Ayoh sometimes visited Ustadz Soh at his pondok. Another informant reported that Ayoh had built a brick meditation cave at this house, with the words "As-salam Alaykum" in front.[37] A coauthor of the booklet *Berjihad di Patani,* Ayoh was seen by some informants as a core leader who would be given a senior post when Patani gained independence.

Groups of men traveled to Kelantan together to procure Ayoh's spells, often spending more than a thousand baht each on transportation, and the costs of the spells themselves—a considerable sum in this low-income area. On March 7 and 8, 2004, Ayoh traveled to Pattani and conducted spell ceremonies at a house near Mae Lan. The March 7 ceremony was attended by more than two hundred people from Pattani, Yala, and Songkhla,[38] including some of the leaders of the April 28 attacks. Ayoh also blessed around thirty or forty knives and swords,[39] "rosaries," shirts, and amulets belonging to the leaders of the group. Most of these items were subsequently found at the sites of the April 28 attacks. Ayoh reportedly went to Kru-Ze and performed a ceremony there after completing his activities on March 7.

Many of those recruited into the movement underwent swearing ceremonies, or *supoh*.[40] One informant explained that the Koran was laid on the floor; they read some verses; then those taking the oath laid hands on the Koran, and one man led the ceremony by reciting a pledge in both Arabic and Malay, which they repeated after him. The oath went: "I promise that I will not unveil the secrets of our group to others. If we unveil the secret we will be *munafik* and we agree to let Allah punish us in perpetuity." They were told the name of the group was Pemuda, meaning youth. But they were not told anything else about the background or leadership of the group. After that they met the recruiter—and sometimes other leaders—regularly to receive instructions and ideological explanations from the recruiter, often in an empty mosque. The recruiter told them that the Thai state had destroyed Muslim youth with many "urinations" such as introducing karaoke, which brought dirtiness to Patani.[41] He asserted that if Southern Muslims did not fight to regain Patani this would be a sin, but if they died fighting they would be with Allah in heaven and would help their parents and families to join them there.

Another magical element in the preparations for April 28 was the use of holy sand. One informant confessed to having dropped holy sand on the roads around Thepa district in Songkhla, apparently in an attempt to block military and police vehicles from accessing the Saba Yoi checkpoint.[42] It is clear that magic formed an integral part of the planning behind the attacks.

Attacks

Accounts by surviving April 28 attackers have a naïve and unreal quality: groups of men, many young, some of them friends, rushed up to military and police posts and district offices, a few with guns,[43] some wielding knives, but others unarmed, chanting Islamic phrases and apparently believing or hoping that magic spells and holy water would make them invisible, invulnerable, or both. Others claimed that they simply had no idea what was going on; one insisted he had just followed one of his relatives: "I didn't have any intention to do bad things when I went to the police station. I had no weapon. Nobody told me anything."[44]

Descriptions of the Than To attacks are particularly chilling; participants and eyewitnesses gave broadly similar accounts.[45] Eight young men rode up to the army post and parked their motorcycles nearby, before forming a line, raising their hands to pray for one minute before the leader, Yukipli Dolloh, led the group toward the base. Ten meters from the gate, Yukipli dashed through the entrance; they all shouted "La ilaha illa Allah," then "Ali Lam." Soldiers shouted at them not to enter the camp, then shot into the air three times, but the militants kept running forward. The soldiers shot at them, leaving five dead and two wounded; one was arrested uninjured. At Than To and elsewhere, militants were shot dead within minutes, by security personnel who could scarcely believe their eyes. A few lucky ones were injured or escaped. In certain spots—notably the Saba Yoi market—militants were shot at point-blank range, execution style. Saba Yoi was a police action. Those who attacked army checkpoints had more chance of survival: the army made arrests at Than To and the Sirindhorn camp, but the police arrested no one.

One informant attended a meeting at Kru-Ze on the evening of April 27, at which thirty to forty men were present. They planned to attack the nearby police checkpoint before retreating into the mosque with any weapons they could seize, believing that the police would not dare to shoot into the mosque.[46] Another informant said that he took part in a meeting on April 26 attended by Ustadz Soh and around thirty men, including core leaders such as Zamsudin Kalor, Asmee Salam, and Toleh Lamo, at which targets for impending attacks were discussed in a brainstorming session. Those proposed were:

1. Checkpoint at Ban Kru-Ze
2. Military base inside Ta Seh irrigation office, annex of Sirindhorn Base, Yala
3. Mae Lan police station
4. Checkpoint, Saba Yoi, Songkhla
5. Bo Thong, Nong Chik checkpoint[47]

Leaders were appointed for each attack. In the end, 105 attackers were killed, along with one civilian and five members of the security forces, following twelve separate incidents.[48] Ya Yi-Eng,[49] an army officer who has written about these incidents, has noted that blaming ustadz was not enough: We have to ask why these young men allowed themselves to die?[50] I have outlined the details of each attack below.

Songkhla

1. Saba Yoi: nineteen killed, aged between sixteen and thirty,[51] all but two local from Susoh village, one from Pattani, and from Narathiwat.

Fifteen had gunshot wounds in the back of the head, some had scars on wrists apparently from being tied up. Two were shot running toward the market checkpoint. The police claimed that the remaining seventeen men refused to surrender their weapons and retreated to a local nearby restaurant; the police then surrounded the place before attacking. Fifteen militants died inside and two outside.

Pattani

2. Kru-Ze Mosque, Muang district: thirty-two killed inside (plus three members of the security forces, thirty-five altogether), aged eighteen to sixty-three. The victims came from mainly from Pattani and Yala.[52] The incident began with an attack on a nearby police post, in which two policemen were killed—the post and police motorbikes were set on fire. The police and army surrounded the mosque into which the attackers had retreated. One Special Forces soldier was killed in the operation.

3. Ko Mo Kaeng checkpoint, Nong Chik, Pattani: two killed.

4. Mae Lan police station: twelve militants killed (aged eighteen to forty-one), nine from Mae Lan, two from Yarang and one from Khok Phoh, and one policeman shot. Around twenty-one men drove up to the police station in a pickup truck just before 6:00 A.M.

Yala

5. Ban Niang police checkpoint—Muang district, Yala: ten killed, aged nineteen to forty-four, all came from Yaha. Many were students from Thamma Wittaya School, Yala. Three police were injured, all ten attackers were killed.[53]

6. Sirindhorn army base, Muang district, checkpoint: one soldier and two militants killed,[54] one survivor arrested.

7. Krong Pinang police station: four men killed.[55]

8. Krong Pinang, army checkpoint: seven killed.[56]

9. Krong Pinang district office: two militants were killed outside a nearby house by Or Sor.[57] Another three were later killed at Ban Kuwa mosque five kilometers away.[58]

10. Ban Ba Ngoy, Raman, Border Patrol Police point: one attacker injured, no deaths.

11. Banang Sata, Border Patrol Police base: eight attackers killed, aged eighteen to thirty, one policeman injured.

12. Than To, Yala, army camp: five killed and three wounded, aged twenty to thirty-two, from Yala's Muang district.

In most cases, groups of young men rode up to checkpoints on motorcycles, dismounted, and then attacked security forces by running up to them wielding knives and machetes. After the events, twenty-four men involved in the attacks found their way into custody.[59] Those arrested were largely bit-players, youths who had little knowledge of what was going on, or those assigned only supporting roles, perhaps because the leaders of the movement did not fully trust them. Statements given by people arrested provided some useful background to the attacks but failed to answer crucial questions about the ideological underpinnings of the militant movement, the relative importance of jihadist versus separatist motives, its relationship with earlier separatist organizations, the whereabouts of Ustadz Soh, and the extent to which he was operating on his own behalf.

Structure

Accounts of the structure of the movement remain sketchy, but a recurrent theme was the use of small cells, locally recruited, who had personal knowledge of only one or two core leaders; and a division of labor between those whose primary duties were observation and intelligence gathering, and those who carried out actual attacks. One informant who was a group leader for the April 28 movement explained that his main task was recruiting new members—he recruited six in his area—and monitoring the movement of officials. In another deposition, he claimed that his team was only involved in helping attackers to escape or hide after operations.[60] His group was known in Malay as *durong-ngae,* or "supporters"; actual operations were carried out by youth groups, or Pemuda, who called themselves *abadae,* or "invulnerable" in Arabic.[61] Abadae, consisting solely of those who had undergone protective spell ceremonies, had the task of attacking state officials. Ustadz Soh did not tell him who to recruit or how,[62] but once they were recruited, Ustadz Soh would decide who was suitable for abadae, and who should be assigned supporting duties.[63] One informant wanted a close friend, Hama, to work with his support group, but Ishad (the leader of the village's parallel Pemuda group) asked Hama to join the operations unit because he was single.

Many active members of the movement who survived the April 28 attacks were "supporters," who carried out noncombat duties such as transporting others or placing holy sand at key locations. One member of the April 28 group confessed that he had been recruited into the BRN in mid-2003 by Hamah Salae (one of those who died inside Kru-Ze);[64] another said that he had been recruited into BRN by Zamsudin Kalor (another Kru-Ze victim).[65] He also claimed that Yuso Mama, another core leader, had held monthly Friday meetings at which he declared that they were part of BRN, but did not specify which group.[66] Yuso mentioned a network of BRN groups in several parts of Mae Lan. The informant stated that all those who took part in the attack on the Ban Kru-Ze checkpoint were BRN members. In Yuso's own depositions, he admitted to leading a small cell of BRN, saying that he had been recruited in January 2002 by Ustadz Ae.[67]

One participant in another component of the operation was told his group was part of BRN.[68] Militants in his area were divided into three groups: one group was ordered to attack Mae Lan police station, another group was ordered to meditate inside Kru-Ze, and a third was ordered to drop holy sand on the roads.[69] He and three others were warned by a core leader on April 26 not to join the attacks two days later, because he had not undergone three rounds of spell ceremonies.[70] However, another informant testified that neither Ustadz Soh nor Ayoh ever mentioned the names of BRN, PULO, Bersatu, or other movements to them; he believed the April 28 operation was not related to BRN. One informant heard Ustadz Soh talk in negative terms about PULO, which he said had a different ideology and was attached to misguided tactics such as kidnap and ransom.[71] He did not know the name of Ustadz Soh's group, but those who had received the spells were collectively known as "Roham tuno hu abada," which meant "if you help Allah, Allah will help you, and you will be immortal."

The available evidence suggests connections between the Kru-Ze, Mae Lan, and Saba Yoi operations, as well as the small Nong Chik and Sirindhorn base attacks. Both Kru-Ze and Mae Lan seem to have been coordinated by "Ustadz Ya," Zakariya Yuso (age forty-one). Other significant figures associated these attacks were Sama-ae Lateh (also known as Ustadz Ae, age sixty) and Zamsudin Kalor (age twenty-seven). These three men died in Kru-Ze; their addresses are given as Khok Poh, but the same village is apparently listed in one key source as being in Mae Lan.[72] Ustadz Soh seems to have personally directed the main Yala attacks, notably those at Krong Pinang and Than To. In other words, the April 28 attacks might be tentatively divided into two closely linked groups: the "BRN" wing (whose attacks were planned at the April 26 meeting), and the "Abadae" wing:

Ustadz Ya, "BRN"—Kru-Ze (32), Mae Lan (12), Saba Yoi (19), Nong Chik (2), Sirindhorn (2), losses 67

Ustadz Soh, Abadae—Ban Ba Ngoy, Raman (0); Banang Sata, Yala (8); Krong Pinang (16), Than To (5), Ban Niang (10), losses 39

Most of the older men—including all those over fifty—were in Kru-Ze, and all but three of those over forty were in the "BRN" attacks. One forty-four-year-old was killed in the Ban Niang attack, along with two men in their early forties at Krong Pinang. By contrast, the average age of those who died inside Kru-Ze was thirty-two; seven were over forty years old, five were fifty or older, and three were in their sixties. The average age of those killed was twenty-nine in "BRN" attacks, versus twenty-four in Abadae attacks.[73] Some of the Abadae attacks were led by young men: Yukipli Dolloh, aged thirty-two, led the Than To attack, while Usman Salae, thought to be about twenty-eight, led the Krong Pinang attacks. While the "BRN" wing under Ustadz Ae emphasized the need to make practical preparations for war—including stocking up on food—Ustadz Soh seems to have placed little emphasis on such activities.

The "BRN" designation was a vague one and might not imply an actual linkage to a wider BRN movement; the name could have been invoked simply to satisfy the curiosity of recruits. Designating some April 28 incidents BRN attacks does not suggest that the operation was carried out by BRN; rather, that some of the recruiters for April 28 invoked the image of BRN for their own purposes—what might be termed a "post-BRN" understanding. Those who claimed that elements of the April 28 movement had BRN connections or lineages may also have done so simply at the behest of their interrogators. Yet it was striking that the April 28 attacks fell firmly within the "older" tradition of separatist struggle in certain respects: the targets were confined to the police and military, no civilians were attacked, and no women or children were involved as either victims or perpetrators. On another level, however, the April 28 attacks were new: many of the leaders, especially on the Abadae side, were young fighters who had no connection with the old movement.

This reading of the April 28 movement is necessarily tentative, since most those who really understood its structure are dead or have disappeared. The structure has been sketched out using tantalizingly incomplete deposition materials that may be highly misleading. Yet the dualism suggested here does have a resonance with the wider militant movement as it emerged later, seen by some as a descendent of "old" groups (especially BRN), but more plausibly understood as a new and rather organic phenomenon.

Analysis

If they were supposed to represent a literal challenge to the Thai state, the April 28 attacks were a dismal failure. The organizers of the attacks devoted more time to the use of spells and magic than to military preparations. Had they been better trained, even lightly armed attackers could have inflicted more casualties on the Thai security forces: many of them sacrificed their lives pointlessly in attacks that were suicidal in effect, if not exactly in intent. As one surviving attacker put it: "My family asked me why I went with them. I would get killed going there with just my bare hands."[74] If the aim of the attacks was to arouse popular resentment against the Thai state by provoking the storming of Kru-Ze, the attackers certainly succeeded, but at a very heavy cost.

The attacks on the other locations were almost entirely in vain. Only one operation, the Krong Pinang attacks, was somewhat "successful." Although sixteen militants were killed, a few attackers survived, and a group of them briefly made off with a large cache of weapons. This operation may have been more effective partly because the attackers launched simultaneous assaults on the army checkpoint and the police station, creating more confusion among the security forces. They were helped by a stroke of luck: a pickup truck at the scene belonging to a defense volunteer had been left with the keys inside, allowing eight attackers to make good their escape: "I guess it's because of that truck we took. It's lucky that the key was in that vehicle."[75] The confidence and strong survival instincts of some of these eight—especially the driver of the truck—were another crucial factor in their success. Five of them later surrendered to the army. The successes of the Krong Pinang attacks illustrated that properly planned raids—using pickups instead of motorcycles to transport weapons seizures, and with escape routes prepared—could produce real results. Yet there is no evidence that the "successes" achieved at Krong Pinang were the desired outcome of the attacks: they may have run entirely counter to Ustadz Soh's cynical expectations. A survivor of the Than To attacks told the authorities that although they hoped to seize guns from the soldiers if their operation was successful, he did not know where they would have taken them; there was no appointment to meet at a particular place after the attack and no plan for where to hide the weapons afterward.[76] They were told that if they died, they would die for God. Ban Niang, where attackers were shot even before getting off their motorbikes,[77] exemplified the most dismal and pointless form of martyrdom, rivaled only by the chilling extrajudicial executions of fifteen men at Saba Yoi.

Coordinated attacks on a series of security checkpoints were an impressive show of force, illustrating that antistate sentiments were not confined to isolated locations or to a narrow set of local grievances, and that a large-scale movement was at work. But it is questionable whether the April 28 attacks strengthened the wider cause; some young men surely hesitated to join militant groups that might send them to their deaths. Although the April 28 attacks could be portrayed by sympathizers as brave and fearless, essentially they were foolhardy and reckless actions: militant losses exceeded those of the authorities by twenty-one to one. What initially looked like a relatively sophisticated set of simultaneous attacks turn out on closer scrutiny to have been very amateurish and inept actions, by naïve and unthinking young men. That Ustadz Soh was able to recruit more than 130 men to participate in the April 28 operations testified to a widespread sense of resentment against the Thai state; it also showed that large numbers of Malay-Muslim men were very easily led and could be readily enlisted to fight for doubtful causes.

One April 28 movement member suggested that Ustadz Soh disappeared to Malaysia (after a brief initial spell in Yala) after the attacks, not because he was avoiding arrest, but because he feared retribution from relatives of those who believed he had deliberately lured men to their deaths.[78] However, Abdulloh Agrul, a former student at the pondok where Ustadz Soh taught, claimed that the ustadz continued to be active in Yaha, Banang Sata, and Yala in the months following April 28 and was responsible for ordering him to attack two soldiers with a pistol on July 22, 2004.[79]

Perhaps the most persuasive reading of April 28 is to cast Ustadz Soh as a deluded freestanding entrepreneur, intent (along with his Kelantan ally and court magician Ayoh) on wreaking havoc and fantasizing that he could trigger the expulsion of Thai state from Patani. As one security official put it: "There was only one man behind the whole incident—Ustadz Soh."[80] Rather than a realistic fighting man, Ustadz Soh was a silver-tongued dreamer who knew better than to place faith in his own spells and medicines, lighting the fires of violent dissent before himself fleeing their scenes—only to appear a few weeks later and declare that a change of tactics was now needed. April 28 was not itself a serious challenge to the Thai state but a spectacular display of wild fury on the part of profoundly disenchanted Malay-Muslim youth. That latent fury signaled serious dangers ahead for Thailand's legitimacy and authority in the Southern border provinces.

Beyond April 28

While the Narathiwat army camp raid of January 4, 2004, marks a convenient date to indicate the resurgence of violence in the South, there is a strong case for believing that the movement had been regrouping for some time. Don Pathan has pointed out that between late 2001 and the first three months of 2003, at least eight policemen were shot by snipers, often using AK–47s from a distance, in poor light, and in what amounted to a series of coordinated and highly professional attacks.[81] In deposition evidence, some suspects admitted involvement in the movement dating back to 2002 or even earlier. January 4 marked the movement's major opening salvo, and April 28 was the date on which the potential scale of rebellion became apparent; but the resurgence of violence was already well under way before 2004.

Recruitment

Where do militants come from? The foot soldiers of the movement are largely young men between the ages of around eighteen and thirty. Most are contacted individually by people who inculcate them with ideas about the struggle. They may then be invited to some training sessions and at some point (not normally straight away) are asked to take part in a supoh, or swearing ceremony.[82] Recruits are usually sworn in in groups, creating a sense of solidarity and mutual moral support, and making participants believe they are taking part in something larger. When one informant took part in physical training exercises organized by the movement, he was surprised to see other youths there whom he knew and had never suspected of involvement in the movement.

Another informant interviewed by a Thai reporter explained that he was a sociable individual who often joined teashop discussions concerning incidents in which Muslims had been victims, such as Tak Bai and Kru-Ze.[83] Initially he was unsure who sympathized with the movement and who did not. Gradually those in his circle became increasingly disturbed by accounts of Muslims being killed by Buddhist state officials and began harboring growing feelings of hatred toward Buddhists:

> A friend of ours said he knew a leader of the movement and offered to take us to meet that leader, and then we went with him. The leader is just an ordinary person but his words were very convincing. The leader said.... "Muslims in this world are brothers, when the infidels attack our brothers we have to protect them, it is a religious matter."

A few days after this meeting, a friend came to see him and told him it was time to fight for Allah. He went with his friend to carry out an attack on a Buddhist.[84] After the attack he lay low in the jungle for a couple of nights. When he returned home, his friend told him to act normal and said no one would arrest him. The friend invited him to take part in shooting practice, and then he was assigned to carry out four further operations. After each operation he escaped into the jungle for a while to avoid arrest or extra-judicial killing. During his uncomfortable stays in the jungle, he consoled himself with the belief that he was fighting for Allah. The sympathizers would meet sometimes in the jungle, and the leader's representative would give them weekly assignments. Most recruits came from broken families, or from big families and had received little attention from their parents; relatively few of them came from happy families. Very few of them took drugs, and there was no relationship between the militant movement and drugs. However, after a while he started to have doubts about what he was doing and declined to take part in further operations. At one point he "surrendered" to the military and took part in a retraining camp. But he was ready to resume his activities when there was another large-scale attack on Muslims by the Thai state.

One sympathizer who had been recruited by Ustadz Soh,[85] but who did not take part in the April 28 attacks, reported that as many as two hundred teachers of religious subjects at Thamma Wittaya school in Yala were connected with different separatist groups, which worked secretly and independently of each other despite their shared aims. Some of these teachers recruited students who were physically fit and indoctrinated them into separatist ideologies before sending them for physical training and weapons training. The main groups represented there were BRN, Barisan, "Abadan," and GMIP. He described Thamma Wittaya as the main base for BRN, and the school principal Sapa-ing Basoe as its head. He identified eight ustadz, mainly overseas-educated, as leading figures in a group called Barisan, which focused on indoctrinating senior students. The informant believed that BRN and Barisan had been involved in major incidents such as the January 4 attacks in Joh-Ai-Rong, while the Abadan group headed by Ustadz Soh was behind the April 28 attacks. He claimed that Abadan dated back to 1999–2000. Two ustadz at Thamma Wittaya had recruited students aged 13–15 into the group, and indoctrinated them during after-class small group activities. The aim was to instill them with a strong ideological commitment before they moved on to physical training and later weapons training, but in fact these two stages had not been reached by 2004. The sympathizer also identified a fourth group of Thamma Wittaya teachers as those from GMIP, but believed this group lacked discipline and now had very little role.

One suspect arrested following the October 2005 attack on Wat Phromprasit in Panare recounted how he had been first recruited into the movement in 1999 by a local ustadz, who had told him about the glorious history of the old Patani state, how their people had been enslaved by the Siamese, and the need to restore the sovereignty of Patani.[86] Another suspect recruited the following year recounted the main points of his indoctrination as follows: "The Siamese people invaded Patani state. Our grandparents were tortured. The Siamese people killed some people, and forbade them to wear sarong or eat betel nut. Those with Muslim names were forced to change their names."[87]

A security official argued that the Patani conflict was a "people's war," based on using a variety of techniques to involve more and more Malay Muslims in the conflict at different levels.[88] These were (1) to create a current of resistance (*sang krasae*), (2) create a way of thinking[89] (*sang naeo khit*),

(3) create beliefs (*sang khwam chua*), and (4) establish principles of struggle (*udomkan*). These principles were based on ethnicity—a sense of being Melayu and forming part of a sophisticated and ancient identity—Islam as the pillar of culture, and the idea of the historical suppression of the Patani state by Siam. Recruiters tended to emphasize these issues above all others: history and identity formed the core material for recruitment propaganda, while ideas of jihad were invoked as a secondary theme, a resource to be mobilized rather than the main focus of the recruitment.

According to one senior police officer, the movement generally avoids recruiting youths who are known for being local troublemakers, petty criminals, or drug users; they generally prefer devout kids with good educational and family backgrounds, who understand that they are taking part in a serious political struggle.[90] An informant stated that the movement distrusted those who used drugs or liked night life, fearing that they lacked discipline and would not follow procedures properly.[91] Another informant stated that they were asked to recruit young men of good character—who did not drink alcohol or take drugs—to join the movement.[92] One low-level recruit stated: "I used to like going to restaurants and listening to songs, but when I joined the movement they told me not to do this, it did not look good."[93] Another informant reported that all those who died on April 28 from his village were good devout young men, who acted under the influence of religious leaders: they were inexperienced, uneducated, and unemployed, and thus easily influenced by elders.[94] Because such youths are well regarded in the local community, they rarely figure as suspects; when evidence against them comes to light, fellow villagers and even their immediate family are usually incredulous.

An informant from Sungai Padi, Narathiwat, reported that he had joined the movement in 2002, taking an oath administered by a former tadika teacher: he had to praise God in Arabic seven times, read five verses from the Koran, and repeat the ten principles of the group:[95]

1. Do good things for Allah
2. Do not disclose secrets to the enemy
3. Respect and adhere to the movement
4. Fighting is beyond personal interests
5. Attend the meetings when summoned
6. Stick with the promises and words
7. Sacrifice life and property when necessary
8. Give and take with sincerity and pure-mindedness
9. Don't be at a disadvantage
10. Must act according to orders when they are issued

This Raman informant stated that they were told by an instructor at a meeting in May 2004 that those who took part in the April 28 incident "were deceived—they didn't respect the rules, they didn't follow the leaders." At the meetings he attended, the emphasis was on the history of the ancient Patani kingdom, which they were told consisted of four and a half modern provinces (Pattani, Yala, Narathiwat, Satun, and half of Songkhla). Thai officials had tortured their ancestors and forced them to dig the Saen Saeb canal in Bangkok.[96] The instructors inspired them with a hatred of Thai officials and a desire to take revenge on behalf of their ancestors. These meetings, never lasting more than half an hour, took place at a pondok; the instructors brought a handbook and documents to the lectures, but never distributed any materials. They were told that the movement had no name. It had a hierarchy, but they were not told the number of levels. He believed that those who passed the first two levels were then permitted to carry out violent attacks.

A participant in an army surrender camp wrote that religion was a key element used in militant indoctrination:

> Two years ago two people entered village and forced us to act a certain way according to religion....I took the wrong direction, many hundreds of thousands of others are afraid. Lots of people in the villages are confused, they are mainly going in the wrong direction, it would be better if there were people who knew the truth about religion. The newspapers are wrong, in fact we had regular meetings in the village, and were taught about religion and jihad.[97]

He implied that the media misrepresented the violence as the result of banditry, failing to see that there was an organized movement with ideological motives.

Another informant reported taking part in a series of ten lunch-break ideological training sessions (conducted by an ustadz who later died in Kru-Ze) at Triam Suksa private Islamic school in Pattani.[98] The ustadz stressed that the state of Patani had been occupied by Siam: so Muslims should join hands to advance the cause of independence by torching the houses of government officials, particularly the police and the military. Impressed by the ustadz's knowledge and status, the informant was persuaded to join the movement. After taking a supoh in mid-2003, another informant attended a series of evening ideological training sessions organized by the movement for a group of participants, at a student house in Yala municipality, between November 2003 and March 2004.[99] Different instructors led the sessions on each occasion, mostly from Thamma Wittaya School; the content emphasized *wayib,* or duty according to Islam;

they were told about the history of Patani, and talked about the need for sacrifices to seize Patani back from Siam. Those attending the sessions donated twenty baht per month to the movement.

Another militant declared that he wanted Pattani to gain independence; his thinking had been shaped by friends and family members, and by stories of abuses by Thai officials.[100] His late grandmother had told him that "in the past Patani was such a pleasant place that belonged to the Melyau. But it was lost to the Thais." A friend in the movement told him that they had to seize back Patani; to do so, they had to start by shooting as many police officers as possible. Masore Jehsani, a suspect in the Wat Phromprasit murders who made a public "confession" for the TV cameras that the authorities later distributed on DVD, emphasized the abuses of officials as a primary motivation:

> I have been taught by the movement that state officials are cruel and look down on villagers, they said we can prove this truth by ourselves. According to my observations at the district office, it is true that villagers are maltreated; the officials never think that villagers pay for transportation to come to see them, but officials shout at villagers in return. The movement regularly points out this problem to young men.[101]

A teenager interviewed by journalists argued that Tak Bai had radicalized his generation more than any other incident, supporting militant propaganda about aggressive Thai forces suppressing Malay Muslims in the South. He described how each recruit, who had already been exposed to critical versions of Patani story at tadika (weekend Islamic schools):

> swears allegiance to his cell on a Koran, then eats a piece of paper bearing 24 vows written in Arabic script, washed down with holy water blessed by the village imam. "After you've drunk it you don't feel fear," says Ma-ae. "You can even withstand the pain of torture without confessing."[102]

On what level recruits actually believe in the efficacy of magic is difficult to ascertain, but deposition evidence from April 28 suggests that some attackers genuinely expected their various preparations to afford a degree of personal protection. New recruits would graduate progressively from distributing leaflets to acts of petty vandalism (such as defacing road signs), serving as a lookout, blocking roads with trees or tires, and then participating in actual attacks. Not all recruits took on these tasks enthusiastically; one sixteen-year-old whose father had been killed by the militants in one of their stronghold villages explained: "They sent me a message through the son of a local imam, telling me that eventually I will have to join the movement or face the consequences."[103] The militants used a range of techniques to recruit and retain members, ranging from emotional appeals to ethnicity, to reciting historical propaganda about the Patani state, deploying the rhetoric of pop jihad, and invoking oaths, holy water, and superstitious rituals linked to traditional Malay folk Islam, all selectively backed up by threats and intimidation in some areas. The movement employed a miscellany of ideas and incentives, essentially characterized by a ruthless pragmatism rather than a systematic ideology.

Demands

A question constantly raised about the Southern conflict was "What do they want?" The militants persistently declined to claim responsibility for their actions or to advance a formal set of demands. One self-proclaimed leader, Hassam, appeared vague about the demands of the movement, telling interviewers that he did not want an independent Islamic state, just a boost in representative politics—"more Muslims in local government"—coupled with reductions in the level of Thai security forces.[104] NRC chair Anand Panyarachun suggested much the same thing. Leaflets apparently produced by the movement were also sketchy about militant demands; their main focus was on demonizing the Thai state and the munafik who supported it, and on regaining Patani from Siamese oppression. Only a handful of leaflets went further. One directly stated, "Our effort is to create an Islamic kingdom in the land of Patani,"[105] while another asserted, "We will construct the Patani state as a righteous palace, and make it safe and peaceful in the desirable way in the sight of God."[106]

Former Narathiwat MP Najmuddin Umar believed that over time two core demands would emerge: negotiations for autonomy, and a referendum on the question of independence.[107] Najmuddin predicted that if such a referendum ever took place, those advocating independence might win by a margin of around two to one. The only detailed elaboration of postindependence political arrangements appears in the appendices to *Berjihad di Patani,* which propose creating a body known as the "Council for Constitution and Traditional Customs of the State of Patani," consisting entirely of ulama from the Shafi'i school of jurisprudence. This ulama council would then appoint a King, a ruler descended from the old Patani sultans. The council would be empowered to remove the King if he behaved unjustly. The ulama council would also appoint a lower council, comprising educated professionals selected by the people, which would serve as a kind of cabinet to oversee the running of the Patani state. The elaborate political structures envisaged in *Berjihad di Patani,* which combine a just monarch, the rule of ulama, and modern notions of managerial rule by popularly selected technocrats, beg more questions than they answer, drawing on multiple competing sources of legitimacy.

In practice, independence for a tiny Patani state sandwiched between Thailand and Malaysia seems a deeply unrealistic prospect, and there are reasons to believe that the militants would settle for some form of autonomy. PULO spokesman Kasturi Makota strongly intimated that the militant movement would interested in discussing such possibilities, if the Thai authorities had a serious proposal to make.[108] He claimed that BRN-C would also be ready to join such talks, which PULO would be happy to facilitate.

Tactics

The militants used a wide range of different tactics, varying from one area to another, which constantly evolved and developed; generalizing about the nature of the violence was therefore fraught with difficulties. The authorities identified three main tendencies in the evolution of movement tactics: mixed tactics, focused tactics (with tight, specific targets in a limited area), and special tactics.[109] The use of mixed tactics began at the outset: the January 4, 2004, attack on a Joh-Ai-Rong army base was preceded by simultaneous arson attacks on twenty schools all over Narathiwat province, so distracting and confusing the authorities, and sending them rushing off in all directions—a hallmark of many subsequent incidents. At the same time, some roads were blocked by trees, or using barriers made from burning tires. The coup de grace—a deadly attack on the base by large numbers of assailants (perhaps a hundred or more)—was coupled with the seizure of a large quantity of weapons. In other words, there were four different modes of activity (arson, obstruction, shooting, and weapons heist) in the same complex attack. April 28, though far less successful and sophisticated, also involved a mixture of targets and tactics. A police lecture dubbed that day's incidents "Duson-nyor Part 2."[110] In many of the larger incidents, scale trumped deadliness: the impact came from the sheer size or number of incidents, rather than overall casualties. Sometimes the impact derived primarily from the symbolic nature of the target, as with a bomb outside the house of a judge in Yala on May 12, 2005, or a series of small bombs on June 15, 2006, at key government installations such as Pattani Provincial Hall. Through the use of "daily killings" and repeated small-scale attacks, the movement created a sense of constant unease among the population.

A new tactic seen in 2005 was the use of bombs in busy areas, set off simultaneously in different places. Examples included the agitation tactics of July 14, 2005, when fires were started all over Yala, bombs were placed in six places, and numbers of security forces proved inadequate to

Fig. 4.1 Cars on fire following an explosion at the Yala provincial hall (Charoon Thongnual)

deal with twenty-three different incidents at once. The aim was to create a sense of anarchy. Military uniforms were later found at the house of one suspect: impersonating the security forces was an occasional tactic. On the night of August 31, 2005, three bombs went off in Sungai Kolok and six in Pattani. Further devices failed to explode in Pattani, and so three targeted road bridges did not collapse. On the same night there were also six shootings (three fatal), three arson attacks, and eighteen tire burnings.

On January 19, 2006, mobile phone masts were attacked in 68 places at once, in four different provinces. In May 2005, weaponry that had been taken on January 4 was used in a variety of attacks. Another new tactic was the use of tripwires across a road to set off a bomb on May 13 in Bacho. Larger and more effective bombs were able to blow large military vehicles off the road, as seen in Sungai Padi on May 15. On June 23, 2005, four separate motorcycle bombs were exploded at four different district offices in Yala. Another innovation was the use of "second bombs": typically the first bomb brought out the security forces to investigate, while the second bomb targeted the army and police. The deputy police commander of Narathiwat province was very seriously injured by one of these bombs in April 2007. A variation was to stage a shooting attack and then lure the authorities to a bomb site. This was done on the evening of May 18, 2005; after a killing and weapons seizure at a teashop in Sungai Padi, spikes in the road prevented the police from taking the main road to the site, forcing them onto a narrow side road flanked by forest, where a bomb was triggered as their vehicle passed a bend.

Beheadings were another shock tactic used by the movement—on thirty occasions by mid-2007.[111] Some victims of beheading were found with notes saying, "You caught someone who was innocent. We killed someone who was innocent." This targeting of civilians who were not working for the state or implicated in the conflict was a new development, as was the targeting of women, children, and monks. While the old separatist groups could legitimate their actions by claiming that they were striking agents of the Thai state, the new militants simply aimed to create a heightened sense of fear.

As the violence continued, numbers of Muslim victims increased, many of them working or associated with the state, or suspected of being informers. One army officer told me how he had visited a village headman at around 6:00 P.M. one evening, wearing his uniform; within two hours of his leaving, the headman had been shot in front of his family.[112] The officer no longer entered villages in uniform. The police were puzzled at how successfully the movement was able to target informers;[113] senior police officers had openly stated that they believed every police station contained at least two militant sympathizers, a statement that really upset Muslim police officers, who found themselves in a terribly difficult position. At the beginning of 2008, seven police officers and three military officers were actually arrested on charges of passing information to the militant movement.[114] Some incidents were actually carried out by the authorities themselves; all sides were spreading disinformation to confuse the situation, which created ample opportunities to settle new and old grievances under the cover of the political violence.

A recurrent feature of the post-2004 violence was a new willingness to kill civilians, including women and children, and an emphasis on the murder of those Muslims who were believed to collaborate with the Thai state; such Muslims were portrayed as munafik, or traitors to their religion. These tactics were sanctioned in the booklet *Berjihad di Patani.* Similar tactics and discourse are common features of the advanced stages of what Hafez terms "Muslim rebellions" and have been seen in many other conflicts. He suggests that the violent groups typically use the rhetoric of ethical justification (violence is justified, for example, with reference to state repression and alien domination), advantageous comparison ("our transgressions are nothing compared what they have done to us"), and displacement of responsibility (we are forced to act to defend ourselves against them).[115] All three forms of rhetoric can be seen in the use of militant violence in Southern Thailand and contribute to a "moral disengagement." This moral disengagement creates a vacuum within which violence against civilians can thrive, often becoming simply an end in itself.[116] Hafez quotes the mantra of the Algerian GIA: "no dialogue, no cease-fire, no reconciliation and no security and guarantee with the apostate regime."[117] By casting the Thai state as an infidel regime, and those Muslims who support it as apostates, the militant movement in Southern Thailand seeks to mobilize Islam as a resource to destabilize the existing political order. This process involves substantial civilian casualties, including the murders of large numbers of Muslims.

A further development in tactics involved the use of bombs and follow-up shootings; on March 27, 2005, a train bomb in Sungai Padi was followed up by five snipers shooting at police officers on board the patrol train: eleven policemen and eleven railway workers were injured. Bombs were devised that employed various forms of trickery and deception. Car bombs were another innovation: on June 13, 2005, a refuse truck was used to deliver a bomb into the compound of Sungai Padi police station. Another variation was the use of bombs above eye level.[118] While the militants tended to avoid direct attacks on well-defended military installations, they did attack more vulnerable army camps, such as an improvised checkpoint in Chuab, Joh-Ai-Rong, on October 5, 2005—striking when soldiers were having their evening meal—and killing one soldier using a bomb hurled at a military construction site camp in Rusamilae, Pattani, in August 2006. An example of a target-specific attack was the shooting of army rangers providing security for teachers in Raman on September 27, 2005: snipers had shot at the rangers' motorcycle from two concealed, raised vantage points in shrubbery along a quiet stretch of road. Similar sniper attacks took place elsewhere in Yala in the weeks and months that followed. Yet snipers were relatively rare in Thailand; typically, the skill of a gunman lay in his daring, his ability to shoot a target at point-blank range, usually from the pillion of a motorcycle when the victim was stopped in traffic or on foot.

It was common practice to warn people who were being targeted for assassination, who would often receive anonymous notes. One such note read as follows:

The First and Last Warning

If you love your wife and children, stop acting like a *spy* and *leaking* information to those stupid policemen and soldiers. Think about it! Do you want to live a *normal* life and be happy, or live a life of *munafik* and *die* like a dog? Stop before your blood turned *halal* (can be killed without any guilt). Test me and you'll see the result! I'll do it *my* way, like I've done with *many* people in many places. Use your *brain*. Is the *small* amount of money worth your *life*? Ha ha haa. Don't you think no one knows! I'll be watching you![119]

Some leaflets gave Muslims serving in positions such as headman three days to resign.[120] Alternatively, warning "funeral" signs such as eggs, rice, or pieces of white cloth would be left outside the houses of prospective victims.

Another tactic was the growing use of disguise and subterfuge: gunmen dressed as Muslim women attacked a police station on March 7, 2005, while men disguised as women played leadership roles in some militant-orchestrated protests.[121] Three Thai policemen were killed in an attack on a Saiburi checkpoint on July 20, 2006, by attackers wearing army uniforms. Most attacks were carried out by young men operating in teams of five or six. Security camera footage of the shooting of two naval personnel at Lalo railway station in Rusoh, Narathiwat, on January 29, 2006, showed how the group of at least ten attackers divided into three units: one unit signaled the presence of the target, a second unit of assailants carried out the attack using M-16 and AK-47 assault rifles, while a third unit kept watch. The attackers also removed some of the station's computer equipment in a failed attempt to disarm the security camera, illustrating a well-planned attack.[122] Favorite targets included government officials living or traveling outside secure compounds. Sometimes compounds themselves were stormed, as in the large-scale attack, by apparently more than a hundred assailants, on the police station and the district officer's house in Banang Sata on November 7, 2005.[123] The district officer, who had previously survived an ambush on his pickup truck on the night of May 9, only escaped with his life after taking refuge in the house of some Muslim neighbors. Backup teams collected the weapons and bodies of some of the militants killed in the attacks.

There were persistent rumors that some small-scale incidents were simply done for money: youths were given as little as three hundred baht to carry out acts of vandalism, for example.[124] These claims resonate with similar accounts found in Iraq, Afghanistan, and other insurgencies. Yet such stories were also a convenient cover for any youths caught in the act, one which obscured the central rationale for the violence and confused listeners about what was really afoot in the region. Three bomb-making suspects who took part in a meeting with Narathiwat imams organized by the provincial governor and the military told the audience that while they had sometimes received token payments for their work, these amounts were very ad hoc and did not provide the motivation for their actions.[125]

"No Go"

How far were some areas of the Southern border provinces effectively "no go" zones for the Thai state? Despite official denials, effective control on the part of the Thai state did not extend right across the three provinces. Some areas of Narathiwat and Yala (notably parts of Betong) had been operating with only marginal intervention from the Thai authorities long before January 2004, in some cases since the Phibun era in the 1950s.[126] Districts such as Sungai Padi and Joh-Ai-Rong in Narathiwat, or Banang Sata in Yala, were generally avoided by most outsiders, including state officials, wherever possible. Such districts were "checkerboard areas" made up of small pockets, some relatively secure, but others under the effective control of criminal or militant groups. As in the Basque country, Iraq, Northern Ireland, and other conflict zones, distinctions between criminal and militant activity are often blurred in Southern Thailand. During the 1980s there was a concerted attempt to open up communications and normalize the subregion. The Southern Border Provinces Administrative Centre exercised a very loose governmental authority over such areas; but as time wore on its jurisdiction grew weaker, and checkerboard squares dominated by criminal activity, militant training camps, and radical ideas began increasingly to outnumber more secure, state-friendly squares. While the military might sometimes drive through these areas in convoys, they rarely stepped out of their vehicles. In effect, these areas were special administrative zones, in which the SPBAC had assumed much of the normal functions of the state.

One informant stated that he knew villages where half of the villagers were in the movement, and most of the rest were sympathizers.[127] In such places, it was impossible for the headmen and kamnan to work normally. When the military went to see them, the movement would visit them afterward to ask what was said. The movement people were known to the headmen and came to them all the time, giving them instructions and telling them not to lean too far in the direction of the state. In some places—such as Ai Batu in Narathiwat, or Banang Sata, state structures were barely functioning. A striking example of a former "no go zone" was Ban Pari and two adjoining villages, Tuekor and Sako, in Chanae, Narathiwat which even before January 2004 had been avoided by state officials because of their reputation as a remote and inaccessible separatist stronghold.[128] When militants attacked the house of the village headman—himself a former separatist—in August 2005, he used all his powers of persuasion to win local youths away from the movement. Many later took part in an army "peace training" reeducation camp in Songkhla.[129] The authorities sought to capitalize on this grassroots rejection of the militants by establishing a strong presence in the village, including creating a large number of development projects and forming a village defense force out of the ex-militants.[130] This experiment, however, proved impossible to generalize. In Ai Batu, for example, there was no headman, no assistant headman, no imam, only one assistant imam, and only one TAO member: people were now afraid to serve in these roles, after the incumbents had been shot or run away.[131] The Chor Ror Bor village defense scheme had also been suspended. While a community leader denied that the village was a "no go" area for the authorities, saying that the military did come round and carry out surveys, the only military vehicles I saw passing through the village were driving at high speed. In February 2006, nine teachers at the local school were taken hostage; following the incident, the military attempted to seal off the village and impose their authority on the community, but this policy ended after a month, apparently because it met with complete noncooperation. Ai Batu was an extreme example of a community over which the Thai state had very little jurisdiction, but similar if less overt local resistance was widespread in several districts of Narathiwat and Yala. In many areas, headmen and assistant headmen existed in name only; they were rarely around, and performed few, if any, official duties.[132] In many cases they had repeatedly tried to submit their resignations to district officers, without success.

Difficulties in operating basic state services went far beyond the security forces themselves, as notes from an interview with two postal workers illustrate:

> We don't wear postal uniforms any more when we deliver the mail—it's too dangerous. Sometimes we wear sarong and cap as though going to the mosque to pray, carry letters on our motorbikes where they are not conspicuous. Most of the post office men killed were wearing uniform—this

has happened in Rusoh, Mayo, and a couple of other places, even one guy close to retirement was shot while emptying a postbox in Yala.

They change their clothes before heading out on deliveries, or cover their uniforms with another article of clothing. There are some places where they don't always deliver the letters, or ask people to come to the post office for registered mail, rather than signing for it at the door.

Usually the security forces around here respond very slowly, so they can't rely on them. They are scared. They use various techniques when delivering mail, changing the time of day they deliver it, sometimes bring it in the evening instead of morning. They claim they still deliver every day. They try not to let people know how they are coming. It depends on their relationship with villagers, okay if they can get on with them. But it's best not to be too friendly either. "We need someone who is not too active to do this job." There are three or four tambon around here that are dangerous.[133]

One Muslim teacher in a relatively peaceful rural area of Narathiwat reported that apart from soldiers escorting teachers to and from school, there were no military patrols in his area, and he had not seen a policeman in the village in years. "Why has the government forgotten my village?" he asked rhetorically. He insisted that the state had effectively abandoned his village many years ago, and that since 2004 even officials from the TAO were scared to travel there.[134] A Pattani academic involved in community research was shocked to discover that many villages she visited were apparently never entered by government officials. Even frontline public servants such as health visitors typically asked villagers to come to them, rather than going out to the communities for which they were responsible.[135]

The notion of "no-go" areas was quite a complex one, starting with the general reluctance of bureaucrats all over Thailand to perform service roles, compounded by fears on the part of officials about the risk of violence, and then exacerbated by actual militant activity. Security officials argued that the militant movement had its own parallel structure in certain areas of the three provinces, with its own headmen (known as ayoh), kamnan, district chiefs, and governors, as well as military commanders.[136] They also suggested that each province was divided into three zones: the movement in Pattani was organized into East, West, and Central divisions, for example.[137] While a compelling narrative, this idea of a "shadow state" seemed somewhat implausible: why would the militant movement, which did not accept the legitimacy of the Thai state, adopt the same arbitrary and essentially fictive division of the region into provinces, districts, and villages that had no historical resonance?

Yet however exactly the movement was organized, the impact on the ground was the same. As one security official put it:

> In the areas that have ayoh, we can't enforce the law. Hence, state power cannot dissolve the influence of the agitation in these regions. This includes many areas of Joh-Ai-Rong, Chanae, Rangae, and Sungai Padi. They won't allow any power from the Thai state to make sure that they have absolute control over the areas.... It's impossible for state power to function: kamnan and phuyaiban are also under their control. Kamnan will be questioned every time they are seen talking with the Thai authorities. Many kamnan and phuyaiban are "naeoruam" of the movement;[138] hence they avoid contact with the military. Some kamnan came to me and said that they didn't want to join the movement, but don't think they could resist their power. Kamnan don't want to die. Many phuyaiban are dead already.[139]

Such pressures applied not only to leadership figures such as headmen. One surrenderee who took part in a military-organized peace camp explained that he was useful to the movement because, as a fish vendor, he traveled outside the village every day. He was told to monitor the movements of officials and report them once a week. He was told that he would be shot if he did not obey. This made him nervous because two of his neighbors had already been killed, and he knew that the militants would not hesitate to kill those who turned their backs on them.[140]

The security official believed that by 2006 the movement had de facto control of around 30 percent of the 1,980 villages in the three provinces: roughly 600 villages. There were over a hundred ayoh, each overseeing three or four villages. In these areas government officials did not operate properly, and social services were not really functioning. If the number of villages under the movement's control ever reached the tipping point of 50 percent, the Thai state would be in serious trouble.[141] One community leader suggested that in his village around 70 percent of people were in the movement, including most of the youth.[142] All the leaders were younger people, most under thirty, none very old. The names of the core leaders were never revealed. In his village, everyone knew who was active in the movement. A young recruit who had dropped out of the movement asserted that in some places they controlled more than 50 percent of the youth.[143] There were already sufficient forces for them to engage in "all-out struggle,"[144] and the militants were simply waiting for the right moment to begin. Nevertheless, the influence and control of the movement was patchy: in some places they could make little or no headway, and so they avoided these areas and concentrated on the zones where they could most readily win people over. In Narathiwat, the movement was probably strongest in Sungai Padi—where it controlled virtually every village—and Rusoh; it was also extremely successful in Joh-Ai-Rong and Rangae. One sign of militant influence was a demand that all shops close on Fridays, usually spread by word of mouth but sometimes in leaflets. Though theologically questionable,[145] the closure of shops on Fridays looked like a symbolic act of resistance to the state. Actually, it showed the success of the movement in putting pressure on small business owners.[146] The pressure for Friday closures was strongest in mid-2005. One local politician in Toh Deng explained that people there were so suspicious of the state that they would not show up for meetings of any kind: when local development projects were set up by the Thaksin government requiring a village-level committee to distribute funds, not a single person volunteered, not even community leaders such as headmen or imams. Politicians had to visit villagers at home to try and get anything done.

An army colonel admitted that no-go zones were quite widespread in areas close to the Malaysian border, though he claimed these were decreasing.[147] However, in many districts the military would be reluctant to stage organized activities—such as "peace training" for local men—which were best held in other areas of the country. This remark illustrated the problem of "degrees of normality"; despite the formal claims of the security forces that they were in control of the three provinces, they could not operate freely anywhere in the border zone. There was not necessarily a direct relationship between the "red zones" designated by the security forces, and these "no-go areas." Real "no-go areas" were relatively small in area, but their continuing presence illustrated the emptiness of comments by Thaksin and other government figures that not one inch of Thai territory would be ceded: what was the use of "holding" territory over which the state had little or no effective control? On the ground, control and jurisdiction were matters of degree, questions of constant renegotiation. Few villages were as inaccessible to the Thai state as Ai Batu, but this was not the point. While one security official referred to conditions in the 30 percent of villages dominated by the movement as "anarchy,"[148] a more accurate way of portraying them might be as "liminal zones." These villages were not precisely part of Thailand—since the state did not function there effectively—and yet not exactly outside it. Within these areas, some children still attended government schools, the military carried out some patrols, and some mail was still delivered. The militant movement was undermining the capacity of the state to function, but was not yet providing alternative services for local communities on any scale. But as fear of violence grew, liminality spread to encompass wider and wider areas, and public services declined even in communities where little violence had taken place.

Some army officers believed that it was necessary first to win the war before negotiations could begin.[149] In other words, the first priority had to be "breaking the structure" of the movement, partly by targeting their community leaders, the ayoh. This was disputed by other security officials, who felt that the two processes had to go hand in hand. In practice, "breaking the structure" was not easily done: if you put pressure on the militants in one area, they would simply decamp to another. Some military officers believed that by taking militant sympathizers out of the "water," they would be unable to live. Other officials felt that this was a false analogy, since everyone had to live somewhere, and unless the underlying grievances of the Malay Muslim community were addressed, more volunteers would come forward to replace any who were won over to the side of the Thai state.[150] In many respects, the views of the military had been shaped by the experience of fighting the Communist Party of Thailand (CPT). The CPT had been defeated after a "political offensive" based on an amnesty and surrender policy.[151] Many officers believed that sooner or later, militants in the South would be forced to give themselves up and return to normal life. In practice, however, most of the militants were already leading lives of relative normality, staying in their home villages, and taking up arms only intermittently; the CPT analogy was dangerously misleading.

Cells

The militant movement is based on village-level cells, with considerable operational autonomy, divided into different units for conducting operations. For some analysts, cells were the key to understanding the conflict. One journalist argued that the militants were not primarily animated by big-picture ideological concerns. The reluctance of the militants to strike outside the three provinces reflected a failure to think big: when they did launch attacks in places such as Hat Yai Airport, their actions were largely symbolic rather than strategic. For the most part, their grievances were immediate and localized: "These guys are doing it out of resentment, hatred and anger":

> What we are seeing now is that the small cells at the very local level are taking a life of their own and declaring, deciding themselves what is "go" or "no go," what is off limits and what is not off limits....A different kind of consciousness exists, not the same kind of consciousness exists across the board. One cell might decide it's okay to do this, this cell might not agree with that. When you have this, you don't have a command structure, any kind of standard operating procedures or rules of engagement, then it's up to the individual cell to decide.[152]

A member of one "New PULO" group stated that his cell had nineteen members: when they prepared for a planned operation against a police box, they divided into three different units.[153] Another informant claimed that there were three operational groups of militants in his area.[154] One was a mobile group of seven who dressed like ordinary villagers and used any vehicles that were available to keep an eye on all the roads. This group sometimes carried weapons and attacked state officials. A second group was responsible for monitoring communities, and had seven members, including some women. They found jobs in restaurants or other central locations and had two tasks: monitoring the movement of officials, and guarding and checking escape routes after operations. Such a role was apparently performed by one suspect in a December 29, 2004, shooting of a Muslim policeman; the suspect had worked as a groundsman at the Pattani Provincial Hall, and confessed to monitoring the movements of the target, including drawing a map of his route home.[155] A third group was the so-called "ninja" group, divided into two teams, with a primary task of killing state officials. According to this informant, the two ninja teams were competing with each other to kill more officials, and received a twenty thousand baht reward each time. He commanded one of the "ninja" teams, receiving orders from another man who was under Masae Useng. The informant met Masae Useng eight times and was trusted by him because his father knew him.[156]

Another informant involved in a Nong Chik group told the authorities that information within the Pemuda was strictly compartmentalized.[157] Members only knew what was going on inside their own team; different teams worked on specific activities such as robberies, car thefts, shooting officials, and arson attacks. Members within the group did not trust one another, and were told that they would gain recognition within the organization by carrying out successful operations. Based on such accounts, there is a wide measure of agreement about the way individual cells operate, but much less consensus about the wider structure of the movement.

Mobilizations

One crucial development was what the police termed "special tactics," the mobilization of large crowds, starting with the notorious Tak Bai incident on October 25, 2004. Such tactics aimed at attracting more attention and sympathy from wider society, both inside Thailand and beyond. Following the arrest of six Muslim men whose weapons had been taken, protestors were summoned from a wide area to surround the Tak Bai police station. By turning water cannon onto the crowds, shooting several men dead, and then piling more than a thousand others onto army trucks, in which 78 more protestors died, the security forces handed the militants an enormous propaganda victory. Narathiwat MP Ariphen Utarasint argued that those who had planned Tak Bai had hoped for precisely such an outcome, playing calculated games with the lives of protestors, most of whom did not understand that they were being used.[158]

After Tak Bai, the movement had persistently sought to repeat this early "success." On June 9, 2005 in Saiburi, another large crowd of three hundred to four hundred people gathered in what the authorities believed was an orchestrated plan to start a riot, after some suspects had been picked up on charges of spraying graffiti. The plans were foiled when the authorities defused the situation peacefully by releasing the suspects. Tanyong Limo in September 2005 was an elaborate and carefully planned attempt to raise the political temperature and provoke the authorities, capitalizing on an evening shooting incident at a village teashop, in which two local Muslim men were shot dead from a passing pickup truck. This incident was highly contested: while locals insisted that the shootings were carried out by the security forces, security sources suggested that they were a cynical ploy executed by the militant movement, for the purpose of blaming the state and triggering a mass protest. Two marines who entered the village to investigate were taken hostage, and women and children set up barricades around the area.[159] The following day, the marines were tortured and killed; the authorities resisted the temptation to storm the village and rescue them. The marines' car had the words "Police kill the people" scratched on one passenger door. Another Tak Bai had been avoided but at significant cost. According to a subsequent official investigation, the authorities had received information a week prior to the incident of high levels of militant activity around the village, including the monitoring of movements by the security forces.[160] The official Tanyong Limo investigation report also identified a clear division of labor between at least six teams of militants who respectively prepared the location for the imprisonment of the hostages by obtaining the key and changing the lock before the teashop incident, took control of the mosque loudspeaker to make announcements to the villagers, seized the hostages, gathered people together to block officials and stall them during the negotiations, organized the provision of food for the community, and actually killed the hostages.

Blaming the authorities for violent incidents was a central element in militant tactics and helps explain why armed groups were so averse to claiming responsibility for attacks. Of course, militant propaganda was fuelled by certain incidents in which the security forces were palpably at fault, epitomized by Tak Bai. After Tanyong Limo, the authorities tried to head off the buildup of large protests by swiftly settling up road blocks

Fig. 4.2 Female protestors and children barricade Tanyong Limo village, Narathiwat, during a hostage siege, September 21, 2005. A poster accuses the Thai security forces of being the real terrorists (Anon)

to prevent people traveling into sensitive areas. A similar protest in Bongor, Rangae, on November 16, 2005—ironically triggered by the appalling shooting of a family, widely viewed as an extrajudicial killing by the security forces—was thwarted when the authorities quickly created three concentric rings of checkpoints around the village.

Similar incidents, involving taking teachers' hostage, or surrounding police stations following the arrest of suspects, became standard operating procedures for the militant movement during 2006. At some protests, elaborate barricades were created: when the Kapoh police station was besieged on January 4, 2007, by protestors demanding the release of a murder suspect, the organizers erected tents and even installed electric lights, showing that they were prepared to be there for the long haul.[161] The following morning, police found groups of men cutting down trees and dropping tire spikes to seal off the area.[162] While police were diverted by pursuing those responsible—even exchanging fire at one point—hundreds of women, walking inconspicuously in groups of two and three, began pouring into the area; they had parked motorcycles and other vehicles at various places within one or two kilometers of the police station and began converging there from all directions. Many were carrying food and water. This protest was only dispersed when the chairman of Pattani Islamic Council told the crowd (without consulting the police) that the suspect would be released.

At Tanyong Limo and subsequent protests, men generally stayed in the background: women assumed leading roles in challenging the authorities, making it very difficult for the security forces to function effectively. "Protestors" came in from a wide area, mobilized though extensive networks; few of them had any direct knowledge of the people or issues at the core of protest. Protests became an increasingly popular strategy: one in 2005, eight in 2006, and twenty-four in the first four months of 2007. A community leader in an area where several demonstrations had been held argued that such protests typically began when members of the movement were arrested;[163] he believed there would be no protests if an ordinary, innocent individual was picked up. Both the militants and the authorities had refined their techniques: the movement by deploying women, the authorities by adopting a softly-softly approach. Protestors who were arrested and interrogated typically told the police that they had been paid to take part, but the community leader believed this was just an agreed line, which they used in response to official questioning. The militants had a budget to support their operations and activities, but this was not the same thing as "rent-a-mob": people joined the protests for other reasons. While some protestors were enthusiastic supporters of the movement, others joined in because of pressure from militant groups.[164]

> Put yourself in their position, what if you don't show up?...at least a hundred villages are like that...where they control the hearts and minds of the people, well, not so much the hearts, but at least the minds of the people. "Heart" meaning that the villagers believed them, maybe not, probably not. But the "mind" is that if I don't go out there and demonstrate in the name of whatever against the state...I'll be a black sheep.[165]

The motivations of those joining in these mobilizations were unclear: resentment against the state, or fear of the insurgents? In all probability, they reflected a combination of the two. A journalist argued that such incidents did not follow standard operating procedures: "I don't think the insurgents have any real grand plan, or "does and don'ts"...there are many victims who are Muslims. It's very hard to rationalize these things."[166]

Groups

Questions concerning the role played by "old" separatist groups, and the degree to which such groups control the Patani violence, are central matters of debate. No organization has formally claimed responsibility for recent incidents. One spokesman for the movement argued that refusing to claim responsibility for incidents was a deliberate tactic,[167] a way to avoid being identified and tracked down by the authorities. Another reading was that by not claiming responsibility, those behind the violence avoided taking responsibility, and so did not have to confront the ramifications of their own actions.

For some analysts, BRN-Coordinate is clearly the leading group behind much of the violence;[168] one security analyst has argued that PULO had been effectively "decapitated" by arrests and surrenders in 1998, and thereafter had been largely usurped by BRN-C, which was the main force behind the violence.[169] But for others, the continuing relevance of BRN-C and other groups was highly contested.

A member of BRN-Coordinate told Human Rights Watch (HRW) that his organization was the main force behind the violence since January 2004, claiming that the Thaksin government's controversial war on drugs had created fear in Malay Muslim communities and given an opening to the militants:

> Out of resentment towards Thai authorities, those villagers were desperate and requested us to give them protection. We gave them training in military and self-defense tactics, in parallel with political indoctrination about the struggle for independence. This is how we re-established control of the population and stepped up attacks on the government. We truly believe in our cause—that we are fighting to liberate our land and protecting our people from the oppressive Thai authorities.[170]

An August 2007 Human Rights Watch report declares starkly that BRN-C "has emerged as the backbone of the new generation of separatist militants." The report claims that BRN-C has cells in two-thirds of the 1,574 villages in the region, and more than seven thousand youth members. Local militants in their network refer to themselves as "Pejuang Kemerdekaan Patani" (Patani Freedom Fighters).[171]

Police commander Adul Saengsingkaew suggested that by mid-2006, there were around three thousand militants organized in roughly five hundred cells of five or six members each, spread across the three provinces. He claimed that the unnamed organization had five divisions: the ulama (indoctrination and recruitment), political (psychological warfare and propaganda), economic (fund-raising), RKK (armed forces), and pe-muda (youth wing) units.[172] HRW offered a slightly different list of five units, in which the ulama and political sections were merged and "women's affairs" constituted a fifth unit. According to former Fourth Army commander Kitti Rattanachaya, intelligence documents seized in 2003 revealed that the militants had devised a seven-point plan to seize power in the South.[173] As Connors notes, different versions of the seven stages have been discussed.[174] One version describes the stages as (1) creating public awareness of Islam, Malayness, and the need for an independence struggle; (2) building mass support through religious teaching; (3) creating a secretive organization; (4) recruiting and training three thousand disciplined youth fighters; (5) building a nationalist ideology among Malay Muslims in the government and those living in Malaysia; (6) launching new waves of attacks; and (7) carrying out a revolution.[175]

An alternative view expressed by some journalists was that the state authorities were "fighting with ghosts" in a "grey jihad": they had been persistently unable to identify the real enemy and characterizations such as Adul's and Kitti's were attempts to conceal the authorities' lack of real understanding of the forces ranged against them. According to this view, the movement was much more amorphous than most security analysts were ready to admit.

> I think they have some idea. I think there is some structure, but I don't think there is one overall leader. I think maybe at the top we have a collective group of people who share the same consciousness, but the question for me is, do these people at the top control the guys on the bottom. I don't think so. I think they have taken on a life of their own.[176]

One leading academic similarly suggested that the movement was organized as a "network without a core," with a "horizontal lattice" instead of a formal leadership structure.[177] For him, to understand the movement properly involved grasping it in its own terms, rather than trying to project onto it externally constructed models that did not accord with local realities.

For the Thai state, however, it was necessary to produce a more solid "reading" of the problem; without believing in identifiable masterminds, the state security operation could not function: "that's what they get paid to do."[178] The persistent claims of senior security officials—and journalists who shared a similar perspective—that they really understood the structure of the militant movement could partly be viewed as necessary, ritual utterances. The regular occurrence of highly coordinated attacks—in some cases as many as a hundred incidents in one night—illustrated that the movement was not simply a collection of isolated cells carrying out local revenge killings.[179] Yet many of the coordinated attacks inflicted relatively few casualties; their primary impact was psychological, a show of force. The question was how far these coordinated incidents reflected an organized political movement as opposed to a loose-knit network that could collaborate selectively in carrying out operations?[180] The journalist argued that the cells shared a common consciousness but not much else: "Every now and then you see a cell that pushes that the envelope, like Kuching Rupa."[181]

Some clues about the nature of the movement may be gleaned from anonymous leaflets apparently distributed by militants in the three provinces, though the provenance and authenticity of these documents is always problematic.[182] One leaflet signed "from Malay Muslims in Patani" stated:

> 2. Our group fights for Malay Muslims against cruel enemies. Allah said in the Koran that "I give permission for you to fight against those who hurt us."
> 3. We are not terrorists, nor separatists. We just try to bring back what belongs to us. Don't ever think that our actions are terrorism.[183]

The rejection of the term *separatists* here is interesting; for those who do not accept the legitimacy of the Thai state's control over Patani, "separatism" is not a legitimate way of understanding their struggle. Another leaflet ended with the succinct declaration, "Matters in history are the source of the consequences in the present."[184] Anonymous leaflets sent out by those purporting to be part of the movement were normally unsigned, or else signed with generic phrases rather than the names of known groups. There was no consistent signature on the leaflets, which included: "Berjihad di Patani group,"[185] "From all the fighters,"[186] "Warriors of Patani,"[187] "Mujahidin Patani,"[188] "Patani State Liberation Movement,"[189] "Patani State Liberators,"[190] and "The Fighters."[191] These designations defined the militants by their deeds: they were fighters, warriors, mujahidin, jihadists, and liberators. The actions of the militants were their core message, speaking much louder than any words. Through their leaflets, they apparently distanced themselves from the old groups and the earlier discourse of "separatism."

Those who questioned the continuing role of the old groups often had close familiarity with their workings. Najmuddin Umar expressed alarm at the growing number of violent attacks, which he argued could not be attributed to old groups such as BRN or PULO—these groups had only fought abusive government officials.[192] Many incidents were now being carried out by youths aged only fifteen to seventeen, another change of tactic. Though recognizing that a new militant movement was behind much of the violence, he also insisted that this movement was unpopular with many villagers.

A former low-level Muslim intelligence operative explained how he had worked secretly for the military from 1980 to 1997, using a variety of covers to track down members of the old insurgent groups.[193] His work often took him to jungle and mountain areas; his main task was to prepare maps showing where the insurgents were based, which he passed to the military. He believed that his information had led directly to the deaths of thirty-two separatists during this period. Over time, the old separatists became weary of staying in the jungle and wanted to come out. Their activities were no longer about politics, but had become a way of life, a mode of criminality. The operative had always communicated with a single army officer who was his handler. But in 2004, someone inside the security services leaked the name of one of his relatives, a fellow operative who had originally introduced him to the work. His relative was shot soon afterward, and the authorities did nothing to help the family. Now the old intelligence operatives did not dare supply information any more. The new militants were really professional and cool-headed, riding up to their targets openly on motorcycles, and not at all scared of the army or police. But despite his deep and longstanding information networks, he had no idea about the identities of the current wave of militants, and he was sure the violence was not being perpetrated by a reconfigured version of the old groups.

Another researcher argued that cells were "loosely structured" and possessed substantial operational autonomy, but were overseen by zone coordinators who were behind collaborative actions.[194] Coordinators were linked to a group of "elders," some of whom were based outside Thailand. He believed that BRN-C was the largest group, but did not have overall control; in some areas, turf wars were taking place between different militant factions. BRN-C had ruffled feathers by moving into zones previously considered PULO strongholds. While acknowledging the decline of PULO, their foreign affairs chief Kasturi Makota claimed that because BRN-C was now the largest active militant group, they tended to receive credit for most of the attacks in the South, regardless of whether or not they were really involved in them.[195]

One journalist argued that in one sense BRN was involved, or what he termed "*luk lan* BRN," the "descendants of BRN"; some of the movement's work was based on reactivating existing BRN networks, which had originally been started by Islamic teachers. But because the new movement lacked the socialist Islamic ideals of BRN, and because the new fighters were not interested in the social mindset of formal institutions as understood by earlier generations of separatists, many security personnel preferred to refer to them simply as "RKK."[196] RKK was not the name of an organization, but simply a description of the small fighting cells used by the movement.[197]

Drawing together these arguments, the new movement could be termed "luk lan BRN," or "post-BRN," a BRN-derived structure bereft of a substantive ideological, societal, jihadist, or organizational core, a network organization that lacked an explicit command structure. As Anthony Davis put it: "The average militant or *juwae* (fighter) is more likely to see himself as a fighter for the separatist front than as a member of BRN-Coordinate or PULO specifically."[198] The insistence of state officials that they could characterize the movement in terms of a revived version of older separatist groups was not entirely without foundation, nor was this view incompatible with readings suggesting that the post-2004 violence was a new and very different phenomenon from earlier modes of violence in the region.

As the level and intensity of attacks continued to escalate in the postcoup period, the frontline fighters of the movement (known internally as juwae and typically referred to by the authorities as RKK, or Pemuda) were largely clueless about the role and identity of old-guard BRN, BULO and BIPP separatists, many of whom had been inactive for years, in some cases living in exile in Sweden.[199] However, some cell leaders on the ground were still in touch with certain members of the old guard, who were trying to revive their former networks. Some of the cell leaders had been active members of these groups in the 1980s or 1990s, had given up the struggle, but had then assumed new roles in the revived movement: in other words, people, organizations, and generations overlapped, even if there was no direct continuity. The tactics of the juwae differed from those of the old groups however: while the old movement had focused its attacks firmly on the police, military, and the Thai state, the new movement selected targets much more opportunistically and did not hesitate to attack schools, women, children, or even monks. Whereas the old militants had based themselves in remote upland areas and carried out raids in the towns, the new militants lived in settled communities, blending in with the rest of the population and closely monitoring the movements of the security forces. In this way, they could easily disappear following attacks. The new militant fighters could collaborate for certain operations but were not subject to the orders of any executive council; their cells had sprung up organically since 2001.

A militant leader calling himself Hassam, giving a press interview in 2006, claimed to control 250 fighters, and stated that 80 percent of villages in the Southern border provinces contained at least one militant cell. According to him, the new militants were more ruthless than the old groups: "While their youthful ranks overlap with PULO and BRN, they refuse to publicly align themselves with any insurgent outfit."[200] While many cell leaders were under thirty, Hassam was in his fifties and had fought with BRN and PULO before accepting an official amnesty in the 1990s. Like some other leaders, he rejoined the insurgency after Thaksin became premier in 2001 and argued that the old groups "belong to the past." The new conflict was far more ruthless; anyone suspected of spying for the Thai authorities would be killed, including women, teenagers, or even Islamic teachers. Hassam mentioned one district in which militants had pledged to kill ten Buddhists for every dead Muslim, a brutal war of vengeance. The same article quotes an "active BRN commander" in Narathiwat as saying, "These youths are different from us....They don't understand how their brutality could undermine the work of other groups seeking Pattani's liberation." At the same time, there was no open split or overt contestation between the juwae and the older groups. Old leaders from PULO, GMIP, BIPP, and BRN interviewed in Kuala Lumpur by *The Nation* in February 2007:

> did not say how the violence in the deep South could be stopped or explain the extent of their influence, if they have any, over the militants referred to locally as *juwae*, or fighters. The most they would say is that they still have their network of supporters and sympathisers in place within the deep South.[201]

Another analyst argued that the insurgents comprised a large number of groups and were especially strong in Yala.[202] They did not talk to each other very much, were highly fragmented and competitive, and used different tactics in different territories. In some places they really controlled their areas and were practically ready to raise their flags.

Governments prior to Thaksin always kept channels of communication with the old separatist groups permanently open and frequently used financial incentives to buy off attacks—a tactic especially favored by former premier Chavalit Yongchaiyudh.[203] Narathiwat MP Najmuddin Umar, a long-time Chavalit loyalist, suggested that if the government wanted to solve the problem, they should provide financial incentives to those connected with the movement, inviting them to come and talk.[204] He also suggested that if the military was given a special budget of 50 million baht per district, they could hire local people who really knew the problem to solve the violence. The clear implication was a return to the tactics of cooptation; this time, however, it would not be enough simply to pay off core leaders, but to channel significant funds right down the village level.

Some well-informed figures—such as Shazryl Eskay Abdullah, the Thai honorary consul in Langkawi, Malaysia—believed that the old groups might still be able to exercise influence over those fighting in Pattani.[205] By contrast, Hassam claimed that the leaders of the old groups had very little control over fighters on the ground, who had no interest in negotiations or dialogue: "They just want to fight."[206] The juwae were clearly unmoved by gesture politics by the Thai state, such as Surayud's Tak Bai apology. He also claimed that the juwae were very decentralized and had little sense of any longer history of struggle.[207] Leaders at his level would meet every six weeks or so to chat, but this did not qualify as a council or a formal forum. Sometimes these "chats" would involve agreeing on a date to carry out coordinated attacks on a specific kind of target. Such attacks could make big headlines, but arguably large-scale pinpointed attacks were more significant: a good example was an attack on an army convoy in Sungai Padi on April 23, 2007, a complex operation that involved an arson attack on a school, bombs along a road, and then follow-up shootings that left eighteen soldiers injured.

On the central question of the role of the old groups and the nature of the movement, positions on the issue can be staked out on a continuum as follows:

1. BRN-C is the leading organization in the violence (Jane's profile, Thai security sources).
2. BRN-C is clearly the biggest player (Human Rights Watch).
3. BRN-C is the biggest player, but beware of overstating their centrality because there are other players involved (Kasturi).
4. Seeing this in terms of BRN-C is not too helpful—think more in terms of "the descendants of BRN" (luk lan) as key players (*The Nation*).
5. Forget BRN and the old groups, it's a "network without a core" (Chaiwat Satha-Anand).
6. This is all localized—don't see it in terms of structures or groups at all (Nidhi).

This range of options offers a preliminary basis for analyzing the militant movement, but some further scrutiny of the alternatives is required.

Dualities

The six alternative readings sketched out above—some of which overlap—can be broadly grouped into two camps. The first three readings emphasize structure, and the second three are primarily concerned with agency. The first three exhibit an almost palpable longing for a substantive militant organization, a longing which is shared by militant leaders (whose information has shaped these readings), by the Thai security forces, and by independent security analysts. The militant "leadership" needs to lay claim to an organization in order to secure political recognition, seats at the negotiating table, and a place in history. The Thai security forces are eager to recognize a militant organization in their own image, with identifiable leaders, forces, goals, and above all hierarchies—hence their endless preoccupation with the naming and locating of "masterminds." Security analysts are also most comfortable with relatively clear-cut organizational enemies. The first three options are a convenient set of readings for a whole range of players. They represent the external construction of the Southern Thai militant movement, the basis of attempts at negotiations—like the ill-fated 2006 Langkawi talks, which were brokered by former Malaysian premier Mahathir Mohamad. If these readings are correct, they could easily be validated through a ceasefire initiative, a common feature of conflict resolution processes. Groups who really control violence on the ground have the capacity to demonstrate that control by bringing it to a temporary halt.

The remaining three options focus on the internal realities of the movement, which somewhat resembles a franchise operation. Trainers—some of whom may have links with old groups such as BRN-C—instruct cohorts of recruits in how to carry out attacks, and indoctrinate them with anti-Thai sentiments. Once trained, these recruits create their own cells and begin a largely freelance campaign of violence, answerable to no one, and animated primarily by hatred and anger.[208] For the most part, they no longer see themselves as part of any formal grouping. Such cells have a degree of contact with each other—mainly because members of different cells previously trained together—and these contacts can be used to orchestrate coordinated attacks. But such intermittent forms of coordination should not be confused with a centralized control and command structure, or a formal militant organization. These readings suggest that those groups who claim to be behind the violence may not have the capacity to deliver a ceasefire, let alone a substantive political settlement of the conflict.

In other words, the militant movement is characterized by an essential dualism, a discrepancy between external constructs and internal realities. Another element of the dualism was a distinction between old groups and their networks, and new, extremely organic cells of young fighters, who take orders from no one. The six readings sketched above are rather revealing about the perspectives, priorities, and objectives of those who script and deploy these interpretations.

Islam

How relevant was Islam to the resurgence of militant violence in the South? The role of Islamic teachers such as Ustadz Soh in fomenting violence was well-documented, as was the use of jihadist rhetoric in anonymous leaflets and in the *Berjihad di Patani*. Wattana Sugunnasil has made a strong case for understanding the conflict in terms of Islamic ideas, notably the claim that the struggle in the South was a jihad, and the view that those Muslims who opposed the struggle were munafik and could justifiably be killed.[209] Nevertheless, it was difficult to extract any clear position from the words and actions of the Patani militants. Michael Connors has suggested that *Berjihad di Pattani* is of questionable authenticity and has been misinterpreted.[210] Malaysian academic Farish Noor argued that there was "no theology" in the text.[211] However, while lacking a coherent theology, the document was nevertheless replete with Koranic references and Islamic terms. Alongside its use of Islamic rhetoric, the document also called for the next ruler of Patani to be a descendant of one of the deposed Patani

Fig. 4.3 Female students seated on the ground as Thai soldiers raid a Narathiwat pondok, July 2, 2007 (Anon)

sultanates—a demand coming from a very different ideological perspective. Certainly, the notion that the militants were *salafi* was very problematic: most of those killed or arrested had links to the traditional pondok system and were not even modernists, let alone ultramodernists.

A security official who had studied the conflict closely argued that the root cause of the violence was the appropriation of grievances by the movement. The crucial issue was the question of history: that "rat Patani" was an Islamic state destroyed by Siam, and that a jihad was needed to restore it and to right past wrongs.[212] In other words, the militant movement was not animated by theology. Rather, it had pragmatically adopted some Islamic language for the purpose of advancing a political cause rooted in history. According to most deposition testimony from suspects, those who recruited them spoke primarily about Patani history and the legacy of abuses committed by Thai officials. The rhetoric of jihad was used by the militants to highlight core concerns about the oppression of Malay Muslim identity in the South. According to this official, if people believed that the old Patani sultanate was an Islamic state that was destroyed by Siam, this potent myth could transcend mere separatism, by fusing—or perhaps confusing—Malayness (atalak Melayu) and Islam.

According to the official, the idea of Patani as an Islamic state had been a controversial one, espoused by BRN but eventually dropped. He argued that when seventeen former BRN fighters surrendered in 2003, a new group took over the old BRN networks and adopted the current strategy and approach.[213] The essence of this approach was to use history to call for a jihad, creating the feeling of not being Thai, and sowing these ideas into kids at the tadika level and also at the pondoks: the revival of the notion of Patani as a lost Islamic state, linked to the claim that the Thai state had limited their freedom of religion and mistreated the Malays, who were like second-class citizens compared to other Thais. Recognizing the impossibility of fighting the Thai state through conventional means, this revived version of the movement developed its own form of irregular warfare using small cells. Central to their strategy was gaining the attention of the international community; events like Kru-Ze and Tak Bai were planned for the purpose of appealing to world opinion, and involving the Organization of the Islamic Conference, the UN, or other external agencies in the conflict.

After concluding that Islam was not the core factor inspiring the insurgency, the same official had abandoned earlier programs to encourage Islamic teachers in the region to teach "correct" religion. He was convinced that the movement's primary goal was simply to create a sense of anarchy, believing that the issue would ultimately be solved through the intervention of external actors. The argument that the old Patani sultanate was an Islamic state was highly tendentious, since the sultanate was ruled for a time by Queens (impossible in an Islamic state), there was no evidence that Patani was ever governed by a council of ulama, and the Koran was never used as the basic law of the country.[214] A similar interpretation was posted on an internet site and later distributed in leaflet form.[215]

Was the Patani conflict a jihad? Lutfi lists five possible justifications for jihad:

1. To respond to injustice or aggression; to protect and defend life, family, property, religion, and the motherland.
2. To guarantee the freedom of faith and religious practice, from anyone seeking to vilify or obstruct freedom of ideas and religious belief.
3. To defend the dissemination of Islam to all humankind, which sustains mercy and peace.
4. To give a lesson to those who betrayed their promises or those who attacked the faithful, or those who opposed the orders of Allah, and rejected justice and compromise.
5. To give those who have been oppressed, no matter where are, liberation and protection from their oppressors.[216]

The themes used in indoctrinating recruits to the movement, like those of many anonymous leaflets, generally emphasized the first of these five justifications: the Siamese had violated the motherland of Patani and were guilty of aggression and injustice. As a typical leaflet, entitled "A Call for Jihad," stated, "We proclaim this statement to the entire peaceful Islamic world. What we are doing is taking back what belongs to us. We are declaring war with Kafir Siam who took away our human rights and the sovereignty of Patani state."[217] Most leaflets raise no specific religious grievances; Siam is rarely directly accused of preventing Muslims from practicing their religion.[218] In the main, grievances relating to territory, aggression, and injustice are painted in jihadist hues. A senior Thai security official argued that none of the justifications applied in the South; he did not accept that Muslims had to defend their motherland, or that they did not enjoy freedom of religion. For him, the jihadist rhetoric of the Southern Thai militants was a crude and unconvincing attempt to capitalize on popular global discourse about jihad. It also exploited the idea that those who took part in jihad were warriors for God, who would be rewarded in heaven. The Patani militants were trading in a simplistic, populist understanding of jihad, which lacked proper historical or theological foundations. The security official argued that the Thai side could only fight the militants effectively if they mobilized ideas, challenging the claim that this was a real jihad. Yet despite these counterarguments, jihadist rhetoric that reduced Patani history to a list of grievances against Bangkok was very compelling to many young Malay-Muslim men.

Resistance?

One reading of the violence in the Southern border provinces was that the militant movement lacked any explicit political objectives but was simply carrying out acts of resistance to the authority of the Thai state. Versions of such arguments were advanced by some commentators and informants, including central Thai Buddhists who were sympathetic to the plight of Malay Muslims in the South but unsympathetic to separatist goals.[219] Prominent Thai historian and left-liberal intellectual Nidhi Aeusrivongse portrayed the militant movement in similar terms, as a "millenarian revolt," whose vision of a separate Pattani was little more than a "fantasy state."[220] Nidhi's reading of the violence was strongly influenced by the April 28 attacks and did not take much account of later developments in the conflict. Yet some of his themes were echoed by a community leader in Tanyong Limo in 2006; when asked whether people in the village were part of the movement, he answered that they were, but in the "positive sense that they encouraged people not to be slaves, to study more, to become politicians, and so on."[221] They were not part of the movement in the sense of being separatists, they simply wanted to create pride in their Malayness, and not to be "coolies."[222] A journalist very familiar with the South similarly argued that the preoccupation of the authorities with the idea of a "separatist" agenda was a major obstacle to understanding the nature of the violence; despite their resistance to Bangkok, the militants knew that they lacked the capacity to create a separate Patani.[223] He argued that the recruitment of militants was based on the same recurrent theme: hatred of officials, based on their oppression of Malay Muslims. Nidhi believed the violence that began in 2004 had little to do with the old separatist groups, although they would naturally want to link themselves with it; "the heart of the movement is the low-ranking small people, and that other parties are only marginally involved." Nevertheless, speaking in Pattani on May 11, 2006, Nidhi acknowledged that few other scholars or analysts had accepted his reading.

In fact, Nidhi's interpretation needs to be unpacked into four major components: (1) old separatist groups were no longer the main actors; (2) "small people" were the protagonists in the violence; (3) the violence was not driven by a separatist agenda, but rather comprised acts of resistance against the Thai state; and (4) a range of socioeconomic grievances underpinned the violence. Nidhi's interpretation reflected his background as an historian of Southeast Asia, who rejected views of history that centered

ation-states and the actions of monarchies and elites.[224] Taken as a
[wh]o[le], though, Nidhi's four points risked neutralizing and depoliticiz-
ing the violence, reducing it to the level of uncivil disobedience, a not-so-
everyday form of peasant obduracy. Of his four points, the first two were
arguably the most persuasive. Just because the violent action had shifted
from old organized separatist groups to new, improvised, bands of sub-
altern fighters did not mean that their attacks were mere acts of resistance.
It is equally possible that the new generation of "small people" fighters did
share on some level the aspiration of an independent Patani state, and that
the continuing violence was ultimately animated by such political dreams,
however third-hand and third-rate these vague fantasies might seem.

This was the view of veteran Wadah politician Najmuddin Umar:[225] he
suggested that those behind the violence were not thinking very deeply
but simply wanted to create incidents and generate confusion. Yet while
Najmuddin questioned whether some of the attackers really subscribed to
coherent separatist ideas, he did believe that "separatist" aspirations were
nevertheless the basic motivation behind the violence: this was not simply a
resistance movement with no focused objective.[226] In other words, the question of whether the violence was essentially "separatist" could not be answered with a simple "yes" or a "no": "separatist" motivation was a matter
of degree. Elements of Nidhi's characterization of the violence—the primacy
of "small people" and marginalization of the old groups—rang true, even if
his overarching reading of the conflict in terms of "peasant resistance" was
flawed. Though not "classically separatist" in the sense of BRN or PULO,
the new struggle was nevertheless a "postseparatist" one.

Conclusion

Most militant actions are carried out by small cells of locally based youths
who see themselves as fighters, *juwae*, typically recruited by older men,
often linked with Islamic schools or *tadika*. The main device for recruitment
is the invocation of political myths concerning Patani history and the oppression of Malay identity by the Thai state; a strong supporting theme is
that of abuse of power by Thai government officials, the military, and especially the police. These themes are sometimes couched in jihadist or Islamic
terminology, but it remains very questionable how far this language reflects
a substantive theological dimension to the struggle. The form of Islam associated with the struggle is a traditionalist Malay form of Islam overlaid with
magical and syncretic practices, not a modernist Islam. In Southern Thailand, Islam is a resource that the militant movement mobilizes for political
ends; the violence is not primarily animated by religious grievances.

Evidence for the idea that the struggle is a reconfigured version of the old separatist movement is patchy. Some of those involved in the movement have faced considerable social pressures to join, while others are actively coerced. There is a strong case for arguing that the violence is "postseparatist"; the fighters do not see themselves as separatist per se. BRN-C has probably been given too much credit for the violence. Some of the fighters are the "descendants of BRN" (luk lan BRN), but this does not make them really "BRN"; they might best be termed "post-BRN." At the same time, in places they may retain some channels of communication to elements of the old groups.

The Patani conflict is a form of irregular network warfare. Ultimately, the militant movement is, to use Chaiwat Satha-Anand's term, "a network without a core": an outfit defined largely by its agency rather than its structure. This is a "postseparatist" movement, in which some "post-BRN" elements are still in circulation, but for which old differences between different militant groups and ideological orientations have become lost in an angry shared cause.

The Patani militant movement could be termed a "liminal lattice." In other words, the movement has two core features: a set of cross-cutting linkages—which can be viewed as a lattice—and a quality of liminality, since the movement exists only at the threshold of what constitutes a tangible organization. While many players and spectators in the conflict would like to firm up the lattice, imagining it as a more solid structure, the movement's pervasive liminality undermines and thwarts these imaginings. The militants on the ground are very real, but their organization is much less so.

CONCLUSION

The Southern Thai conflict is a war over legitimacy. For significant numbers of Patani Malays, Thai rule over their region has long lacked legitimacy; over the past century, rebellious leaders and militant groups have periodically sought to nudge legitimacy strain toward legitimacy crisis. In their attempts to fuel uprisings against Thai rule, rebels have been aided and abetted by the inept repression to which Bangkok has regularly resorted. During the second half of the twentieth century, the Thai state sought to manage the provinces largely through the imposition of virtuous monarchical and bureaucratic rule, a mode of legitimacy predicated on the shared shibboleth "Nation, Religion, King." This shibboleth failed to resonate in Patani.

Since the Prem initiatives of the early 1980s, Bangkok has approached the deep South using two simple interlocking strategies: co-opt and control Islamic leaders and teachers, and co-opt and control the Malay-Muslim political elite. Those who had taken up arms were persuaded instead to buy into a modus vivendi with the Thai state. These processes were managed through the use of representative bodies, including provincial Islamic councils, parliamentary seats, and elected subdistrict organizations. Because Malay Muslims constituted only around a fortieth of Thailand's population, they were structurally doomed to impotence within the country's Buddhist-dominated political order. Bangkok sought to use representative politics to relegate Malay Muslims to permanent marginality within the Thai state, while lionizing the virtuous tokenism of individual leaders such as former interior minister Wan Muhammad Nor Matha. Yet these strategies of co-optation were fraught with danger, since the co-opted elites gradually became alienated from the ordinary people of the region.

Prominent Islamic leaders found themselves major beneficiaries of the Thai state, especially those who tapped into the lucrative business of running "private" Islamic schools that lived on public funds. While the Malay Muslim political class emulated their counterparts in the rest of Thailand by building powerful networks of vote-canvassers and phuak, these networks were focused on securing periodic and nominal electoral support rather than on incorporating villagers into wider Thai society. The political space offered by the Thai state turned out to be largely ornamental, rather than providing real opportunities for local popular participation.

As the Prem-era social compact began to unravel, Patani militant groups began to prepare for a fresh attempt to "out" the Thai state as an illegitimate power. When Thaksin Shinawatra became prime minister, the militants were handed new opportunities to foment rebellion; major security incidents took place regularly from December 2001 onwards. Thaksin ousted the pragmatic accommodationists of the Southern Border Provinces Administrative Centre and the Fourth Army who had managed security in the deep South for two decades, and gave a bunch of vicious and incompetent Bangkok police officers what amounted to a license to kill. Mayhem quickly ensued, and during the Southern annus horribilis of 2004, militant groups staged three major actions designed to humiliate and discredit the Thai state: January 4, April 28, and October 25. The first of these actions demonstrated the complacency and incompetence of the Thai military; the second showed up the excessive eagerness of the infidel Thai authorities to violate the ancient mosque of Kru-Ze; and the third illustrated the cruelty and thirst for vengeance of the security forces. All three actions were revealing about the scope, depth, and determination of the resurgent militant movement.

When these disasters struck, the Malay-Muslim elites on whom the Thai state had been relying to manage the region's population were nowhere to be seen. Islamic leaders had precious little to say about the violence, and Wan Nor and his fellow Wadah group politicians were so compromised that they failed effectively either to represent the fury of the South to Bangkok, or to communicate Bangkok's position to the South. The Thaksin government even tried to blame the Wadah group for what had happened, putting MP Najmuddin Umar on trial for treason, in a tragicomic attempt to teach Wadah a lesson. In the February 2005 elections, all the Malay Muslims who stood in border province constituencies for Thaksin's Thai Rak Thai Party lost their seats. Unhappy with the failure of the provincial Islamic councils to toe Bangkok's line and condemn the violence, Thaksin loyalists, elements of network monarchy, and the military joined forces to try and manipulate the outcomes of the November 2005 Islamic council elections. They had limited success.

Meanwhile the violence continued unabated. There were no more incidents on the scale of Kru-Ze or Tak Bai, but daily killings increasingly targeted civilians and Muslims rather than members of the security forces. Antisystem violence began to take on a cruel logic of its own, as the militants deployed the idiom of Islam to justify beheadings, killings of monks, and other grotesque actions that fed on themselves. The security forces adopted a more outwardly conciliatory posture, trying to prevent any major confrontations that would attract critical international coverage. Nevertheless, an informal policy of selective extrajudicial killings still operated in certain areas, and both Muslim and Buddhist communities were rife with rumor and fear. Adopting muddled royal-speech-derived notions of the need to distinguish between "good" and "bad" Muslims, the security forces made matters on the ground worse with a range of ill-conceived schemes. Among the worst of these was the "surrender program," which forced thousands of innocent men to spend time undergoing nationalist indoctrination in army camps in central Thailand. The security forces proved terminally incompetent in their day-to-day operations, and persistently failed to grasp that most Malay Muslims were neither "good" nor "bad," but simply trying to survive in a murky environment where they feared antagonizing either the state authorities or the burgeoning militant movement.

During his last months in office, Thaksin lost all interest in the South as he concentrated on trying to shore up his own flagging legitimacy as prime minister. The National Reconciliation Commission he had created under pressure from his liberal and royalist critics published a rather mild report in June 2006, which defined the Southern conflict largely in terms of justice issues and failed to acknowledge either the strength of the militant movement, or the essentially political nature of its cause. Following an aborted April 2006 snap election and interventions by the King and Prem, Thaksin was finally ousted in the September 19, 2006, military coup. The loyal monarchists who staged the coup and led the interim government hoped that their restoration of virtuous rule would lay the foundations for a return to peace in the deep South. But the cat was out of the bag: militant cells had been established across much of the three provinces, and the Surayud Chulanont government had nothing new to offer the mainly young fighters who had increasingly grown angry and bloodthirsty. Stuck in a strategic time warp, the government talked of offering the militants an amnesty—failing to understand that concessions used to neutralize the Communist Party of Thailand and an earlier incarnation of the Southern militants twenty-five years earlier were no longer appropriate. In the post-coup elections of December 23, 2007, Wadah tried to stage a comeback by joining the People's Power Party, but gained only two of the twelve constituency seats in the three provinces.

The militants are now in the ascendant. Ultimately, the fighters are defined by their actions, not by formal designations. While some militant actions are coordinated, this does not imply that all the fighters are subject to central control. Much of the violence is carried out on the basis of local initiatives, sometimes opportunistically or for purposes of revenge. Fighters are supported by a much larger community of sympathizers who can be mobilized for protests and other support activities. In some areas, movement sympathizers constitute more than half or two-thirds of the population, though some of these are passive sympathizers who are playing along largely as a survival strategy. In many parts of the three provinces, the Thai state has little real authority: local leaders such as village headmen must live in constant fear of the movement, with which they sometimes also sympathize. Evidence that the movement is trying to develop administrative structures parallel to the state is patchy, and this argument has probably been overblown by security officials.

Their incompetence and lack of stomach for fighting exposed, the Thai military sought to subcontract and privatize the conflict, delegating front-line security duties to rangers, volunteers, and militias wherever possible. By 2007, there were signs that communal violence was beginning: attacks on mosques and Islamic schools bore all the hallmarks of actions by rogue militias or revengeful Buddhists. The government wanted to negotiate, and self-proclaimed leaders based in Sweden and elsewhere professed themselves ready to talk. But there was little evidence that anyone could stop the militant violence. The movement was no longer a reconfigured version of old groups such as BRN-Coordinate, whatever the Thai authorities preferred to believe. Rather, it was a liminal lattice, not so much an organization as a set of intangible connections that grew more liminal and less latticelike as time went on. Despite occasional coordinated attacks, most of the incidents were conducted by self-managed violence franchises. The fighters had gone feral. There were no real masterminds.

Under these circumstances, a solution is extremely elusive. Some have argued for an Iraq-style "surge" in the Thai south, the creation of a "security grid" that would dramatically curtail levels of violence and limit militant activity. But given the terrible limitations of the Thai security forces, boosting troop numbers would probably make matters worse, and any grid would surely prove completely useless. Since the conflict is essentially about the perceived illegitimacy of the Thai state in the deep South, any solution needs to focus primarily on the legitimacy crisis. Thai-style virtuous legitimacy will not wash in Patani, while representative legitimacy on Thai terms has been tested and discredited. The only way forward is to try some form of participatory legitimacy: to give Malay Muslims substantial control over their own affairs, while retaining the border region as part of Thailand. In other words, substantive autonomy—probably called something else—is probably the only long-term solution that might satisfy most parties to the conflict. To broker this settlement, ensure the peace, and marginalize the extremists who would seek to subvert it, new political and security arrangements will be needed. Some kind of third party assistance to reach a settlement, perhaps under UN or Association of Southeast Asian Nations (ASEAN) auspices, might help move matters forward. Understandably, most Thais would not welcome such developments. But it has come to this. The militant movement is unlikely to overpower the Thai state by military means in the foreseeable future. The formation of a civilian coalition government in February 2008—led by pro-Thaksin parties and headed by veteran politician Samak Sundaravej—offered Thailand a fresh opportunity to pursue ways of resolving the Southern conflict. The question for Bangkok is a simple one: preserve nominal Thai rule in the Southern provinces at the price of potentially indefinite daily killings and bombings, or seriously consider some very unpalatable alternatives? Peace will likely only be restored in the South of Thailand when political legitimacy has been firmly established.

This study has shown the limitations of cookie-cutter readings of "ethnic conflicts" based on troubling terms such as "Islamic violence" and "international terrorism." Like Muslims in the other countries discussed in the Hafez study, Patani Muslims do not rebel because of deep-rooted socioeconomic or psychological grievances, and nor are they primarily animated by jihadist ideologies. Their cause is a political one that centers on local questions of legitimacy; they want to regain control of territory they believe to be theirs, and doing so involves violently rejecting the claims of the Thai state on that territory. Understanding such conflicts involves a central focus on political process and opportunities, for which Islam serves simply as a mobilizing resource and a means of framing increasingly shrill justifications for the anticivilian violence that all too often develops a chilling momentum of its own.

For some readers, the most striking features of this book will be two "negative findings." First of all, the Southern Thai conflict is not centrally about Islam. It is certainly true that the militants have capitalized on the way the religious elite have suffered a loss of authority, and that the Thai state has exacerbated matters by meddling with Islamic provincial councils and conspicuously co-opting the owners of private Islamic schools. This loss of authority by older imams and school owners has created a gap into which younger, more aggressive men have stepped. It is equally true that pondok teachers and ustadz have played pivotal roles in recruiting young men to militant activity. In addition, much of the recruitment and training has employed Islamic rhetoric: swearing ceremonies, magic rituals, and talk of jihad. This talk of jihad spills over into some of the anonymous leaflets and public discourse of the movement. But none of this makes the Patani conflict a religious conflict. The primary emphasis of the militants is on historical and political grievances, not religious ones. Islam has something to do with it, but the conflict is not about Islam.

Second, the Southern Thai conflict is not really part of a global conflict, a global jihad, or a global war on terror. In any case, the Islam underlying the Southern Thai conflict is local, "traditionalist" Islam, not Islam of the Salafi-"Wahhabi" variety. And while the insurgency has regional connotations—especially in relation to Thailand's border with Malaysia—nor is the Patani conflict a regional one. Yes, some ustadz in the deep South have trained abroad, in Pakistan, the Middle East, and Indonesia. Yes, there is some traffic between the Thai South and places such as Cambodia and Aceh. Yes, many Malay Muslims in Southern Thailand have dual Malaysian citizenship, and many more have spent time working, legally or illegally, in Malaysia. Militant groups undoubtedly have cells in Malaysia, and some leaders of the old "armed groups" are based there. But the prime movers in the recent fighting are firmly based in Southern Thailand itself. Engaged in a fiercely nationalist struggle, they do not solicit much support from outsiders. This is a conflict between Patani and Bangkok. In that sense, it differs greatly from better known, more internationalized and more explicitly "Islamist" conflicts such as those in Afghanistan and Iraq; a familiarity with these conflicts may not always help to explain what is happening in Southern Thailand. However, as my use of Hafez has shown, many elements of the Patani conflict have strong parallels with other "Muslim rebellions" across the world. While the narrative presented here has been overwhelmingly indigenous, the story of the Southern Thai conflict is replete with resonances: a legitimacy deficit and some ham-fisted repression can all too readily fuel a backlash against unpopular rule.

These two conclusions—that this is not a jihad, and it is not regional or global—may disappoint readers who are hoping for neater and more satisfying explanations, which would allow them to frame the Southern Thai conflict more readily and conveniently. But this is a messy, awkward, in-your-face conflict—not the type favored by generic experts. The conflict in Thailand's Southern border provinces is unlikely to be readily resolved by any postcoup government. A return to relative political normalcy in Bangkok—whatever that may mean—is a necessary but not sufficient condition for the beginnings of a solution. But thinking toward a solution will involve a realistic understanding that the war in the South cannot be won by military means, especially if the Thai security forces remain inept at best, and abusive at worst. Nor will soft Thai language about "justice" and "reconciliation" convince ordinary Malay Muslims, if not backed up by real changes to the culture of impunity, and real proposals for establishing participatory rule and participatory bureaucracy in the deep South. Southern militants thrive because the Thai state lacks sufficient legitimacy: to defeat them, that legitimacy must first be established.

Glossary

Abadae/Abadan: "Invulnerable" in Arabic; militant group led by Ustadz Soh

amphoe: District

ayoh: Local leader of militant network, equivalent to "headman"

barami: Usually translated as "charisma," though the Thai meaning refers more broadly to an individual's positive attributes

babor: The founder, owner, or head teacher of a pondok

Chor Ror Bor: Village security volunteer program, overseen by the Interior Ministry

Chularajamontri: Thailand's royally appointed state counselor for Islamic affairs, also known as the Shaikh al-Islam

fatwa: Formal pronouncement by an Islamic scholar or scholars

hua khanaen: Vote canvasser

hadith: Collected oral traditions related to the words and deeds of the Prophet

Isan: The northeastern region of Thailand

jao muang: Formerly, the ruler of a local area

juwae: Frontline fighters in the Southern militant movement

kamnan: Headman of a subdistrict, oversees a number of village headmen

khana kao: The "old school" (*kaum tua* in Malay): "traditionalist" Islam, less doctrinaire and prescriptive than newer forms

khana mai: The "new school" (*kaum muda* in Malay): "modernist" Islam, tends to emphasize more standardized beliefs and practices

luk nong: Subordinates

munafik: Those who have betrayed Islam

naewruam: Those who sympathize with the militants

nakleng: Tough guy

nayok TAO: Head of a tambon (subdistrict) administrative organization

Or Ror Bor: Predominantly Buddhist local defense volunteer program supported by the Queen

Or Sor: Paramilitary "volunteers" employed by the Interior Ministry

Patani: Alludes to an older and larger area than the modern-day Thai province of Pattani, may have Malay nationalist connotations

Pemuda: Youth wing of militant movement

phu di: "Gentleman," politician who cultivates a respectable image

phuak/phakphuak: Clique

phuyaiban: (Village) headman

pondok: Literally, "hut"; simple Islamic boarding schools teaching only a religious curriculum, "ponoh" in Thai

Saudara: A Malay-identity-oriented student group at PSU's Pattani campus

supoh: Swearing ceremony used by militants in recruitment

tadika: Extracurricular Islamic schools, often teaching at weekends

tambon: Subdistrict

thahan phran: "Rangers," paramilitary force overseen by the army

than siang: Electoral support base, or core vote

tok guru: Islamic teacher

Tor Ror Chor: A community protection scheme organized by the police

ustadz: Islamic teacher

Wadah: Literally, "solidarity"; a faction of Malay-Muslim politicians led successively by Den Tohmeena and Wan Muhammad Nor Matha

Wat: Buddhist temple

Notes

Preface and Sources

1. For a critical view of the way Islam and terrorism are commonly conflated and confused in academic literature and beyond, see Richard Jackson, "Constructing Enemies: Islamic Terrorism in Political and Academic Discourse," *Government and Opposition* 42, 3 (2007): 394–426.

2. Michael Connors, "War on Error and the Southern Fire: How Terrorism Analysts Get It Wrong," in *Rethinking Thailand's Southern Violence,* ed. Duncan McCargo (Singapore: NUS Press, 2007), 145–64 (also in *Critical Asian Studies* 38, 1 [2006]).

3. See Natasha Hamilton-Hart, "Terrorism in Southeast Asia: Expert Analysis, Myopia, and Fantasy," *Pacific Review* 18, 3 (2005): 303–26.

4. John T. Sidel, *The Islamist Threat in Southeast Asia: A Reassessment* (Washington, DC: East-West Center, 2007), 3.

5. Ibid., 3–4.

6. These incidents are reviewed in some prescient articles by Anthony Davis, including "The Complexities of Unrest in Southern Thailand," *Jane's Intelligence Review,* September 2002, 16–19, and "Thailand Faces Up to Southern Extremist Threat," *Jane's Intelligence Review,* October 2003, 12–15. Davis catalogued twenty-five serious incidents in the first seven months of 2002 alone.

7. Interview, May 16, 2006.

8. Srisompob Jitpiromsri, Faculty of Political Science, Prince of Songkhla University, Pattani, "Southern Violence 2008," undated statistical document, sent as personal communication, May 29, 2008.

9. More than 100 men died on April 28, 2004, and over 80 on October 25.

10. Srisompob Jitpiromsri, "ข้อมูลเชิงประจักษ์ภาคประชาสังคม สถานการณ์ชายแดนใต้ 'ดีขึ้น' จริงหรือ?" ["Empirical Data from Civil Society: Has the Southern Border Situation Really 'Improved?'"], August 11, 2007, http://www.deepsouthwatch.org/.

11. Thailand is a violent society, with the highest homicide rate in Southeast Asia and the second highest in Asia (8.47 per 100,000 in 2000), well above the United States (5.5), and far higher than most developed countries (typically between 2 and 3). See http://en.wikipedia.org/wiki/List_of_countries_by_homicide_rate.

12. Two tourists, one Malaysian and one Canadian, were killed in bomb incidents in Sungai Kolok and Hat Yai.

13. A lower-level OIC delegation did visit the South in June 2005.

14. I witnessed this exchange (cited by Wheeler) in Pattani on November 11, 2005.

15. Matthew Wheeler, "U.S. and Southern Thailand Conflict," unpublished paper presented at seminar on "Southern Violence and the Thai State" organized by Chaiwat Satha-Anand, Sirindhorn Anthropology Centre, Bangkok, August 18–19, 2006.

16. Major fieldwork was conducted from September 2005 to September 2006.

17. A handful of informants, mainly academics, preferred to be interviewed in English.

18. When encountering locals who presented themselves as non-Thai speakers, I would normally inflict on them a few phrases of my execrable elementary Indonesian. In most cases, this would quickly elicit responses in quite passable Thai.

19. Most of the interviews using a Pattani Malay translator were initiated by ICG.

20. These were mainly with lawyers, journalists, monks, and victims of violence. At these interviews, Pat generally shared in the questioning, as well as taking notes.

21. There are less than ten of these, which are referenced as "BA interview." Most of Pat's interviews were with journalists. Two interviews were conducted by Kaneeworn (Pim) Opetagon, who also took notes at a number of my interviews.

22. Most staff did not use parking permits, which were never checked; I requested the permit solely in order to badge my identity and name outside the PSU campus.

23. This did not always apply to joint interviews initiated by ICG.

24. My interview notes alone total more than 320,000 words.

25. On the shortcomings of Thai media coverage in the South, see Duncan McCargo, "Communicating Thailand's Southern Conflict: Media Alternatives," *Journal of International Communication* 12, 2 (2006): 19–34.

26. These include Don Pathan of *The Nation,* Anthony Davis of *Jane's Defence Weekly,* and contributors to the March 2006 special issue of *Critical Asian Studies* (also published as *Rethinking Thailand's Southern Violence,* ed. Duncan McCargo [Singapore: NUS Press, 2007]). Some useful papers on the conflict have recently been published by the East-West Center in Washington, DC.

27. Anonymous leaflets and essays have been numbered in the footnotes according to my own reference system.

28. These documents were obtained from a range of anonymous sources. In no case did I make payments of any kind in exchange for official documents.

29. While deposition testimony is inherently problematic, it has been extensively used as a key source on similar conflicts by organizations such as International Crisis Group, notably by prominent Indonesia analyst Sidney Jones.

Introduction

1. See Thongchai Winichakul, *Siam Mapped: A History of the Geo-Body of a Nation* (Honolulu: University of Hawaii Press, 1994).

2. For a discussion of Patani-Siamese relations, see Tamara Loos, *Subject Siam: Family, Law, and Colonial Modernity in Thailand* (Ithaca: Cornell University Press, 2006): 77–88.

3. David Brown, *The State and Ethnic Politics in Southeast Asia* (London: Routledge, 1994): 158–205.

4. Confusingly, Pattani does not have a border with Malaysia.

5. On the 2004 violence, see especially สุภลักษณ์ กาญจนขุนดี และ ดอน ปาทาน, สันติภาพในเปลวเพลิง [Supalak Ganjanakhundee and Don Pathan, *Peace in Flames*] (Bangkok: Nation Books, 2004); and International Crisis Group, *Southern Thailand: Insurgency, not Jihad. Asia Report 98* (Jakarta: May 2005), http://www.crisisgroup.org.

6. Loos, *Subject Siam*, 186.

7. See Michael J. Montesano and Patrick Jory, eds., *Thai South and Malay North: Ethnic Interactions on the Plural Peninsula* (Singapore: NUS Press, 2008). Their volume sets out to question the dominant term for the region, "the Malay peninsula."

8. Michael J. Montesano, "Beyond the Assimilation Fixation: Skinner and the Possibility of a Spatial Approach to Twentieth-Century Thai History," *Journal of Chinese Overseas* 1, 2 (2005): see especially figures on pages 196 and 203.

9. For details of some of these schemes, see สรุปสาระสำคัญ แผนพัฒนาการเศรษฐกิจและสังคมแห่งชาติ ฉบับที่ ๒ (๒๕๑๐-๒๕๑๔) [*Summary of the Second National Economic and Social Development Plan (1967–1971)*] (Bangkok: National Economic Development Board, July 1968), 32, 63–67. The NEDB was later renamed the National Economic and Social Development Board (NESDB).

10. Some prominent Malay Muslim politicians are said to hold dual citizenship. Interview, March 7, 2006.

11. Hasan Madmarn, *The Pondok and Madrasah in Patani* (Bangi: UKM Press, 1999), 75.

12. The most influential text of this kind is Ibrahim Syukri, *History of the Malay Kingdom of Patani*, trans. Conner Bailey and John Miskic (Chiang Mai: Silkworm, 2005). For a relevant discussion, see Patrick Jory, "*From Melayu Patani to Thai Muslim: The Spectre of Ethnic Identity in Southern Thailand*," *South East Asia Research* 15, 2 (July 2007): 255–79.

13. Davisakd Puaksom, "Of a Lesser Brilliance: Patani Historiography in Contention," in *Thai and South and Malay North*, ed. Montesano and Jory, 71–88.

14. Montesano and Jory, citing Milner, state that the *Hidakyat Patani* mentions the term *Melayu* only once, in relation to Johor. This is not to suggest that the people of Patani were not "Malay," but that in previous centuries they did not imagine themselves as "Malay" in any modern sense. Montesano and Jory, "Introduction," in *Thai South and Malay North*, ed. Montesano and Jory, 41n3.

15. Quantifying Thailand's Malay Muslims is tricky. These figures are based on an estimated 1,387,229 Muslims in the three provinces, from a total Thai population of 64.63 million. If Malay Muslims in the adjoining four Songkhla districts of Chana, Na Thawi, Saba Yoi, and Thepa are added, Malay Muslims may amount to around 2.5 percent of Thailand's population. However, Songkhla informants suggested that they were not regarded as part of the same "in-group" by people from the three core Malay Muslim provinces.

16. Interview, March 3, 2006.

17. Srisompob Jitpiromsri, speaking at a seminar at the Institute of Southeast Asian Studies, Singapore, June 21, 2007. In the context of Indonesia, John Sidel refers to some comparable Muslim worldviews as "fantasies," "in the sense of understandings of [the] matrix of social relations and the role of religion within it." John T. Sidel, *Riots, Pogroms, Jihad: Religious Violence in Indonesia* (Ithaca: Cornell University Press, 2007), 16.

18. หะสัน หมัดหมาน, "ความมองสังคมมุสลิมอย่างไร: กรณีสังคมจังหวัดชายแดนภาคใต้," *ทักษิณคดี* [Hasan Madmarn, "How to View Muslim Society: The Case of the Southern Border Provinces," *Southern Studies*] 3, 2 (1994): 51.

19. Academic interview, January 6, 2006.

20. Village visit, November 29, 2005.

21. See Duncan McCargo, "Southern Thai Politics: Some Preliminary Observations," in *Dynamic Diversity in Southern Thailand*, ed. Wattana Sugunnasil (Chiang Mai: Silkworm, 2005), 26–30.

22. Marc Askew, *Conspiracy, Politics, and a Disorderly Border: The Struggle to Comprehend Insurgency in Thailand's Deep South* (Washington, DC: East-West Center, Policy Studies 29, 2007), 12–38.

23. There is no doubt that the Thai authorities have sometimes fabricated arson attacks and other incidents for purposes of their own.

24. See, for example, the NRC's repeated references to conflicts over "natural resources" in the deep South: คณะกรรมการอิสระเพื่อความสมานฉันท์แห่งชาติ, *รายงานคณะกรรมการอิสระเพื่อความสมานฉันท์แห่งชาติ เอาชนะความรุนแรงด้วยพลังสมานฉันท์* [National Reconciliation Commission (NRC), *Report of the National Reconciliation Commission: Overcoming Violence through the Power of Reconciliation*] (Bangkok: NRC, 2006), 3, 17, 25–26, 27, 74–76, 99, and 107 (English version).

25. Srisompob Jitpiromsri with Panyasak Sobhonvasu, "Unpacking Thailand's Southern Conflict: The Poverty of Structural Explanations," in *Rethinking Thailand's Southern Violence,* ed. Duncan McCargo (Singapore: NUS Press, 2007), 89–111 (also in *Critical Asian Studies* 38, 1 [2006]).

26. See Duncan McCargo, "Thaksin and the Resurgence of Violence in the Thai South," and Ukrist Pathmanand, "Thaksin's Achilles' Heel: The Failure of Hawkish Approaches in the Thai South," in *Rethinking Thailand's Southern Violence,* ed. Duncan McCargo (Singapore: NUS Press, 2007), 35–68 and 69–88 (also in *Critical Asian Studies* 38, 1 [2006]); and Puwadol Songprasert, "Chronic Conflict in the Three Southern Border Provinces of Thailand," in *Knowledge and Conflict Resolution: The Crisis of the Border Region of Southern Thailand,* ed. Uthai Dulyakasem and Lertchai Sirichai (Nakhon Si Thammarat: Walailak University, 2005), 173–200.

27. Arguments of this kind are discussed by Zachary Abuza, *Militant Islam in Southeast Asia* (Boulder: Lynne Rienner, 2003), 171–73, and Kavi Chongkittavorn, "Thailand: International Terrorism and the Muslim South," in *Southeast Asian Affairs 2004* (Singapore: ISEAS, 2004), 267–75, though neither makes any grand claims for such an interpretation.

28. On JI, described as a Southeast Asian "terrorist network" linked to al-Qaeda, see Greg Barton, *Jemaah Islamiyah: Radical Islamism in Indonesia* (Singapore: Singapore University Press, 2005).

29. Such arguments were a regular theme in my conversations and interviews with Malay Muslim informants in the South from January 2004 to September 2006.

30. http://singapore.usembassy.gov/president_at_nus.html. It was my privilege to be present when President Bush delivered this speech.

31. For a classic discussion of these earlier movements, see Wan Kadir Che Man, *Muslim Separatism: The Moros of Southern Philippines and the Malays of Southern Thailand* (Quezon City: Ateneo de Manila University Press, 1990).

32. See Duncan McCargo, "Network Monarchy and Legitimacy Crises in Thailand," *Pacific Review* 18, 4 (2005): 499–519; and Duncan McCargo, "A Hollow Crown," *New Left Review* 43 (2007): 135–44.

33. On Thaksin, see Pasuk Phongpaichit and Chris Baker, *Thaksin: The Business of Politics in Thailand* (Chiang Mai: Silkworm, 2004); and Duncan McCargo and Ukrist Pathmanand, *The Thaksinization of Thailand* (Copenhagen: NIAS Press, 2005).

34. The junta was initially known as the Council for Democratic Reform under the Constitutional Monarchy, but soon changed its name to avoid implicating the monarchy in the coup.

35. บารมี [*barami*] is usually translated as "charisma."

36. Conversation with well-placed informant, June 8, 2006.

37. For an elaboration of this analysis, see Duncan McCargo, "Thaksin," 39–71.

38. Mohammed M. Hafez, *Why Muslims Rebel: Repression and Resistance in the Islamic World* (Boulder: Lynne Rienner, 2003). Many thanks to my Leeds colleague Clive Jones for sending me to Hafez.

39. In fact, many of Hafez's arguments could be applied with almost equal force to militant movements in the non-Muslim world, as he himself recognizes.

40. This paragraph draws on Hafez, *Why Muslims,* 17–19.

41. This paragraph draws on ibid., 21–22.

42. Sidel, *Riots*, 217.

43. Interview notes, TAO nayok, December 11, 2005.

44. Buranuddin Useng interview, January 31, 2005. Another source argued that the militants mobilized villagers to reject TRT in the February 2005 elections. Academic, January 30, 2006.

45. Muthiah Alagappa, "Part I, Legitimacy: Explication and Elaboration," in *Political Legitimacy in Southeast Asia: The Quest for Moral Authority,* ed. Muthiah Alagappa (Stanford: Stanford University Press, 1995), 11–65.

46. Ibid., 29.

47. Robert W. Hefner, "Introduction: Modernity and the Remaking of Muslim Politics," in *Remaking Muslim Politics: Pluralism, Contestation, Democratization,* ed. Robert W. Hefner (Princeton: Princeton University Press, 2005), 22.

48. Alagappa, "Legitimacy," 40.

49. Muhammad Qasim Zaman, "Pluralism, Democracy, and the 'Ulama,'" in *Remaking Muslim Politics,* ed. Robert W. Hefner, 67.

50. See Pnina Werbner, "Divided Loyalties, Empowered Citizenship: Muslims in Britain," in *Political Loyalty and the Nation-State,* eds. Michael Waller and Andrew Linklater (London: Routledge, 2003): 105–22.

51. Zaman, "Pluralism," 60–65.

52. Alagappa, "Legitimacy," 46.

53. Ibid., 59.

54. David Beetham, *The Legitimation of Power* (Basingstoke, UK: Macmillan, 1991), 205–42.

55. The idea of a "legitimacy continuum" does not imply that maximum legitimacy is always secured by maximizing participation.

56. The idea of King Bhumibol as *dhammaraja* is a major theme of Paul Handley, *The King Never Smiles* (New Haven: Yale University Press, 2006).

57. Literally "royal-people-mutuality," which Connors defines as "the mythic belief of the mutuality of king and people." Michael K. Connors, "Article of Faith: The Failure of Royal Liberalism in Thailand," *Journal of Contemporary Asia* 38, 1 (2008), 150.

58. In the Thai context, many prominent bureaucrats, academics, and public figures combine some "progressive" social views with conservative, royalist core beliefs, without seeing these contrasting orientations as contradictory. Anand Panyarachun and Dr. Prawase Wasi are leading examples of this tendency.

59. เฉลิมเกียรติ ขุนทองเพชร, *ทะยีสุหลง อับดุลกาเดร์: กบฏ... หรือวีรบุรุษแห่งสี่จังหวัดภาคใต้* [Chalermkiat Khunthongpetch, *Haji Sulong Abdul Gade: Rebel or Hero of the Four Southern Provinces?*] (Bangkok: Matichon Publishing, 2005), 87.

60. Theera was appointed governor of Yala by the Surayud government in 2006. Born in Pattani, he had spent his entire Interior Ministry career in the three provinces, and previously served as deputy governor of both Narathiwat and Pattani.

61. เด่น โต๊ะมีนา, "ส.ส.มุสลิมเป็นแค่ไม้ประดับ," *หนังสือพิมพ์มุสลิม* [Den Tohmeena, "Muslim MPs are Mere Ornamental Plants," *Muslim Newspaper*], December 20, 1997–January 20, 1998.

Chapter 1. Islam

1. Conversation, April 23, 2006.

2. For details of this shrine, see อ.บางนรา (เรียบเรียง) *รามันในประวัติศาสตร์เปรัค, สารวัฒนธรรมประวัติศาสตร์* [Ajarn Bangnara (pseud.), "Raman in the History of Perak," *Historical Culture Journal*], undated, 11–20.

3. Conversation, Khota Baru, May 29, 2006.

4. Visit made on April 10, 2006.

5. Imam, April 15, 2006

6. เฉลิมเกียรติ, *หะยีสุหลง* [Chalermkiat, *Haji Sulong*], 15–16; also James Ockey, "The Religio-Nationalist Pilgrimages of Haji Sulong Abdulkadir al Fattani," unpublished paper, n.d., 22.

7. Umar interview, June 11, 2006.

8. Ibid.

9. Nayok TAO, November 22, 2005.

10. Academic, August 15, 2006.

11. Umar, June 11, 2006.

12. ดอเลาะ เจ๊ะแต, มะรอนิง สาแล, อับดุลเลาะห์ ดือเระห์, กอเซ็ง ลาเต๊ะ, ซารีฟะห์ สารง, ซารีฟ บุญพิศ, มุฮัมหมัด อาดำ และ รอไกยะ อาดำ. *รายงานวิจัยฉบับสมบูรณ์ โครงการอบรมและวิจัยเชิงปฏิบัติการทางประวัติศาสตร์ โบราณคดี และชาติพันธุ์ การศึกษาการเปลี่ยนแปลงทางสังคมและวัฒนธรรม: กรณีศึกษาบ้านดาโต๊ะ และ บ้านภูมิ อำเภอยะหริ่ง จังหวัดปัตตานี* [Dolah Jetae, Maroning Salae, Abdulloh Dure et al., *Final Research Report, Training and Action Research Project in History, Archaeology and Ethnicity, Study of Social and Cultural Change: Case Study of Ban Dato and Ban Phumi, Yaring District, Pattani*] (Thailand Research Fund, December 2004), 182.

13. Imtiyaz Yusuf, "The Ethno-Religious Dimension of the Conflict in Southern Thailand," in *Understanding Conflict and Approaching Peace in Southern Thailand*, ed. Imtiyaz Yusuf and Lars Peter Schmidt (Bangkok: Konrad Adenauer Stiftung, 2006), 181.

14. For a critical view of the emergence of Wahhabism and what he terms "puritanical Islam," see Khaled Abou El Fadl, *The Great Theft: Wresting Islam from the Extremists* (New York: HarperCollins, 2005), 45–109.

15. Academic, January 9, 2006.

16. Academic, August 19, 2006.

17. Academic, August 15, 2006.

18. Noorhaidi Hasan, *Laskar Jihad: Islam, Militancy, and Quest for Identity in Post-New Order Indonesia* (Ithaca: Cornell Southeast Asia Program, 2006), 33.

19. Umar, June 11, 2006.

20. Academic conversation, November 14, 2005.

21. Nayok TAO, November 22, 2006. Most informants who were not themselves Islamic teachers looked askance when I asked them whether they considered themselves old or new school, and plumped for the old school without hesitation.

22. Fieldnotes, August 13 and 19, 2006.

23. When I visited Bamrung Islam School on August 19, no one spoke to me at all, whereas later that morning at Pattani Central Mosque I was greeted by numerous people, several of whom shook my hand and chatted to me.

24. Conversation, August 13, 2006.

25. Academic, June 13, 2006.

26. ดอเลาะ ฯลฯ, *รายงานวิจัยฉบับสมบูรณ์* [Dolah et al., *Final Research Report*], 44.

27. Dawah Tabligh, or Tablighi Jamaat, is a reformist Islamic movement originally from India, which started working across Thailand in the early 1980s, and had a popular *markaz* (center) in Yala. For some details see Ernesto Braam, "Travelling with the Tabilighi Jamaat in South Thailand," *ISIM Review* 17 (2006): 42–43.

28. บุฆอรี ยีหมะ, อะห์มัด ยีสันทรง, มะรอนิง สาแลมิง และ อับดุลฮาฟิซ หิเละ, *โครงการศึกษาความคิดของ "อุลามะอ์:" ความสัมพันธ์กับสุขภาวะชุมชนในสังคมมุสลิมจังหวัดชายแดนภาคใต้* [Bukohri Yimah, Ahmad Yisunsong, Maroning Salaeming, and Abdulhafiz Hileh, "Study Project on the Ideas of Ulama: Relations with Community Health in Muslim Society of the Southern Border Provinces"], Unpublished draft research paper, undated, ca. September 2006, 4–5.

29. They defined *klum sunah* as "a group that supported the idea of using the Koran and sunah for daily life in terms of faith and daily practice, to create morality, and curtail unacceptable behavior." บุฆอรี ฯลฯ "อุลามะอ์" [Bukohri et al., "Ulama"], 5. No one mentioned the term *klum sunah* to me during my interviews.

30. August 15, 2006.

31. Nayok TAO, November 22, 2006.

32. Islamic teacher, June 6, 2006.

33. Academic, October 11, 2005.

34. Academic, October 8, 2006.

35. Lutfi had earlier been viewed with intense suspicion by the Thai authorities, particularly following intelligence reports that he had met leading JI suspect Hambali. Former Wadah MP Muk Sulaiman claimed that he and then interior minister Wan Nor had persuaded Thaksin to reject a U.S. request to have Lutfi arrested following these revelations. Interview, June 10, 2006.

36. Conversation, October 13, 2005.

37. Academic, October 11 2005.

38. Nayok TAO, October 22, 2005.

39. Academic, August 15, 2006.

40. Academic conversation, October 13, 2005.

41. "เสียงโต้จากกลุ่มส่งเสริมศิลปะและวัฒนธรรมมุสลิมจังหวัดชายแดนภาคใต้," (เซาดารอ), *ประชาไท* ["Response from the Group for Supporting Muslim Arts and Culture in the Southern Border Provinces," (Saudara) *Prachatai*], August 18, 2006, www.prachatai.com.

42. Originally, Saudara members came mainly from six schools: (1) Saeng Tham, in Sungai Kolok; (2) Darusa Withaya, in Saiburi, owned by Nimukhtar Waba; (3) Darusalam, in Tanyong Mas, owned by Fakhruddin Boto; (4) Saiburi Islam Witthaya, in Saiburi, owned by Nideh Waba; (5) Thamma Wittaya in Yala; (6) Asisan Tham in Na Pradu, Khok Poh. Four more were later added: (7) Triamsuksa, Pattani, owned by the President of Pattani Islamic Council; (8) Chongratsapwitthaya, near Kru-Ze, Yaring; (9) Sasurupatham in Bana, near Pares; and (10) Somboonsat.

43. Academic, August 22, 2006.

44. "เจาะวงใน "นักศึกษามุสลิม"กับสถานการณ์ร้ายชายแดนใต้," *ประชาไท* ["Inside the World of Muslim Students and the Violence on the Southern Border," *Prachatai*], August 11, 2006, www.prachatai.com. Following complaints about the accusations it contained, this article was subsequently removed from the website.

45. Academics, June 13, 2006, August 19, 2006.

46. Noorhaidi offers a detailed discussion of how Salafi thinking could be transformed from an "apolitical" set of doctrines to "jihadic activism," *Laskar Jihad*, 129–55.

47. Strictly speaking, the *khatib* was responsible for leading Friday prayers, and the *bilal* for making the calls to prayer, but in practice these roles were often interchanged, and those holding these positions were commonly considered "assistant imam."

48. According to one Narathiwat informant familiar with this process, mosque construction funds were normally initially generated locally, especially from MPs or politicians, and foreign funding was normally solicited only in for the final stages of the building. There were large numbers of unfinished mosques in the area. Interview, April 15, 2006.

49. Academic, August 15, 2006.

50. Academic, March 6, 2006.

51. Interview, March 3, 2006. One of the primary requirements for building a mosque was land: in order for the mosque to gain approval, it needed at least two rai of land, which it was assigned as a juridicial person, or to have received proper permission to build on public land. Interview, April 15, 2006.

52. Village visit notes, November 15, 2005.

53. Interview, March 3, 2006.

54. Workshop, Narathiwat, March 15, 2006.

55. ดอเลาะ ฯลฯ, *รายงานวิจัยฉบับสมบูรณ์* [Dolah et al., *Final Research Report*], 23.

56. Imam, April 14, 2006.

57. Interview, March 3, 2006.

58. ดอเลาะ ฯลฯ, *รายงานวิจัยฉบับสมบูรณ์* [Dolah et al., *Final Research Report*], 30.

59. Interview, April 15, 2006. The idea that prayers performed in congregation are twenty-seven times more effective than those performed individually appears in some hadith. See, for example, *Translation of Salih Muslim, Book 4, The Book of Prayers (Kitab Al-Salat)*, no. 1365, available at: http://www.usc.edu/dept/MSA/fundamentals/hadithsunnah/muslim/004.smt.html#004.1365.

60. Seminar, March 14, 2006; interview, April 15, 2006.

61. Conversations, March 19 and 20, 2006.

62. Academic, August 15, 2006.

63. Some of those I interviewed had not completed primary schooling.

64. Imam workshop, March 15, 2006.

65. Such "privatized" donations might be seen as valid forms of zakat but failed to create or foster Islamic institutions at the community level.

66. Interview, August 4, 2006.

67. Focus group, March 28, 2006.

68. Academic, March 6, 2006.

69. The process by which the Thai state suppressed "Northeastern" (in fact, Lao) forms of Buddhism is described in detail in Kamala Tiyavanich, *Forest Recollections: Wandering Monks in Twentieth Century Thailand* (Honolulu: University of Hawaii Press, 1997).

70. Imam, April 15, 2006.

71. ลูกน้อง.

72. Imam and ustadz workshop, March 15, 2006.

73. Leaflet 53. Leaflet 98 makes a similar point.

74. Strictly speaking, a *shahid* (martyr) dies while fulfilling a religious command, or during a war for religion. In practice, the term is often applied more broadly in Patani to those who die violent deaths.

75. Interviews with families of men killed on April 28, 2004; conducted May 10, 2006; May 17, 2006.

76. The 4,500 baht scheme was a job creation program launched in 2004, under which large numbers of Malay Muslims were hired to work on government projects, often as village defense volunteers. Some of those who took part were targeted by the militant movement as collaborators and munafik.

77. Leaflet 49.

78. For a discussion of the politics surrounding the role of the Chularajamontri and the 1997 Islamic Organizations Act, see Imtiyaz Yusuf, "Islam and Democracy in Thailand: Reforming the Office of the Chularajamontri/Shaikh Al-Islam," *Journal of Islamic Studies* 9, 2 (1998): 277–98.

79. The thirteen functions of Islamic Provincial Councils are specified in Article 26 of the พระราชบัญญัติการบริหารองค์กรศาสนาอิสลาม พ.ศ. ๒๕๔๐ [Islamic Organizations Administration Act 1997].

80. Interview, August 7, 2006.

81. Panu interview, May 25, 2006.

82. Interview, August 7, 2006.

83. Interview, August 16, 2006.

84. Around two thousand U.S. dollars.

85. Interview with Pattani Islamic Council President, September 1, 2006.

86. Den's family had long been involved in Islamic council matters: his father Haji Sulong headed the Pattani Islamic Council in 1945 and his brother Ameen was a member in the 1950s.

87. At the time, Den chaired the house committee on religious affairs.

88. เต็งกู อารีฟิน บินเต็งกูจิ อัลฟาฏอนี, "เลือกตั้งกรรมการอิสลาม: ปัญหาการเมืองในองค์กรศาสนา," *ศูนย์ข่าวอิสรา* [Tenggu Arifin Bintengguji Al-Fatani, "The Islamic Council Elections: A Political Problem in Religious Organizations"], *Isara News Center,* November 18, 2005. www.tjanews.org.

89. In 2000, numbers of registered mosques were: Pattani 551, Narathiwat 487, Yala 316. Michel Gilquin, *The Muslims of Thailand* (Chiang Mai: Silkworm 2005), 40.

90. Interview, May 23, 2006.

91. Interviews, January 23, 2006; June 2, 2006.

92. Interview, March 3, 2006.

93. Nideh interview, March 29, 2006.

94. Abdul Rahman interview, June 7, 2006. He was ousted following the November 24, 2005, elections.

95. Academic, March 23, 2006.

96. Nideh, March 29, 2006.

97. See, for example, สัมภาษณ์พิเศษ อัฮหมัด สมบูรณ์บัวหลวง, "วัดระดับคลื่นการเมืองสนามเลือกตั้งกรรมการอิสลาม," *ศูนย์ข่าวอิสรา* [Ahmad Somboon Bualuang, special interview, "Measuring the Political Degree of the Islamic Council Elections"], *Isara News Center,* November 20, 2005. www.tjanews.org.

98. Interview, January 24, 2006.

99. "เรื่องกีฬา."

100. Interview, September 1, 2006. Had the rival team really used 20 million baht to buy votes, they could have given each eligible voter more than 30,000 baht—an extremely large sum of money.

101. Interview, May 23, 2006.

102. "ละคร."

103. Interview, June 2, 2006.

104. Abdul Rahman, June 7, 2006.

105. สัมภาษณ์พิเศษ "อับดุลเระห์มาน อับดุลสอมัต." ประธานคณะกรรมการอิสลามประจำจังหวัดนราธิวาส, *ศูนย์ข่าวอิสรา* [Abdul Rahman Abdul Shamad, chairman of Narathiwat Islamic Council, special interview], *Isara News Center,* November 22, 2005, www.tjanews.org.

106. Academic, March 6, 2006.

107. Interview, March 3, 2006.

108. The literal meaning of pondok, pronounced "pondoh" in Pattani Malay, is "hut."

109. For more details on pondok, see Hasan, *Pondok and Madrasah,* and Ibrahem Narongraksakhet, "Educational Change for Building Peace in Southern Border Provinces of Thailand," in *Understanding Conflict and Approaching Peace in Southern Thailand,* ed. Imtiyaz Yusuf and Lars Peter Schmidt (Bangkok: Konrad Adenauer Stiftung, 2006), 128–47.

110. For example, leading babor Ismael Sapanyan in Yaring taught classes of all his 700 students together for some sessions.

111. For a detailed discussion of typical daily routines, see Hasan, *Pondok and Madrasah,* 58–67.

112. Interview, August 8, 2006.

113. On the merits and shortcomings of this comparison, see Robert W. Hefner, "Introduction: The Culture, Politics, and Future of Muslim Education," in *Schooling Islam: The Culture and Politics of Muslim Education,* ed. Robert W. Hefner (Princeton: Princeton University Press, 2007), 8–9.

114. Conversation, November 15, 2005.

115. Interview, school, June 7, 2006.

116. Ustadz interview, January 30, 2006.

117. Umar, June 11, 2006.

118. Ibid.

119. In practice babors can receive some income from donations, from the sale of agricultural produce, and by selling food and other items to their pupils.

120. Interview, August 8, 2006. There were actually many parallels between pondok and Thai Buddhist temples, which also traditionally provided education for poor boys. The difference was that in Thai Buddhist society, temple schools had been displaced by modern secular education decades earlier.

121. Interview, August 8, 2006.

122. Based on figures cited by Ibrahem, "Educational Change," 141. He cited figures of 249 registered pondok with enrollments of 15,071 students in 2004, a figure which later increased. In practice many pondok were very small, and average figures were inflated by a limited number of much larger institutions.

123. Tayun Islam School, Bacho, June 7, 2006. This school has now become a private Islamic school and expanded greatly. In recent years, applicants from other places have begun to exceed those from their traditional catchment areas.

124. Similar families of Islamic schools exist in Java; see Zamakhsyasri Dhofier, *The Pesantren Tradition* (Tempe, AZ: Southeast Asian Studies Program, Arizona State University, 1999), 73.

125. For details on the history of pondok registration, see Hasan, *Pondok and Madrasah,* 72–79. Interview, August 8, 2006.

126. Ockey, "Religio-nationalist Pilgrimages," 22; เฉลิมเกียรติ, หะยีสุหลง [Chalermkiat, *Haji Sulong*], 19–21.

127. A few private Islamic schools are registered simply as ordinary private schools under Category 15 (1), while others are registered as charitable schools under Category 15 (3).

128. These schools should not be confused with the 319 schools officially registered as pondok from 2004 onward.

129. Academic, August 15, 2006; Interview, August 8, 2006.

130. ดอเลาะ ฯลฯ, *รายงานวิจัยฉบับสมบูรณ์* [Dolah et al., *Final Research Report*], 200.

131. Fieldnotes, June 8, 2006.

132. Interview, June 6, 2006.

133. Interview, March 3, 2006.

134. Interview, August 4, 2006. According to government scales, the teachers concerned—who held teaching diplomas in addition to their degrees—should have been paid 7,900 baht per month. A group of teachers signed a letter requesting a pay rise to 5,000 baht; they were given a choice between retracting their claim and being instantly dismissed. Those who refused were fired the next day. Salaries of 3,000 baht a month were not uncommon.

135. I have previously described this understanding as a "social contract," but have reconsidered this usage because of the elite nature of the bargain. Thanks to Michael Connors for this point.

136. Nideh interview, March 29, 2006; academic, August 15, 2006.

137. Interview, March 3, 2006.

138. Conversation, January 28, 2006.

139. In Thai, "ทางเดิม" and "บาบอภาพนิ่ง." Academic, June 13, 2006.

140. Umar, June 11, 2006.

141. Hefner, "Muslim Education," 18.

142. Workshop, March 14, 2006.

143. Academic, August 15, 2006.

144. Interview, August 8, 2006.

145. Interview, June 6, 2006.

146. The fact that Lutfi chose to subsume his small group of schools within Nideh's association showed that Lutfi's influence as an Islamic teacher and a leader in higher education

was not matched by a parallel dominance in the school sector; Nideh had better bargaining power with the Thai authorities.

147. The election was annulled by the September 19, 2006, military coup.

148. Interview, August 8, 2006.

149. Academic, August 15, 2006.

150. These are my own terms, coined here.

151. Interview, May 25, 2006.

152. The party presented its candidates for the expected forthcoming election at a seminar I attended in Phang-nga on September 3, 2006. Several candidates were either ustadz or had close connections with leading Islamic schools. In the event, the September 19, 2006, military coup led to the cancellation of the election originally planned for mid-October. Field-notes, September 2–3, 2006.

153. Leaflet 124. In Islam, individual ulama have considerable scope to offer their own interpretations of the Koran and other scriptures, and to issue their own fatwa.

154. Academic, June 13, 2006.

155. The question of monks is complicated by a notorious Algerian case, in which a prominent Islamic jurist (actually the most famous of all jurists whose writings are favored by the Wahhabiyya) was cited in support of the killing of monks. See Ibn Taymiyya, *Le statut des moines* [On the Status of Monks] (Beirut, El-Safina Éditions, 1997), with a controversial introduction by Nasreddin Lebatelier (a.k.a. Yahya Michot).

156. Journalist, personal communication, April 27, 2007.

157. Academic, June 13, 2006.

158. Malika Zeghal, "The 'Recentering' of Religious Knowledge and Discourse: the Case of al-Azhar in Twentieth-Century Egypt," in *Schooling Islam: The Culture and Politics of Muslim Education,* ed. Robert W. Hefner (Princeton: Princeton University Press, 2007), 125.

159. Cited in บุฆอรี และ ฯลฯ, "อุลามะอ์" [Bukohri et al., "Ulama"], 2.

160. Academic, June 13, 2006.

161. Ibid.

162. Ibid.

163. Ustadz and imam workshop, March 14, 2006.

164. Interview, August 22, 2006.

165. Academic, June 13, 2006.

166. Interview, August 22, 2006. There is a clear overlap here with ideas of "natural" leadership.

167. บุฆอรี ฯลฯ, "อุลามะอ์" [Bukohri et al., *Ulama*], p. 3.

168. This is a pun on the real title "Chularajamontri," suggesting that he is in effect a government minister rather than a Muslim spiritual leader.

169. Leaflet 100.

170. Interview, June 6, 2006.

171. Ibid.

172. Leaflet 11, Translation from Malay to Thai; the Jawi text was attached. Found in Amphoe Mayo, Pattani, May 16, 2005.

173. One trigger for this protest was the searching of the Yala Islamic Council president's school by the army. Interview, May 23, 2006.

174. Pisan became Fourth Army Commander on April 1, 2004. Though selected for his compromising character, he presided over the two most controversial recent episodes in Thai military history. This issue is discussed in อัฮหมัด สมบูรณ์ บัวหลวง, "บทบาทและอัตลักษณ์ทางศาสนากับความไม่สงบในภาคใต้: อำนาจ บารมี หรือภาพหลอน" [Ahmad Somboon Bualuang, "Religious Roles and Identity, and the Unrest in the South: Power, Charisma or Illusion?"] paper presented at Lowy Institute, Sydney, November 9, 2006, 4–5. Somboon asked rhetorically

whether Kru-Ze and Tak Bai were not in some way the outcomes of the February 2004 intervention by religious leaders, 6.

175. "เลือกกรรมการอิสลามในสายตาชาวบ้าน: แค่ปรับคนแต่ไม่เปลี่ยนแนวทาง," ศูนย์ข่าวอิสรา ["Islamic Council Elections from Villagers' Points of View: Changing the People, not the Direction"], *Isara News Center,* November 23, 2005, www.tjanews.org

176. Abdul Rahman interview, June 7, 2006.

177. Interview at hustings of Islamic council elections, Pattani, November 24, 2005.

178. "อึดอัด," Conversation, December 3, 2005.

179. Fieldnotes, November 13, 2005.

180. Nideh later "withdrew" this call, but the impact had already been felt.

181. "Ignorance 'Cause of Unrest,'" *Bangkok Post,* May 12, 2006.

182. Imtiyaz Yusuf, *Faces of Islam in Southern Thailand* (Washington, DC: East-West Center, Working Paper 7, 2007), 11–12. In a footnote, Imtiyaz notes that Lutfi rejects the term "Wahhabi" in favor of his preferred description of his movement as "Ahl al-Sunna." Imtiyaz playfully glosses "the term Wahhabi is used here for the purpose of identification," fn. 39, 23.

183. Other NLA members from the three provinces included the presidents of the Pattani, Yala, and Narathiwat Islamic councils; PSU College of Islamic Studies director Ismail Ali; and 2006 Narathiwat senate race winner and former "JI" suspect Dr. Waemahadi Wae-dao.

Chapter 2. Politics

1. See Nirmala Rao, "The Changing Context of Representation," in *Representation and Community in Western Democracies,* ed. Nirmala Rao (Basingstoke, UK: Macmillan, 2000), 1–4.

2. See Somchai Pathatharananunth, *Civil Society and Democratization: Social Movements in Northeast Thailand* (Copenhagen: NIAS, 2006), 15–16; and Naruemon Thabchumpon, "Contesting Democracy: Thailand's Forum of the Poor," Ph.D. diss., University of Leeds, 2006. Both studies use case material from Isan, but many of their findings also resonate in the deep South.

3. "In fact, representative democracy has not failed in Thailand, simply because it has not yet been established here as a country-wide polity." Michael Nelson, personal communication, January 4, 2007.

4. On legitimacy deficits, see David Beetham, *The Legitimation of Power* (Basingstoke, UK: Macmillan, 1991), 205–42.

5. ชาญวิทย์ เกษตรศิริ, "เหตุการณ์ความไม่สงบในจังหวัดชายแดนภาคใต้" กับ "ประวัติศาสตร์บาดแผล," ศิลปวัฒนธรรม [Charnvit Kasetsiri, "Violent Incidents in the Southern Border Provinces and the History of Wounds," *Art and Culture Magazine*] (February 2005): 152.

6. Imam, February 21, 2006.

7. Community leader interview, November 15, 2005.

8. คณะกรรมการอิสระเพื่อความสมานฉันท์แห่งชาติ, เอาชนะความรุนแรง [NRC, *Overcoming Violence*], 17–18 [18].

9. Ibid., 96 [106].

10. In other words, the NRC had not fully grasped the idea of "representative bureaucracy," let alone more genuine localization under elected governors.

11. District officer conversation, August 25, 2006.

12. "ปลัดอำเภอ," District permanent secretary.

13. Traditionally, senior positions in the Interior Ministry were dominated by political science graduates from Chulalongkorn (sing dam, black lion) and Thammasat universities (sing daeng, red lion); Ramkhamhaeng graduates were an emerging rival clique.

14. District officer conversation, August 25, 2006.

15. "งานมวลชน."

16. District officer conversation, August 25, 2006. Pracha was removed as Narathiwat governor following the September 19, 2006, military coup.

17. See Ora-orn Poocharoen, "Representative Bureaucracy: An Alternative for Bridging the Gap between the State and Citizen," draft research paper, Faculty of Political Science, Chulalongkorn University, December 24, 2006.

18. These complaints were supported by the Interior Ministry's own surveys of villagers' attitudes to the state bureaucracy. District officer conversation, August 25, 2006.

19. Nayok TAO, December 22, 2005.

20. Interview, March 3, 2006.

21. Nayok TAO, December 22, 2005.

22. Academic, September 15, 2006.

23. Shop owner conversation, October 17, 2006.

24. เฉลิมเกียรติ, *หะยีสุหลง* [Chalermkiat, *Haji Sulong*], 87.

25. Ockey, "Religio-nationalist Pilgrimages," 25. Ockey argues that Sulong's political goals were inseparable from his aspiration to revitalize and purify local Islam.

26. For a discussion, see James Ockey, "Elections, Political Integration, and Cultural Pluralism in the Lower South of Thailand," in *A Plural Peninsula,* ed. Michael Montesano and Patrick Jory (Singapore: NUS Press, 2008), 125–35.

27. Ockey, "Religio-nationalist Pilgrimages," 32.

28. This was the impression I gained from hundreds of conversations and interviews, though few informants expressed the sentiment directly. A common refrain was that the form of autonomy did not matter—the point was to secure the substance.

29. Workshop, March 2006.

30. Ockey, "Elections," 45.

31. Workshop discussion, Pattani, December 2005.

32. This point draws on conversations and interviews with several NRC members.

33. Conversation with Anand, September 7, 2006.

34. Gothom interview, November 16, 2005.

35. "New Thai Govt To Consider Self-rule for Muslim South: Minister," Agence France Press, February 12, 2008.

36. "'ประเวศ' หนุนใต้ปกครองตัวเอง ยันไม่กระทบพระราชอำนาจ และไม่ใช่ไม่รัก 'ในหลวง'" [Prawase Encourages South To Govern Itself, Says It Won't Affect Royal Powers, and Doesn't Mean We Don't Love the King], http://www.prachatai.com, 10 November 2007.

37. Nayok TAO, November 28, 2005.

38. For example, nayok TAO interview, December 13, 2005.

39. Interview, April 7, 2006.

40. Born 1934.

41. The Thai term *trakun* has been rendered here as "clan"; another possible translation is "dynasty."

42. พิชัย เก้าสำราญ, สมเจตน์ นาคเสวี และ วรวิทย์ บารู *การเลือกตั้งปัตตานี ปี 2529 ศึกษากรณีกระบวนการหาเสียง และระบบหัวคะแนน* [Phichai Kaosamran, Somjet Naksewi, and Worawidh Baru, *1986 Elections in Pattani: Case Study of the System of Campaigning and Vote Canvassers*] (Bangkok: Foundation for Democracy and Development Studies, 1988), 27–28.

43. Den Tohmeena interview, August 22, 2006.

44. Den was successively an MP for the Democrat, Prachachon, Solidarity, and New Aspiration parties.

45. Michael Nelson has persuasively argued that "Phakphuak [cliques] fill the void left by political parties, public and citizens" in the Thai electoral context: see his *Analyzing Provincial Political Structures in Thailand: phuak, trakun and hua khanaen* (Hong Kong: Working Paper No. 79, Southeast Asia Research Centre, City University of Hong Kong, August 2005), http://www.cityu.edu.hk/searc, p. 9.

46. พิชัย ฯลฯ *การเลือกตั้งปัตตานี ปี 2529* [Pichai et al., *1986 Elections in Pattani*], 29.

47. Den's *than siang* was probably strongest in Nong Chik and Khok Pho, but he had pockets of strong *phuak* spread across various noncontiguous areas of Pattani province.

48. Interview, January 23, 2006.

49. Den Tohmeena interview, August 12, 2006. Den claimed that manipulation of the voting process by government officials, especially the district officer in Saiburi, cost him the election. Den apparently also believed that then former Islamic Council president Abdulwahab Abdulwahab played a key role in his losing the 1995 election, hence his support for Waedueramae Mamingchi to oust Abdulwahab in the 1999 Islamic council elections. See สัมภาษณ์พิเศษ อัฮหมัด สมบูรณ์บัวหลวง [Ahmad Somboon Bualuang, special interview].

50. The document "ปฏิบัติการเจาะไอร้อง" [Operation Joh-Ai-Rong] (unpublished, anonymously written intelligence dossier, title page missing, undated but internal evidence suggests c. February 2004), 53, offers a very different explanation reflecting Bangkok security perspectives. It argues that Wan Nor and Den fell out because of Den's support for separatism. This speculative and fanciful document is discussed and summarized in Askew, *Conspiracy*, 15–24.

51. Wan Nor was minister of transport and communications in the Banharn government (1995–96); he then served as president of parliament (1996–2000), before returning to the communications portfolio under Thaksin (February 2001–October 2002), then became interior minister (from October 2002) until March 2004, when he became deputy PM until October 6, 2004, then agriculture minister until February 2005.

52. Den interview, August 12, 2006.

53. Thanks to Michael Nelson for this suggestion.

54. This was the explanation given to me by Den, interview August 12, 2006.

55. Letter dated March 19, 2003, to the governor of Pattani, signed by Chana Barami, deputy secretary general to the Royal Household. This covering letter asks the governor to look into complaints made in an attached three-page letter to the palace, apparently penned anonymously, dated January 24, 2003.

56. Letter from Den to the governor of Pattani, dated May 5, 2003.

57. เด่น โต๊ะมีนา, *เลือดเนื้อใช่เชื้อไฟ* [Den Tohmeena, *My Family (Flesh) is not Behind the Southern Fires*] (Bangkok: Working Experience, 2004), 78. I am indebted to Michael Connors for this translation of Den's essentially untranslatable book title.

58. The final phrase means "made me aware that I was being constantly accused" เด่น, *เลือดเนื้อใช่เชื้อไฟ* [Den, *My Family*], 83.

59. The term Pechdau used—*metta*—is replete with Buddhist overtones.

60. เด่น, *เลือดเนื้อใช่เชื้อไฟ* [Den, *My Family*], 104.

61. Ibid., 108.

62. Unpublished document entitled "ข้อเท็จจริงปฏิบัติการก่อความไม่สงบ 3 จังหวัดชายแดนใต้" ("Truth about the Operation of the Unrest in the Three Southern Border Provinces"), undated, 1. The source was a very well-informed Malay-Muslim political figure, but the document is unsupported by other evidence.

63. However, the document also assigned much of the blame to one "Theptheuk," apparently referring to Democrat Party secretary-general Suthep Theuksuban, whose Democrat-military network (including privy councilors Surayud Chulanont and Palakorn Sunwannarat) was improbably held responsible for the January 4 arms raid. See ปฏิบัติการเจาะไอร้อง [Operation Joh-Ai-Rong], 89.

64. A PULO spokesman doubted Den was actively involved in the BRN-Coordinate, since the group did not permit those who worked with the Thai state to become members. Kasturi Makota, PULO Foreign Affairs chief, interview in Sweden, May 10, 2007.

65. Den interview, August 22, 2006. The claim that Den wanted to be Chularajamontri also appeared in ปฏิบัติการเจาะไอร้อง (Operation Joh-Ai-Rong), 57.

66. Morton Grodzins, *The Loyal and the Disloyal: Social Boundaries of Patriotism and Treason* (Chicago: University of Chicago Press, 1956), 208–16.

67. Pechdau was very clear that the seven points remained the core agenda for the Tohmeena *trakun*'s political work and stressed that the first point (autonomy) and the seventh (the shariah court) still needed work. Interview, January 6, 2006.

68. Phichet's opponents accused him of receiving backing from Thaksin for the Islamic Council post, claiming that he had admitted this on a Channel 11 television interview on November 4, 2005. For details, see หนังสือพิมพ์มุสลิมไทย [*Muslim Thai Newspaper*], 7, 21; April 15–May 14, 2006.

69. Den interview, August 22, 2006.

70. Pechdau Tohmeena interview, August 31, 2006.

71. พิชัย ฯลฯ, *การเลือกตั้งปัตตานี ปี 2529* [Phichai et al., *1986 Elections in Pattani*], 29.

72. The group was wiped out at constituency level in the February 2005 election, following a backlash against the hardline security policies of the Thaksin government.

73. Daungyewa Utarasint, "Wadah: The Muslim Faction in Thai Political Party [*sic*]," paper presented at the Ninth International Conference on Thai Studies, DeKalb, Illinois, April 3–6, 2005, 6. Daungyewa does not name the original members of the group, but it is clear that several MPs took part in initial meetings in 1986.

74. Sudin was a veteran Pattani MP who had joined numerous parties; though he claimed to be a founder member of Wadah, he was only formally aligned with the group from September 1992. Sudin interview, August 17, 2006.

75. Daungyewa, "Wadah," 11.

76. พิชัย ฯลฯ, *การเลือกตั้งปัตตานี ปี 2529* [Phichai et al., *1986 Elections in Pattani*], 63–64.

77. ข้อบังคับกลุ่มเอกภาพ (วะห์ดะห์) [Rules and Regulations of the Wadah Group], undated leaflet.

78. Despite his background as a former army commander, Chavalit had long flirted with the left and consistently cultivated support from poor peasants, organized labor, Muslim communities, and other "underdog" interests.

79. From December 9, 1990 to February 23, 1991.

80. Wan Nor stepped down on December 17, 1994, when New Aspiration withdrew from the coalition. During this period, Den and Wan Nor served under a Democrat-led government headed by Chuan Leekpai.

81. Islamic dress was made officially acceptable in government educational institutions on October 1, 1997, when Ariphen was serving as deputy education minister. On the hijab issue, see articles in หนังสือพิมพ์มุสลิม [*Muslim Newspaper*], October 20–November 20, 1997.

82. Born 1951.

83. Den described Ariphen and Najmuddin as his subordinates, "ลูกน้อง"; interview, August 12, 2006.

84. Interview, June 15, 2006.

85. Ariphen interview, August 12, 2006. The other 10 percent of incidents were ordinary crimes.

86. Ibid.

87. Anonymous document, 2, describes Ariphen as a supporter of BRN-Coordinate.

88. Interview, November 1, 2006. Anuphong claimed his interrogators—who took him up in a helicopter and threatened to push him out—wanted him to confess that in an independent Pattani, Den would be the governor, Ariphen the interior minister, and Najmuddin the finance minister, with Anupong the army commander.

89. Imam, April 15, 2006. See also *The Nation*, March 23, 2004: "[Ariphen] has made tremendous political gains from his associations with influential figures from the state apparatus, including senior police and military officers."

90. A warrant was issued for Romali's arrest in 2005 (*Bangkok Post,* August 18, 2005); Ariphen claimed that the accusations against his brother were "politically motivated": see, for example, *The Nation,* February 16, 2006.

91. Imam, April 15, 2006; politician, August 26, 2006.

92. Buddhist, August 24, 2006. อารีเพ็ญ อุตรสินธ์, *การปกครองท้องถิ่นในเขตพื้นที่พิเศษ: ศึกษากรณี 5 จังหวัดชายแดนภาคใต้* [Ariphen Utarasint, *Local Administration in Special Areas: Case Study of the Five Southern Border Provinces*] (Nonthaburi: King Prachadipok Institute, 2002). Despite the provocative title phrase "special area," the paper advocated only modest regional variations in the form of local government, which "should still be connected with central state authority," 19.

93. Sudin interview, August 18, 2006.

94. "ไม่เล่นกับประชาชน," politician, August 26, 2006.

95. Ariphen interview, August 12, 2006.

96. Born 1960.

97. ใจนักเลง.

98. He was defeated in September 1992 and 1995, 1996; he also won in 2006, but the election was invalidated.

99. Politician interview, August 26, 2006; *กรุงเทพธุรกิจ* [*Krungthep Thurakit*], December 26, 2003; *สยามรัฐสัปดาห์วิจารณ์* [*Siam Rat Weekend*], March 19–25, 2004; *กรุงเทพธุรกิจ* [*Krungthep Thurakit*], February 17, 2004; *มติชน* [*Matichon*], February 11, 2004; *ประชาคมท้องถิ่น* [*Prachakhom Thongthin*], No. 35, January 2004.

100. Born 1949.

101. For details see Ockey, "Elections."

102. See *สยามรัฐสัปดาห์วิจารณ์* [*Siam Rat Weekend*], March 19–25, 2004; *สยามรัฐ* [*Siam Rat*], March 3, 2004; *ประชาคมท้องถิ่น* [*Prachakhom Thong Thin*], 35, January 2004.

103. Muk Sulaiman interview, June 10, 2006.

104. Daungyeewa, "Wadah," 10.

105. Muk Sulaiman interview, June 10, 2006.

106. In Pattani, local Malay is normally written in Arabic script, known as Jawi, rather than following the Malaysian practice of romanization.

107. Muk Sulaiman interview, June 10, 2006.

108. Nayok TAO interview, December 22, 2005.

109. Faced with growing calls for his resignation, Thaksin called a snap election early in 2006. The election was boycotted by the opposition and later nullified by the courts. Najmuddin was very proud of gaining 25 percent in this election; he claimed to be the only TRT candidate in the South to beat the "no" vote. Rather like Dr. Waemahadi Wae-dao in the Nararathiwat Senate elections, Najmuddin benefited politically from his perceived victimization by the Thai state. Interview (with MC and FLD), April 22, 2006.

110. Ariphen interview, August 12, 2006.

111. Born 1944.

112. A classic *phu di* politician; see James Ockey, "Thai Society and Patterns of Political Leadership," *Asian Survey* 36, 4 (April 1996): 345–60.

113. "บุคลิก." However, some informants argued that Wan Nor was not a particularly devout Muslim. Interview, December 3, 2005.

114. The Thai term *barami* is often loosely translated as "charisma," but also suggests a high level of "credit" based on attributes such as wealth, power, wisdom, or virtue.

115. Interview, June 10, 2006.

116. This funding was provided via Wan Nor, Phaisan Yingsaman, and Buranuddin Useng. Reported in เดน โต๊ะมีนา, "ส.ส.มุสลิม" [Den Tohmeena, "Muslim MPs"].

117. Palat TAO interview, November 28, 2005.

118. "อิทธิพล."

119. The other Yala Wadah MP, Buranuddin Useng, also had good ties with Den.

120. Interview, May 30, 2006.

121. สยามรัฐ [*Siam Rat*], March 12, 2004; Interview, June 10, 2006. Dawut acted for a time as deputy leader of the Mahachon Party before returning to the Democrats in 2006.

122. Academic, August 10, 2006.

123. NAP was intimately entwined with TRT from February 2001, and formally merged with Thaksin's party on January 27, 2002.

124. "โจรใต้."

125. Wan Nor held no national position from several months from late June 2000 to February 2001, after resigning from the presidency of parliament to serve as the NAP's secretary-general.

126. Notably Muk Sulaiman's beautiful riverside property in Pattani. Den Tohmeena, by contrast, lived in a large shophouse behind his bus company office near Pattani central market.

127. Umar Tayib interview, June 11, 2006.

128. *Bangkok Post,* May 22, 2004. Wan Nor was investigated by the National Counter-Corruption Commission in 2003 and faced tough questioning and a call for his impeachment during a 2004 no-confidence debate.

129. Interview, September 15, 2006. Textual source unknown.

130. Interview, June 15, 2006.

131. Interview, June 10, 2006.

132. Academic, November 9, 2005.

133. ปฏิบัติการเจาะไอร้อง [*Operation Joh-Ai-Rong*], 54, claims that after Wan Nor became interior minister, Den complained he no longer listened to Muslims and had been captured by his officials. Den had wanted Ariphen to act as Wan Nor's ministerial secretary in order to feed him information, but Wan Nor instead selected Muk.

134. Brad Adams, "Thailand's Crackdown: Drug 'War' Kills Democracy, Too," *International Herald Tribune,* April 24, 2003. While the war on drugs was primarily implemented by the police, as interior minister Wan Nor was responsible for the policy, and he made several similar strong statements supporting it.

135. Interview, January 9, 2006. Though clearly not a complete explanation for the violence, a desire to humiliate Wan Nor was probably one factor behind the upsurge.

136. Anonymous leaflet 19, dated September 30, 2005. "Manor" is a play on the name "Wan Nor."

137. A PULO spokesman argued that Wan Nor could not have become interior minister if he were not already 120 percent Thai, or more Thai than the Thais themselves. Kasturi Makota, PULO Foreign Affairs chief, interview in Sweden, May 10, 2007.

138. For a detailed discussion of decentralization in Thailand, see Michael H. Nelson, "Thailand: Problems with Decentralization?" in *Thailand's New Politics: KPI Yearbook 2001,* ed. Michael H. Nelson (Bangkok: White Lotus Press, 2002), 219–81.

139. Nayok TAO interview, Narathiwat, December 13, 2005.

140. Ibid., December 7, 2005.

141. Ibid., November 22, 2005.

142. Interview, March 3, 2006.

143. On one occasion, I went to a Chinese-owned Narathiwat restaurant with a senior Thai Buddhist official. His Muslim driver declined to eat with us, saying that the food there was not halal. Puzzled, the official asked the waitress about another group of customers, who appeared to be Muslim; the waitress confirmed that they were Muslims, but had not ordered any food. "They are only drinking beer…" she explained. Fieldnotes, August 28, 2006.

144. Nayok TAO, December 13, 2006.

145. I observed this firsthand at a seminar in Pattani on December 3, 2005, where two locally well-known Bangkok speakers, senator Suphon Suphapong and NRC member Naree

Charoenpolpiriya were completely overshadowed by Muslim academic Chaiwat Satha-Anand, who based his entire presentation on Koranic references. Everyone I spoke to afterward praised Chaiwat and seemed unmoved by the others.

146. Most nayok whom I interviewed had secular educational backgrounds and had worked in businesses such as construction and trading. Few had high levels of Islamic knowledge.

147. Nayok TAO interview, Narathiwat, December 7, 2005. Similar arguments are made by conservative Thais, for whom local elections politicize supposedly harmonious traditional communities.

148. The responsibilities of TAOs are specified in the Tambon Council and Tambon Administrative Authority Act, 1994, section 67.

149. Nayok TAO interview, Narathiwat, November 22, 2005.

150. One nayok complained that Pracha seemed unaware of the realities on the ground: the militant movement did not support its members to run for elected office. Conversation, December 10, 2005. Coup leader Sonthi Boonyaratglin echoed Pracha's claims in December 2006, sparking heated debate in the columns of มติชน (*Matichon*) December 20 and 21, 2006.

151. Nayok TAO, December 2005.

152. Nayok TAO, conversation, December 10, 2005.

153. Based on notes from a workshop discussion in Pattani, March 5, 2006.

154. See Tambon Council and Tambon Administrative Authority Act, 1994, section 71; in practice, these "tambon regulations" are subject to the scrutiny of district officers.

155. Lunch discussion, TAO workshop, Pattani, March 5, 2006.

156. Focus group discussion, Raman, March 28, 2006.

157. Chandra-nuj Mahakanjana, *Decentralization, Local Government, and Sociopolitical Conflict in Southern Thailand,* Working Paper 5 (Washington, DC: East-West Center, 2007), 27.

158. This "position summary" is my own extrapolation, not one based on a single source.

159. In some comparable conflicts such as Kashmir, different members of the same family have chosen to pursue their grievances through politics and through violence. Thanks to Anthony Davis for this point.

160. See, for example, Omar Farouk Bajunid, "Islam, Nationalism and the Thai State," in *Dynamic Diversity in Southern Thailand,* ed. Wattana Sugunnasil (Chiang Mai: Silkworm, 2005).

161. Surin was deputy foreign minister from 1992 to 1995, and foreign minister from late 1997 to the beginning of 2001. In the Thai context, the Foreign Affairs ministry is considered a "B" grade post, in contrast with the "A" grade ministries of Communications, Interior, and Agriculture successively headed by Wan Nor.

162. เด่น โต๊ะมีนา, "ส.ส.มุสลิม" [Den Tohmeena, "Muslim MPs"].

163. This was acknowledged by one of those MPs, Pattani District 2's Ismael Yidoromae. He argued that the political dominance of Thai Rak Thai had left the Democrats with little room for maneuver. Interview, April 16, 2006. By contrast, another informant argued that he had begged the 2005 parliamentary intake to be more proactive—visiting the sites of violent incidents, for example—but they refused to listen. Interview, September 15, 2006.

Chapter 3. Security

1. I am indebted to Marc Askew for this point; see Askew, *Conspiracy*, 5–12.

2. คณะกรรมการอิสระเพื่อความสมานฉันท์แห่งชาติ, *เอาชนะความรุนแรง* [NRC, *Overcoming Violence*], 2 [3].

3. *Thailand: "If You Want Peace, Work for Justice,"* Amnesty International, ASA 39/001/2006 (London: Amnesty International, 2006).

4. "ผลงาน."

5. Charges against the Tak Bai protestors were finally dropped on November 2, 2006, after Surayud made a public apology for the episode.

6. Lawyer interviews: March 13, 2006; June 4, 2006; June 18, 2006.

7. Interview with prisoner in Pattani jail, March 17, 2006.

8. BA interview with prisoner in Pattani jail, March 17, 2006.

9. Ibid.

10. Anonymous source, August 31, 2006.

11. Security official interview.

12. Lawyer, March 13, 2006.

13. Lawyer, June 18, 2006.

14. Untitled DVD featuring Wat Phromprasit suspects along with security officials, including Pattani governor Panu Uthairat, issued by SBPPBC, November 20, 2005. Five of the suspects were convicted in February 2008 and sentenced to life imprisonment.

15. ผู้ว่าราชการจังหวัดนราธิวาสและโฆษก กสส.จชต. พบปะผู้นำศาสนาและผู้ต้องหาผลิตวัตถุระเบิด [*Narathiwat Provincial Governor and Spokesman of the Southern Border Provinces Peace-Building Command Get Together with Religious Leaders and Suspected Bomb-makers*], DVD issued by Narathiwat Province, undated but apparently produced ca. January or February 2006.

16. *The Nation*, November 27, 2005. The previous month, Thaksin made similar comments about the Koran to the head of the Organization of Islamic Countries.

17. See discussion in *More Power, Less Accountability: Thailand's New Emergency Decree* (Geneva: International Commission of Jurists, August 2005), 10–13. The full text of the decree is available in International Crisis Group, *Thailand's Emergency Decree: No Solution*, Asia Report No. 105 (Jakarta: ICG, 18 November 2005), http://www.crisisgroup.org, 25–29. Under the decree suspects could also be invited for questioning without a warrant, which was often requested later.

18. Lawyer, June 5, 2006.

19. *Emergency Decree on Public Administration in Emergency Situation, B.E. 2548 (2005)*, Section 12.

20. Activist, April 10, 2006.

21. In this context, the term *prisoner* covers both those held in regular custody, and those held in administrative detention under the emergency decree. The latter were often housed in a special secure unit at the Yala Police Academy, or in military camps.

22. Interviews with Narathiwat prisoners, February 20, 2006.

23. BA interview with Pattani prisoner, March 17, 2006.

24. Pattani prisoner interview, March 17, 2006.

25. Lawyer, March 13, 2006.

26. Security official, January 10, 2006.

27. Justice official, August 25, 2006.

28. Interviews with prisoners at Narathiwat jail, February 20, 2006. Prisoners at Pattani jail were allowed visits from Monday to Friday.

29. Conversation, February 20, 2006.

30. Justice official, August 25, 2006.

31. Lawyer, August 14, 2006.

32. Lawyer, March 13, 2006; justice official, August 25, 2006.

33. Court observations, Pattani, February 22, 2006.

34. Local lawyer Anukul Awaeputeh argued that prosecutors might take on additional functions in the South, working with the police on sensitive security cases. คณะทำงานสื่อสารกับสังคม กอส., *วิพากษ์รายงานคณะกรรมการอิสระเพื่อความสมานฉันท์แห่งชาติ "เอาชนะความรุนแรง ด้วยพลังสมานฉันท์* [Media and Society Working Group, NRC, *Critiques of the*

National Reconciliation Commission Report "Overcoming Violence through the Power of Reconciliation"] (Bangkok: NRC, 2006), 161.

35. Prosecutor, August 2006.

36. Anukul Awaeputeh, a Pattani lawyer involved in defending a number of security cases, argued in an interview responding to the NRC report that more experienced judges were needed to work on cases in the South to protect the interests of defendants. See วิพากษ์รายงาน กอส. [*Critiques of the National Reconciliation Commission*], 161.

37. Lawyer, March 13, 2006. Lawyer conversation, February 19, 2006.

38. Lawyer conversation, August 16, 2006.

39. Lawyer, March 13, 2006.

40. Justice official, August 25, 2006.

41. *The Nation,* December 16, 2005.

42. "จับมาก่อน," justice official, August 25, 2006.

43. Lawyers: March 13, 2006; June 4, 2006.

44. Police major-general Korkiat Wongvorachart interview, April 21, 2006.

45. The popularity of the American TV crime series *CSI* may also have played a part.

46. Sherry Ann Duncan, a young Thai-American, was murdered in Samut Prakan in 1986. Four men were convicted of killing her, but then acquitted on appeal in 1993. The case was the subject of a 2001 movie, *Sherry Ann.*

47. Lawyer, August 14, 2006.

48. Lawyer, March 13, 2006.

49. Lawyer, August 14, 2006. The Tak Bai case was one where some observers believed "professional" witnesses had been deployed by the prosecution; these witnesses had allegedly studied video footage of the incident closely, in order to testify convincingly.

50. Lawyer, November 25, 2006.

51. Lawyer, January 27, 2006.

52. A similar view was expressed by another lawyer, June 6, 2006.

53. Lawyer, August 14, 2006.

54. Justice official, August 25, 2006.

55. Lawyers: August 14, 2006; March 13, 2006.

56. One example was the murder of a Buddhist monk at Wat Phromprasit in October 2005. Lawyer, March 13, 2006.

57. Lawyer, January 27, 2006.

58. The official name of the center was ศูนย์นิติธรรมสมานฉันท์ 3 จังหวัดชายแดนภาคใต้, or the Center for Justice and Reconciliation in the Three Southern Border Provinces. Curiously, this was normally rendered into English as the "Rule of Law Center."

59. Report on the Center's First Anniversary, presented August 14, 2006, 6–7.

60. Equally problematic was the informal postcoup policy of granting bail to people facing even very serious charges, apparently as part of the Surayud government's preference for "reconciliation."

61. คณะกรรมการอิสระเพื่อความสมานฉันท์แห่งชาติ, *เอาชนะความรุนแรง* [NRC, *Overcoming Violence*], 74–80 [80–87].

62. Interview with Lieutenant-General Vaipot Srinual, former head of the National Intelligence Agency, May 17, 2007.

63. "'If you have a whole battalion there and you're still negligent, then you deserve to die,' Thaksin said." *The Nation,* January 6, 2004.

64. For rare critical discussions of the Thai military, see Duncan McCargo, "Security, Development, and Political Participation in Thailand: Alternative Currencies of Legitimacy," *Contemporary Southeast Asia* 24, 1 (2002): 50–67; and James Ockey, "Thailand: The Struggle to Redefine Civil-military Relations," in *Coercion and Governance: The Declining Political Role of the Military in Asia,* ed. Muthiah Alagappa (Stanford: Stanford University Press, 2001), 187–208.

65. This happened in 1973, 1976, 1992, and at Tak Bai in 2004.

66. "สร้างสถานการณ์." Interview with senior army officer, Pattani, November 23, 2005. The officer cited parallels with the CPT, whose struggle had been fueled by other government agencies for thirty years, but was ended by the army.

67. Fieldnotes from visit to Tak Bai district, October 4–6, 2005.

68. Senior army officer, Pattani, November 23, 2005.

69. *มติชน* (*Matichon*) July 19, 2005.

70. The discussion in this paragraph draws on details from รุ่งรวี เฉลิมศรีภิญโญรัช, "การคัดเลือกและการปฏิบัติหน้าที่ของเจ้าหน้าที่ทหารตำรวจ กับปัญหาการละเมิดสิทธิมนุษยชนในสามจังหวัดชายแดนภาคใต้." [Rungrawee C. Pinyorat, "Recruitment and Performance of Soldiers and Police Officers: The Problem of Human Rights Violations in the Three Southern Border Provinces"], unpublished paper presented at seminar on "Southern Violence and the Thai State" organized by Chaiwat Satha-Anand, Sirindhorn Anthropology Center, Bangkok, August 18–19, 2006, pp. 6–9.

71. A Muslim local politician from a red zone of Narathiwat expressed admiration for the work of these "Red Berets," whom he described as friendly, helpful, and well-behaved compared with other soldiers, especially rangers. Conversation, August 27, 2006.

72. I have followed convention by translating the Thai phrase "ทหารพราน" (*thahan phran*) as "rangers," but the English term is rather misleading: whereas the U.S. Army Rangers are a highly disciplined elite special operations force, Thai rangers are an ill-disciplined and nonprofessional militia, originally created in 1978 as bounty-hunters to rid Thailand of communists. In Desmond Ball's classic understatement, "The rangers in the South do not seem to have managed to win the affection or confidence of the local population." Ball concluded that the rangers should be abolished. *The Boys in Black: The Thaharn Phran (Rangers), Thailand's Para-Military Border Guards* (Bangkok: White Lotus, 2004), 111.

73. *มติชน* (*Matichon*), April 26, 2007.

74. However, soldiers I spoke to admitted that they had not learned enough Malay to communicate effectively. Conversation with low-ranking soldiers at temple, Pattani, April 23, 2006. These soldiers had received three months of training (including combat skills) before being deployed in the South. They had been issued with phrasebooks and copies of the emergency legislation.

75. Found displayed at a TAO office, November 2005. Following abuses by rangers in early 2007, Fourth Army commander Lieutenant-General Viroj Buacharoon issued a new set of instructions, containing ten "dos" and ten "don'ts" for troops in the South. Viroj's cover note stressed the need to use a "military-political strategy" to achieve victory in the conflict, which involved leading by example and learning from past mistakes.

76. Abbot interview, August 11, 2006.

77. Informant conversation, October 5, 2005.

78. Thais use a formal and hierarchical hand greeting known as the *wai;* many Malay Muslims are uneasy with this custom, and prefer to shake hands.

79. Quoted in กิ่งอ้อ เล่าฮง, "มิตรภาพในสมรภูมิแดง," *ศูนย์ข่าวอิสรา* [King-or Laohong, "Friendship in the Red Zone"], *Isara News Center,* October 26, 2005, www.tjanews.com.

80. รายงานของคณะกรรมการอิสระสอบข้อเท็จจริง, "กรณีมีผู้เสียชีวิตในเหตุการณ์อำเภอตากใบ จังหวัดนราธิวาส เมื่อวันที่ ๒๕ ตุลาคม ๒๕๔๗" ["Report of the Independent Commission to Investigate the Deaths in the Tak Bai Incident," October 25, 2004] (Bangkok 2004), 44–45.

81. รุ่งรวี, "การคัดเลือกและการปฏิบัติหน้าที่." [Rungrawee, "Recruitment and Performance"], 8.

82. For a detailed discussion of rangers, see International Crisis Group, *Southern Thailand: The Problem with Paramilitaries* (Jakarta: ICG, October 2007), 4–14, http://www.crisisgroup.org.

83. Leaflet 28, also 53.

84. พันโทหญิง พิมลพรรณ อุโฆษกิจ, "วัฒนธรรมองค์กรของหน่วยงานทหารในภูมิภาคต่างๆ ที่มีผลต่อก
ารแก้ปัญหาความไม่สงบใน 3 จังหวัดชายแดนภาคใต้" [Lt. Col. Pimonphan Ukhotkij, "Organisational
Culture of Military Units from Different Regions and the Effect on Conflict Resolution in
the Southern Border Provinces"], unpublished paper presented at seminar Southern Violence
and the Thai State organized by Chaiwat Satha-Anand, Sirindhorn Anthropology Center,
Bangkok, August 18–19, 2006, especially 105–9. The study correlates incident statistics for
the period October 2004 to September 2005 with troop assignments. Central region troops
were assigned to Tak Bai, Sungai Kolok, Waeng and Sukirin, all in Narathiwat; northeastern
units were sent to Chanae, Narathiwat, and Muang and Nong Chik in Pattani, while Southern units covered Banangsata, Raman and Krong Pinang in Yala, as well as Jo-Ai-Rong and
Sungai Padi in Narathiwat, and Yaring, Panare and Mayo in Pattani.

85. พิมลพรรณ, "วัฒนธรรมองค์กร" [Pimonphan, "Organizational Cultures"], 106.

86. This was presumably because many government officials in the three provinces
shared similar backgrounds to the Southern soldiers.

87. พิมลพรรณ, "วัฒนธรรมองค์กร" [Pimonphan, "Organizational Cultures"], 107.

88. Ibid., 109.

89. See statement on zoning by the SBPPBC in *มติชน (Matichon)*, February 27, 2005;
and quotes from defense minister Sampan Bunyanan's statement to the Senate Defense Committee, *สยามรัฐ (Siam Rat)*, March 2, 2005.

90. Cited in *โพสต์ ทูเดย์ (Post Today)*, April 4, 2005.

91. *สยามรัฐ (Siam Rat)*, March 1, 2005.

92. "Thai Senator Alleges 'Inappropriate Conduct' of Buddhist Troops in South," *Bangkok Post*, May 25, 2005.

93. "Southern Thai Tensions Will Escalate if Soldiers Have Sex with Local Muslim
Women, Clerics Say," *Associated Press*, May 24, 2005.

94. "Thai Army Launches Probe into 'Inappropriate Conduct' of Troops in South,"
Bangkok Post, May 26, 2005.

95. Conversations with local Muslim women, November 29, 2005.

96. Leaflet 65, found in Raman, Yala, June 8, 2005. This leaflet was also distributed in
a variety of other locations.

97. Leaflet 9, Raman faxed May 27, 2005.

98. ลูกไก่ในกำมือ, "baby chicks in the fists of their hands," a Thai idiom.

99. Abbot interview, August 11, 2006.

100. One officer based in Narathiwat stated quite directly that he saw his assignment
there as the key to rapid promotion—though only a major, he hoped to become a general
within ten years. Conversation, August 27, 2006.

101. Junior army officer, December 17, 2005.

102. Edited fieldnotes, TAO Bukit, Narathiwat, December 13, 2005.

103. Senior army officer, November 23, 2005.

104. For example, nayok TAO interview, December 11, 2006.

105. Visits to Ban Pari and Ban Samo, April 20, 2006.

106. This took place at the university auditorium on May 24, 2006.

107. I observed these procedures followed daily while living in Belfast, Northern Ireland,
1992–93.

108. Three policemen were shot dead at a Pattani checkpoint in broad daylight on July 20,
2006, by militants wearing army uniforms; two more policemen were shot at a checkpoint
on May 11, 2007.

109. David Fullbrook, journalist, personal communication June 23, 2007.

110. "I'd say the Thais take their bunker construction from Hollywood." Fullbrook
communication.

111. Fullbrook communication.

112. Foot patrols became more common during 2007, as tactics changed; they were regarded by rangers and Border Patrol Police as essential in order to ensure that roads were not booby-trapped.

113. Fullbrook communication. One group of seven soldiers, traveling in an ordinary pickup truck, were killed in a roadside explosion in Rangae on May 9, 2007; the militants were so confident there was no backup vehicle that they came out and shot all the soldiers on the road to ensure they were dead. "Seven Killed in Brutal Attack," *The Nation*, May 10, 2007.

114. Army major interview, May 11, 2006.

115. The figure of fifty men came from the interviewee; some analysts suggest that a hundred or more militants must have taken part in the January 4 incident.

116. Major, May 11, 2006.

117. มติชน (*Matichon*), July 12, 2005.

118. "ลูกผู้ชาย," "หน้าตัวเมีย," "รบอยู่ใต้กระโปรง," Major interview, May 11, 2006.

119. Ironically, the Thai security forces did not always perform well when rare "straight fights" took place. On October 11, 2007, six militants fended off around 150 soldiers and police who had surrounded a house in Rusoh for twenty minutes; one militant was killed, but the other five escaped.

120. The independent Kru-Ze report states that four lots of grenades were hurled into the mosque, tear gas grenades at 10:00 A.M., then others at 11:00 A.M., 12:30 P.M., and then at 2:00 P.M., when nine grenades were thrown in just prior to the storming. รายงานคณะกรรมการอิสระไต่สวนข้อเท็จจริงกรณีเหตุการณ์มัสยิดกรือเซะ (ภาคแรก) [*Report of the Independent Fact-Finding Commission on the Kru-Ze Mosque Incident (Part I)*] (Bangkok, July 26, 2004), 12–18.

121. รายงานกรณีเหตุการณ์มัสยิดกรือเซะ [*Kru-Ze Report*], 2004, 19, 14, 17.

122. Major interview.

123. "แผ่นดิน," colonel interview, May 19, 2006.

124. Conversation with BA, June 14, 2006.

125. พลเอกพัลลภ ปิ่นมณี นายพลแม็คอาเธอร์แห่งเมืองไทย, *ผมผิดหรือ? ที่ยึดกรือเซะ!* [General Panlop Pinmani, The General McArthur of Thailand, *Was I Wrong to Seize Kru-Ze?!*] (Bangkok: Good Morning Publishing, 2004).

126. "งานมวลชน," major interview.

127. Leaflet 14. Thrown in front of the Nongrad Health Center at Yaring, Pattani on April 24, 2005 at 9:00 P.M., by two youths riding a grey Honda Wave motorcycle.

128. Leaflet 99.

129. Panlop was rumored to have received a large bouquet of flowers the day after the storming, sent by a member of the royal family.

130. รายงานกรณีเหตุการณ์มัสยิดกรือเซะ [*Kru-Ze Report*], 2004, 33–35. One member of the committee submitted a minority report exonerating the security forces of all blame.

131. The Kru-Ze and Tak Bai reports were released together. Both reports had some details blacked out: very few in the Tak Bai report, while most erasures in the Kru-Ze report were names of witnesses cited in the footnotes.

132. Interview, June 6, 2006.

133. The widow of one man killed inside Kru-Ze said that the condition of her husband's body showed he had been tortured: "They were so brutal, they treated him as though he was an animal, not a human being." Interview, May 10, 2006.

134. Lawyer interview, June 17, 2006.

135. Vendor near Kru-Ze, December 14, 2004, interview cited in May Tan-Mullins, "Voices from Pattani: Fears, Suspicion, and Confusion," in *Rethinking Thailand's Southern Violence*, ed. Duncan McCargo (Singapore: NUS Press, 2007), 147 (also in *Critical Asian Studies*, 38, 1, March 2006).

136. This process is clearly shown on one of the videos circulating after the incident.

137. The Tak Bai enquiry report found that while official military sources claimed that trucks took around three hours to reach their destinations, drivers and detainees argued that their journeys took around five hours. By car, the journey can easily be made in two hours. Even after the trucks arrived at the army camp, there were long—possibly fatal—delays before detainees were unloaded. รายงาน กรณีเหตุการณ์อำเภอตากใบ [*Tak Bai Report*], 2004, 25–28.

138. Ibid., 2004, 30.

139. Interviews with relatives of Tak Bai victims and protestors, June 2, 2006.

140. Army captain, December 17, 2005.

141. รายงาน กรณีเหตุการณ์อำเภอตากใบ [*Tak Bai Report*], 2004, 28.

142. Interview with Tak Bai protestor, June 2, 2006.

143. Chermsak Pinthong, "The Truth about the Tak Bai Incident," *The Nation*, November 8, 2004.

144. Conversation with Tak Bai victim, November 5, 2005.

145. General Motors military truck.

146. Graveyard.

147. Leaflet 106, undated.

148. Army captain, December 17, 2005.

149. รายงาน กรณีเหตุการณ์อำเภอตากใบ [*Tak Bai Report*], 2004, 22.

150. Army captain, December 17, 2005.

151. Colonel interview, December 12, 2005.

152. *The Nation,* October 27, 2004.

153. รายงาน กรณีเหตุการณ์อำเภอตากใบ [*Tak Bai Report*], 2004, 31–32.

154. Ibid., 2004, 47, 51. In addition, the report singles out Major-General Chalermchai Wiroonphet, then commander of the Fifth Infantry Division, as the officer responsible both for the crackdown and for the transportation of prisoners. Chalermchai left the Tak Bai police station at 7:30 P.M. to meet the prime minister. Also criticized is Major-General Sinchai Nutsatit, the then deputy commander of the Fourth Army Region, who failed to take adequate care of the prisoners who arrived at the Inkhayut camp in Pattani (see 49–51).

155. Chermsak, "The Truth."

156. Fieldnotes, visit on January 14, 2006.

157. Fieldnotes, Ban Pari visit, April 20, 2006.

158. Nayok TAO conversation, August 27, 2006.

159. I visited the scene on the morning of February 20, with a group of four NRC members. We found a large number of spent bullets at the site, all marked "RTA" (Royal Thai Army). Fieldnotes, February 20, 2006.

160. BA conversations, March 10, 2006.

161. Human Rights Watch (hereafter HRW), *"It Was Like Suddenly My Son No Longer Existed": Enforced Disappearances in Thailand's Southern Border Provinces* (New York: Human Rights Watch, March 2007), http://www.hrw.org.

162. Six of them disappeared before January 4, 2004 (four in 2002, two in 2003), six soon after the January 4 incident, another six in 2005 (five of them in one incident), and two in 2006. The additional victim was Bangkok lawyer Somchai Neelaphaichit.

163. HRW, *Enforced Disappearances,* 6. Compensation of 100,000 baht was paid following investigation by a low-profile special government committee in late 2005.

164. รุ่งรวี, "การคัดเลือกและการปฏิบัติหน้าที่" [Rungrawee, "Recruitment and Performance"], 26–27.

165. A border patrol police officer told an academic researcher that some Buddhist and Muslim villagers had volunteered to "take out" a person they believed was responsible for militant violence; he claimed he talked them out of it. Interview on December 12, 2005, cited

in ชิดชนก ราฮิมมุลลา, *ระดับการเรียนรู้และเข้าใจการจัดการความขัดแย้งด้วยสันติวิธีของเจ้าหน้าที่ทหาร ตำรวจ และฝ่ายปกครอง ในพื้นที่จังหวัดยะลา ปัตตานี และนราธิวาส (คำสั่งสำนักนายกรัฐมนตรี 187/2546).* [Chid-chanok Rahimmulah, *Level of Learning and Understanding in Managing Conflict using Peaceful Means among Military, Police, and Civil Officials in Yala, Pattani, and Narathiwat (Prime Minister's Order 187/2546)*] (Bangkok: NRC Working Group on Peaceful Resolution of Conflicts, 2006), 44.

166. "Family's Murder Carefully Planned," *Bangkok Post,* November 17, 2005.

167. Fieldnotes, visit to Bo-ngor January 14, 2006.

168. Senior security official, September 6, 2006, believed the attack was to avenge five rangers killed by militants on October 5, 2005. Another theory linked the attack to troops from the nearby marine base, presumably in revenge for the Tanyong Limo kidnap deaths.

169. Leaflet 59, same as Leaflet 116, fax dated August 8, 2005.

170. He used the phrase "สุดยอด." Conversation, June 15, 2006.

171. Pasuk Phongpaichit, Nualnoi Treerat, Yongyuth Chaiyapong, and Chris Baker, *Corruption in the Public Sector in Thailand: Perceptions and Experience of Households* (Bangkok: Chulalongkorn University, Political Economy Center, 2000), 27. Police shared worst place in the rankings with MPs.

172. As Cynthia Enloe observes, troubled relationships between the police and military are leading causes of ethnic conflicts; see her *Ethnic Soldiers: State Security in Divided Societies* (Harmondsworth, UK: Penguin, 1980), 108.

173. สุภลักษณ์ กาญจนขุนดี และ ดอน ปาทาน, *สันติภาพในเปลวเพลิง* [Supalak Ganjanakhundee and Don Pathan, *Peace in Flames*] (Bangkok: Nation Books, 2004), 302–5.

174. This section draws on a conversation with a group of low-ranking policemen in Chana, Songkhla, September 10, 2006.

175. "ทหารสบาย สบาย…ตำรวจอยู่ประจำ." Comments by Police General Seripisut (aka Seri) Temiyavej, seminar at CS Pattani Hotel, April 6, 2006. In February 2007, Seripisut was appointed Thailand's national police chief.

176. "Police barber" (shop name), Bacho, Narathiwat, January 5, 2006.

177. Discussion at CS Pattani Hotel, April 6, 2006.

178. Senior security official, January 10, 2006.

179. Senior security official, March 9, 2006; *Bangkok Post,* January 27, 2006.

180. Korkiart interview, April 21, 2006.

181. I was briefly stopped and informally detained by such a unit in Pattani province on January 30, 2006.

182. Interview with police commander, Kapho, January 20, 2007; on Than To, see Reuters report, May 3, 2004.

183. Teacher conversation, March 19, 2006.

184. Korkiat interview, April 21, 2006.

185. Conversation with group of policemen, September 10, 2006.

186. CS Pattani police seminar, April 6, 2006.

187. Interview, November 9, 2005.

188. Training session at the Yala Police Academy, March 16, 2006.

189. Academic, October 11, 2005.

190. April 28 suspect interviews, June 16, 2006.

191. Academic, March 6, 2006.

192. Interview, June 6, 2006.

193. Ibid.

194. Lawyer, June 5, 2006.

195. ชิดชนก, *ระดับการเรียนรู้* [Chidchanok, *Level of Learning*], 44, citing interview with senior police officer, Pattani, December 27, 2005. The language used was rather crude: "จะไม่สันติกับมัน." The lack of a subject—"เมื่อก่อนเคยฆ่าลอโจรมายิงวิสามัญ"—makes it unclear

whether he was admitting having previously ordered or taken part in any extrajudicial killings, or whether he was just describing what used to happen. However, active involvement is implied.

196. Again, the statement was ambiguous, but could be read as implying a gap between policy and practice as concerns extrajudicial killings.

197. Police conversation, September 10, 2006.

198. Police Region 9 covers Pattani, Narathiwat, and Yala, as well as Satun, Songkhla, Phatthalung, and Trang.

199. Senior security official, September 6, 2006.

200. Yala had a regular allocation of 3,300 police officers, but as of December 2005 only 2,300 were in post; in Pattani, the figures were 3,023 and 2,581 respectively. รุ่งรวี, "การคัดเลือกและการปฏิบัติหน้าที่" [Rungrawee, "Recruitment and Performance"], 12.

201. รุ่งรวี, "การคัดเลือกและการปฏิบัติหน้าที่" [Rungrawee, "Recruitment and Performance"], 13.

202. *Bangkok Post*, November 27, 2006.

203. Senior security official, September 6, 2006.

204. Replaced in November 2006 by the reformed SBPAC.

205. In Thai, ความสงบและความเรียบร้อย.

206. This was clearly illustrated in the Kuching Rupa incident of May 19, 2006, when two teachers were taken hostage; the Rangae district officer failed to notify his police or army counterparts, and the procedures were ignored.

207. The "Or Sor" date back to 1954; on their deployment in the South, see Desmond Ball and David Scott Mathieson, *Militia Redux: Or Sor and the Revival of Paramilitarism in Thailand* (Bangkok: White Lotus, 2007), especially chapter 6.

208. Ball and Mathieson give details of 37 Or Sor killed between 2001 and 2005, 243–45.

209. Former Yala official conversation, August 31, 2006.

210. ชุดรักษาความปลอดภัยหมู่บ้าน (village security defense team). This scheme was not confined to the South, but also operated in other border areas.

211. Ball and Mathieson, *Militia Redux,* 260.

212. Leaflet 91. Fax sheet dated August 2005.

213. Conversation, August 27, 2006. The politician used the term "ลูกพี่" (literally, "big brother").

214. For example, more than a hundred weapons were seized in coordinated attacks on October 26–27, 2005.

215. Fieldnotes and interview notes, visit to Ban Pakdi, July 2007.

216. "นอนหลับสบาย." Fieldnotes, May 20, 2006.

217. Panu interview, May 23, 2006.

218. For example, surrender camp essay 4/32, September 19, 2005.

219. For example, surrender camp essay 4/9, essay 4/13, September 19, 2005.

220. อาสาสมัครรักษาหมู่บ้าน (village defense volunteers).

221. Interview with head of Or Ror Bor unit, April 23, 2006.

222. Ball and Mathieson, *Militia Redux,* 241. They cite examples of Muslim Or Ror Bor.

223. ตำรวจรักษาชุมชน.

224. Interview with deputy head of community police in one tambon, Yala, December 1, 2005.

225. The program hired large numbers of locals on one-year contracts from October 2004; a second, smaller program operated from October 2005.

226. I observed this training at an army base in Songkhla province, December 14, 2005. The plan was to train around 20,000 people in 34 centers; the 21-day training included military drilling and shooting practice. Those I saw mainly looked bored and indifferent to the training.

227. "หมู่บ้านสันติสุข" Fieldnotes, April 11, 2006.

228. Panu interview, May 23, 2006.

229. In principle, this policy was not the responsibility of subdistrict organizations but that of the provincial governors. In practice, however, the district offices put pressure on TAOs to implement the policy, perhaps since the work involved was difficult and potentially dangerous.

230. Interview, April 13, 2006.

231. To my surprise, one very down-to-earth local Muslim politician told me quite seriously that muban santisuk was an excellent program. Fieldnotes, หัวคะแนน (vote canvasser) conversation, May 20, 2006.

232. Interview, community activists, May 15, 2006.

233. Colonel interview with BA, August 27, 2006.

234. TAO official interview, April 13, 2006.

235. Police colonel Phitak Iadkaew interview, July 23, 2007. For more details, see International Crisis Group, *Southern Thailand: The Problem with Paramilitaries*, 20–21.

236. Interview with Somsak, head of justice maintenance section, SBPAC, January 27, 2007. At the time only 80 of the 200 staff slots had been filled.

237. Interview with Jiraporn Bunnag, deputy secretary-general of National Security Council, May 17, 2007.

238. Somsak interview; see International Crisis Group, *Southern Thailand: The Impact of the Coup*, Asia Report No. 129 (Jakarta: ICG, 15 March 2007), at http://www.crisisgroup.org, 13–15. ICG suggested that SBPAC seemed unable to respond effectively to a case in which the military were accused of torturing a suspect, pp. 17–18.

239. My analysis of essays written by 96 participants at one surrender camp between August and October 2005 shows that 30 insisted they were completely innocent of all militant sympathies, 57 acknowledged some level of involvement, 4 were ambiguous, and 5 illegible. Of those who admitted some activity, the great majority (42) said they had served as lookouts for the movement; 8 admitted swearing oaths, and only 4 admitted to acts of arson or vandalism.

240. Senior security official, March 9, 2006. Several peace trainees wrote about conflicts with community leaders, or believed their unusual lifestyles made them suspect. Batch 5, September 26, 2005.

241. Colonel interview with BA and DM, August 27, 2006.

242. "เอาใจรัฐมนตรี สร้างข่าว."

243. Senior security official, March 9, 2006.

244. Interview, December 15, 2005.

245. Interview, April 16, 2006.

246. Fieldnotes, August 27, 2006.

247. Journalist conversation, May 16, 2006.

248. Chidchai was a former police general who served successively as interior minister, justice minister, and deputy prime minister during Thaksin's 2005–6 government. He was distinguished mainly by his sheer mediocrity.

249. Vaipot conversation, September 16, 2006.

250. Conversation, February 15, 2006.

251. Thailand possessed 4 UAVs, all Israeli in origin. *The Nation*, April 5, 2006.

252. Academic interview, April 12, 2006.

253. Interview, November 19, 2005.

254. Academic interview, April 12, 2006.

255. Panitan, November 19, 2005.

256. Interview, October 16, 2005. Both Pichai and Jiraporn had retired by 2007.

257. See Askew, *Conspiracy*, 15–26.

258. Interview, April 16, 2006.

259. Army colonel, March 13, 2006.

260. Senior security official, March 9, 2006.

261. Conversation notes, September 14, 2006.

262. Senior security official, September 6, 2006.

263. Fieldnotes from visit to village, August 24, 2006.

264. It is debatable how far those who planned Tak Bai could have anticipated such large-scale fatalities, but the tragic outcome was a huge propaganda boost for the movement, and one that subsequently disabled the security forces.

265. Duncan McCargo, "State of Denial," *Time* [Asia], September 11, 2006. In the latter part of 2007, construction of the school did finally resume.

266. This section draws on interviews with key figures involved in these incidents, January 20 and 21, 2007.

267. Such arguments were summarized in an undated paper circulated by Zachary Abuza in March 2007, entitled "Wake Up Call," and echoed by *Jane's Defence Weekly* correspondent Anthony Davis.

268. Jiraporn interview, May 17, 2007.

269. Conversation, May 16, 2007.

270. See Daniel Ten Kate, "Thailand's Southern Rebels Return to Spotlight," *Asia Sentinel,* January 17, 2008.

Chapter 4. Militants

1. A leading group in earlier waves of violence, associated with a mixture of socialist ideology and Islam.

2. The term *separatist* is problematic, and militants in Patani reject it. The hard-to-translate Thai equivalent "แบ่งแยกดินแดน" (something like "tearing apart the land") is replete with intensely nationalist sentiments.

3. How far all 105 actually were "militants," and whether some of those who died—especially at Kru-Ze—may have been innocent, remains unclear.

4. Colonel interview, May 19, 2006.

5. Community leader interview, June 16, 2006.

6. A booklet entitled *Berjihad di Patani,* found on the body of a militant inside the Kru-Ze mosque, has been the subject of much analysis. The document is rich in jihadist language and sentiments, along with Patani nationalist rhetoric. Don Pathan has cautioned against reading too much into the text (*The Nation,* August 6, 2004), but Wattana Sugunnasil sees it as a crucial source on the thinking of the movement. Wattana Sugunnasil, "Islam, Radicalism, and Violence in Southern Thailand: *Berjihad di Patani* and the 28 April 2004 Attacks," *Rethinking Thailand's Southern Violence,* ed. Duncan McCargo (Singapore: NUS Press, 2007), 112–36 (also in *Critical Asian Studies* 38, 1 [2006]).

7. Fourth suspect, June 16, 2006.

8. Third suspect, June 16, 2006. M6 is short for Mathiyom 6, or the twelfth grade of schooling in Thailand.

9. Fourth suspect, June 16, 2006.

10. Confusingly, this school is also known as Pondok Melayu Bangkok (because of its proximity to this well-known intersection), as well as by its official name, Rong Rian Tabiya Tuwata.

11. AW deposition 1, May 1 and 2, 2004. In this and subsequent notes, initials are used to protect the anonymity of deposition informants.

12. AW deposition 4, May 18, 2004. Soh roused the boys daily for morning prayers, hitting them with a *tasbeh* ("rosary") if they did not stir. He was reportedly fired from the school about five months before April 28, apparently for striking students. PM deposition 1, May 12, 2004.

13. YM deposition 4, July 7 and 15, 2004. According to various depositions, Ustadz Soh was 165 cm (5 feet 5 inches) tall, and aged around 30. He played football on the school pitch every day. He had no mobile phone—receiving telephone messages via his brother—and could not drive himself, using his nephew as a driver; he rode a green Honda Wave motorbike. Ustadz Soh, who smoked hand-rolled cigarettes, maintained two houses—one at the pondok and another in a nearby village, where his wife and young child lived.

14. MD deposition 1, June 11–12, 2004.

15. Ibid.

16. First suspect, June 16, 2006.

17. AS deposition, June 3, 2004.

18. Fourth suspect, June 16, 2006.

19. Second suspect, June 16, 2006.

20. P deposition 2.

21. IHYK deposition, May 12, 2004.

22. AJ deposition 1, June 7, 2004.

23. AA deposition 2, July 27, 2004.

24. TL deposition 1, June 16–17, 2004.

25. AD deposition, May 15 and 16, 2004. Ustadz Soh told another informant he would become president. YM deposition 4, July 7 and 15, 2004.

26. AS additional deposition 1, May 20, 2004.

27. In an interview, the same informant said he had taken part in a swearing ritual about a month before the incident, which contradicts his deposition testimony.

28. In Thai, เกรงใจเพื่อน. IM deposition, May 12, 2004.

29. AS deposition 1, June 18, 2004.

30. Fermented fish sauce.

31. A similar claim appears in YM deposition 1, June 17–20, 2004.

32. YM deposition 2, June 20 and 21, 2004.

33. AM deposition 2, July 27, 2004.

34. AW deposition 3, May 16, 2004.

35. AS deposition, June 3, 2004.

36. YM deposition 3, 27 June 2004.

37. AS deposition 4, 23 June 2004.

38. Summary of depositions by YM, DY, DL and NT, dated June 22, 2004.

39. AW deposition 4, May 18, 2004.

40. YY deposition 1, April 28 and 29, 2004.

41. YY deposition 2, May 8, 2004.

42. MKD deposition 2, July 3, 2004; deposition 3, July 11 and 12, 2004.

43. Eight Yala attackers were reported to have had automatic rifles. Police in Songkhla alleged that the Saba Yoi militants had pistols, but when asked by the father of one victim to show him the gun allegedly used by his son, failed to produce it. International Crisis Group, *Southern Thailand: Insurgency not Jihad*, Asia Report No. 98 (Jakarta: ICG, March 2005), http://www.crisisgroup.org, 24. For a photograph of a dead Saba Yoi militant apparently holding a pistol, see ยะ ยี่เอ็ง, *คม...เสธ.แดง ภาค 4 ตอน เบื้องหลังสันต์ถูกปลด ตามปืนไปอาเจะห์ พลีชีพที่กรือเซะ* [Ya Yi-Eng (pseud.), *Khom Sae Daeng, Part Four, Behind The Dismissal of Sant, Following the Guns to Aceh, and Suicides at Kru-Ze*] (Bangkok: Ya Yi-Eng, 2004), 204.

44. Third suspect, June 16, 2004.

45. AW deposition 1, May 1 and 2, 2004; deposition 3, May 16, 2004; YM, deposition 1, April 28 and 29, 2004.

46. NT deposition 1, June 10, 2004.

47. No attack took place there; the attackers apparently switched to the Mo Kaeng checkpoint instead.

48. Details here from ICG, *Insurgency not Jihad*, 24–25, and ยะ ยีเอ็ง, *คม...เสธ.แดง* [Ya Yi-Eng, *Khom Sae Daeng*], 196–21.

49. Ya Yi-Eng is a pen-name used by Major-General Khattiya Swasdipol, a maverick cavalry officer who has published several books dealing with the South, strongly critical of the police.

50. ยะ ยีเอ็ง, *คม...เสธ.แดง* [Ya Yi-Eng, *Khom Sae Daeng*], 205.

51. ICG, *Insurgency not Jihad*, but Bhumiputra gives the youngest as 18, and one as unknown. ภูมิบุตรา, *106 ศพ ความตายมีชีวิต: เรื่องจริงไทยมุสลิมผู้เสียชีวิตในเหตุการณ์ 28 เมษายน 2547.* [Bhumiputra (pseud.), *106 Corpses, Living Death: A True Story of Thai Muslims Who Died in the 28 April 2004 Incident*], Bangkok: Khien Paendin, 2004, 252–53.

52. Plus three from Songkhla and one from Narathiwat, though the identities of seven remain unknown.

53. There is no sign of heavy weapons in Ya Yi-Eng's pictures—one dead attacker holds a small knife.

54. One aged 23 from Yarang, the other unknown.

55. The Krong Pinang attacks were a complex incident, in which 16 men between 18 and 43 were killed altogether. Simultaneous attacks were launched at three adjoining locations, and some attackers died elsewhere. A group of the attackers escaped in a pickup truck with a sizeable cache of weapons from the police station.

56. All came from nearby villages.

57. ยะ ยีเอ็ง, *คม...เสธ.แดง* [Ya Yi-Eng, *Khom Sae Daeng*], 199, claims these militants were using an M–79, but a survivor insisted at least one wounded militant there was the subject of an extrajudicial killing.

58. They had fled there with other weapons seized earlier. Some others in this group later surrendered.

59. ICG, *Insurgency not Jihad*, 24.

60. AS deposition, June 3, 2004.

61. AS additional deposition, May 20, 2004.

62. AS deposition, June 3, 2004.

63. AS additional deposition, May 25–26, 2004.

64. AS deposition 3, June 20, 2004.

65. NT deposition 1, June 10, 2004.

66. The term *BRN* has been used by various factions: the original BRN founded in the early 1960s, and its later derivatives BRN Congress, BRN Ulama, and BRN Coordinate. BRN Ulama pursued the idea of an Islamic state, which was rejected by BRN Congress; BRN Congress is believed to have been defunct since around 2003; and the only active "military wing" of BRN is thought to be BRN Coordinate.

67. YM deposition 2, June 20 and 21, 2004.

68. AS deposition 1, June 18, 2004.

69. AS deposition 3, June 20, 2004.

70. AS deposition 4, June 23, 2004.

71. AW deposition 4, May 18, 2004.

72. Village 3, tambon Kuannori. See ภูมิบุตรา, *106 ศพ* [Bhumiputra, *106 Corpses*] compare pages 249, 250, and 251.

73. Calculated from detailed list of victims, ภูมิบุตรา, *106 ศพ* [Bhumiputra, *106 Corpses*], 246–53. Average ages of those who died in the various incidents were as follows: Kru-Ze 32, Mae Lan 30.3, Saba Yoi 24, Nong Chik 21, Sirindhorn camp 23, Krong Pinang 27, Banang Sata 21.75, Than To 26.6, Ban Niang 25.5.

74. Second suspect, June 16, 2006.

75. Fourth suspect, June 16, 2006.

76. YY deposition 3, May 8, 2004.

77. Ya Yi-Eng states that the police shot the youths immediately, because they had heard the news of attacks in other places on their radios, ยะ ยีเอ็ง, *คม...เสธ.แดง* [Ya Yi-Eng, *Khom Sae Daeng*], 211.

78. AS, additional confession 2, May 25–26, 2004.

79. Abdulloh Agrul, undated deposition. Abdulloh was subsequently the focus of extensive media attention, but his rather convenient claims that Ustadz Soh was alive and still ordering attacks have never been verified.

80. Security lecture, March 16, 2006.

81. Don Pathan, "South Militancy Has Been Years in the Making," *The Nation*, May 30, 2006.

82. Youth, August 23, 2006. This informant dropped out at an early stage and never actually took the supoh.

83. *ศูนย์ข่าวอิสรา* [*Isara News Center*], August 29, 2006, http://www.tjanews.org/.

84. The interviewee apparently revealed nothing about the nature of this attack.

85. AA deposition 2, July 27, 2004.

86. AA deposition, undated.

87. AS deposition, undated. These references to being forbidden from wearing sarong or eating betel nut apparently refer to the policies of the Phibun government in the 1930s, which demanded that all Thais adopt Western norms of "civilized" behavior.

88. Security lecture, March 16, 2006.

89. สร้างกระแส, สร้างแนวคิด, สร้างความเชื่อ, อุดมการณ์.

90. Senior security official, January 10, 2006.

91. MD deposition, March 13 and 14, 2004.

92. TL confession 1.

93. Essay 4/23, surrender camp, September 19, 2005.

94. PS deposition 2, June 19, 2004.

95. Undated interview with unnamed suspect, arrested 2004.

96. Another informant reported that Ustadz Soh had made the same point about the canal. AA, undated deposition.

97. Essay 1/1, surrender camp, August 26, 2005.

98. Unnamed source, undated deposition, circa August 2004.

99. MS undated deposition.

100. MJ deposition, December 29, 2004.

101. Masore Jehsani, Wat Phromprasit suspects untitled DVD, November 20, 2005.

102. Andrew Marshall with Don Pathan, "In Death's Shadow," *Time* (Asia), November 26, 2006. This article contains some important interview sources.

103. Don Pathan, "Alone in the Shadow of the Militants," *The Nation*, May 21, 2006.

104. Marshall and Pathan, "In Death's Shadow."

105. Leaflet 34, found inserted into the journal of Thamma Witttaya Foundation, September 28, 2004.

106. Leaflet 53, fax dated August 4, 2005.

107. Najmuddin Umar interview, August 18, 2006.

108. Kasturi Makota, PULO Foreign Affairs chief, interview in Sweden, May 10, 2007.

109. This section draws heavily on notes from a lecture on militant tactics given at the Yala Police Academy, March 16, 2006.

110. The lecture apparently sought to draw parallels between the "magical" elements used in the two events, as well as the idea of April 28 as the anniversary of Dusun-nyor. For a relevant discussion, see Chaiwat Satha-Anand, "The Silence of the Bullet Monument: Violence and 'Truth' Management, Dusun-nyor 1948, and Kru-Ze 2004," in *Rethinking Thailand's Southern Violence*, ed. Duncan McCargo (Singapore: NUS Press, 2007), 11–34 (also in *Critical Asian Studies* 38, 1 [2006]).

111. Beheadings to date have been "postmortem"; heads were chopped off already-dead victims.

112. Colonel interview, May 19, 2006.

113. Conversation, March 16, 2006.

114. *The Nation,* January 8, 2008.

115. Hafez, *Why Muslims Rebel,* 158–59.

116. Ibid., 161.

117. Ibid., 160. A similar mantra of "five no's" was widely used in the Southern Thai conflict.

118. Bombs are normally at, or close to, ground level; rooftop bombs contain an additional element of surprise.

119. Leaflet 12, found in Kirikate, Than To, Yala on May 16, 2005. The pronouns used here for you and I, *ku* and *mung,* are very vulgar.

120. The headman in Ai Batu had received similar notes shortly before he was murdered. Interview, April 24, 2006.

121. Police arrested one such man at Khopho police station in January 2007.

122. The arrest of a suspect in the Lalo station attack formed a trigger for the events leading to the Kuching Rupa school hostage incident, and the subsequent death of Khru Juling.

123. Interview, November 20, 2005.

124. Conversation, August 30, 2006.

125. One suspect said that he had been given a computer and motorcycle by the movement. ผู้ว่าราชการจังหวัดนราธิวาส [*Narathiwat provincial governor*], DVD.

126. Interview, November 19, 2005.

127. Conversations, March 16, 2006, April 24, 2006.

128. Journalist interview, January 29, 2006.

129. Army officer interview, September 14, 2005.

130. Fieldnotes, visit to Ban Pari, April 20, 2006.

131. Interview, Ai Batu community leader, April 24, 2006.

132. For example, Tanyong Limo interviews, January 14, 2006. In theory there was a headman, two regular assistant headmen, and two additional assistants, but in practice only one of these five men stayed regularly in the village. One assistant headmen had been shot twice (but survived), while an imam was shot dead on December 10, 2005.

133. Postal worker interviews, May 29, 2006.

134. Interview, March 19, 2006.

135. Conversation notes, December 3, 2005.

136. Security lecture, March 16, 2006.

137. Security official, March 16, 2006.

138. Meaning allies or supporters.

139. Security lecture, March 16, 2006.

140. Surrenderee essay 2/3, August 26, 2005.

141. Colonel interview, January 10, 2006.

142. Interview, January 21, 2007.

143. Youth, August 23, 2006.

144. "รบเต็มที่."

145. Many religious authorities argue that there is no requirement to close shops for the whole of Friday, so long as they are closed during prayers. Seminar with Islamic teachers, Narathiwat, September 11, 2005.

146. In Toh Deng sub-district, Narathiwat, I observed one shop displaying three separate signs indicating that the business was closed on Fridays.

147. Colonel interview, BA and DM, August 27, 2006.

148. Colonel interview, January 10, 2006.

149. Ibid.

150. Senior security official, March 16, 2006.

151. This process is discussed in Chai-Anan Samudavanija, Kusuma Snitwongse, and Suchit Bunbongkarn, *From Armed Suppression to Political Offensive* (Bangkok: ISIS, Chulalongkorn University, 1990). Most Thai academic commentary on the CPT "defeat" overstates military successes, and underplays how the CPT simply collapsed of its own internal contradictions.

152. Interview, June 5, 2006.

153. AM deposition, January 27, 2004. "New PULO" was a 1995 offshoot of the original Patani United Liberation Organization.

154. ASB depositions from April 10 to May 15, 2004, and undated later deposition.

155. MJ deposition, December 29, 2004.

156. Then Fourth Army Commander Lt-General Ongkorn Thongprasom suggested that militants often worked in three teams: one team to scope out the target, another to place weapons in position, and a third group to carry out the actual attack. Don Pathan, "South an Elusive 'Spider's Web' for Generals," *The Nation*, September 6, 2006. The "spider's web" could be a useful analogy for the structure of the militant movement, but is misleading because it suggests that there is only one spider.

157. MH deposition, August 11, 2004.

158. Ariphen, August 12, 2006. A PULO spokesman believed Tak Bai was a BRN-C operation: Kasturi Makota, PULO Foreign Affairs chief, interview in Sweden, May 10, 2007.

159. Security officials insisted that the marines were regular visitors to the village and had been asked to come to Tanyong Limo that night as part of a deliberate plot. Lectures, March 16, 2006. This was contradicted by my interview with a community leader in the village, who insisted that the marines were based in Bo-ngor, had not worked in Tanyong Limo, and did not know anyone there. The same source did not believe that the marines were involved in the teashop shooting. Interview, February 1, 2006.

160. เหตุการณ์ที่บ้านตันหยงลิมอ อำเภอระแงะ จังหวัดนราธิวาส [*Incident at Tanyong Limo Village, Ra-ngae District, Narathiwat Province*], Official report of investigation committee chaired by Police Major-General Woraphong Chiawprichai, Deputy Head of the Southern Border Provinces Peace Building Command (Police) (Yala: SBPPBC, 2005).

161. Police commander interview, January 20, 2007.

162. Militants often placed spikes on roads, so as to burst the tires of passing vehicles.

163. Community leader interview, January 21, 2007.

164. "Former hostages, such as the teachers who were held at Joh-Ai-Rong district's Ban Chor Koh School by hundreds of villagers, warn against implicating the entire community. Dire consequences face those who ignore commands and demonstrate in the streets, say the former hostages, who refuse to point out the five people who attacked them." Don Pathan, "Hopelessly Adrift in the Stormy South," *The Nation*, May 23, 2006.

165. Interview, June 5, 2006. The figure of a hundred villages deeply penetrated by militants was given by the Fourth Army in mid-2006 and appears to be a serious underestimate.

166. Interview, June 5, 2006.

167. Kasturi Makota, PULO Foreign Affairs chief, interview in Sweden, May 10, 2007.

168. This is the view of many Thai military and security officers and is strongly made in the detailed group profile "Barisan Revolusi Nasional Patani-Melayu (BRN)," *Jane's World Insurgency and Terrorism,* posted April 27, 2007. This profile suggests that at least a third of villages in the three provinces have been "seriously infiltrated" by the group.

169. Journalist, May 16, 2007.

170. Human Rights Watch, "*Suddenly My Son,*" 14, citing anonymous interview, July 25, 2006.

171. Human Rights Watch, *No One is Safe: Insurgent Violence against Civilians in Thailand's Southern Border Provinces* (New York: HRW, August 2007), http://www.hrw.org, 7–8, 18–28.

172. *The Nation,* June 23, 2006.

173. พลเอกกิตติ รัตนฉายา, *จุดไฟใต้ ตั้งรัฐปัตตานี* [Kitti Rattanachaya, Igniting the Southern Fire, Establishing the Pattani State] (Bangkok: n.p. 2004), 119–21.

174. Connors, "War on Error," 157–59.

175. Human Rights Watch, *No One is Safe,* 18–19.

176. Interview, June 5, 2006.

177. Conversation, Chaiwat Satha-Anand, November 9, 2006.

178. Interview, June 5, 2006.

179. Examples include 23 separate incidents around Yala town on the night of July 14, 2005, more than 40 bombs on June 15, 2006, simultaneous explosions at more than 100 locations on the night of August 1, 2006, and bombs at 22 Yala banks on August 31, 2006.

180. Kasturi argued that this kind of coordinated attack meant the movement had effective control of fighters on the ground, but admitted that some violent incidents could be characterized as "revenge attacks" outside the control of movement leaders. Kasturi Makota interview, May 10, 2007.

181. Two Buddhist schoolteachers were taken hostage and beaten in this May 2006 incident; one of the teachers subsequently died.

182. For a preliminary discussion of leaflets in the conflict, see สะรอนี ดือแระ, *ความเห็นของคนท้องถิ่นต่อสถานการณ์ความรุนแรงภาคใต้: ศึกษาจากใบปลิว ข้อเขียนข้างอาคาร สื่อท้องถิ่น* [Saronee Duerae, *Perceptions of Local People concerning the Southern Violence: A Study from Leaflets, Graffiti, and Local Media*] (Bangkok: NRC, 2006), 21–26.

183. Leaflet 3, fax date June 14, 2004.

184. Leaflet 14, distributed in Yaring, April 24, 2005.

185. Leaflet 1, date June 1, 2005.

186. Leaflet 58, fax dated August 2005.

187. Leaflet 51, date unclear.

188. Leaflet 62, Yaha, August 10, 2005.

189. Leaflet 81, Raman, Yala, March 21, 2005.

190. Leaflet 88, Panare, Pattani, June 13, 2005.

191. Leaflet 117, fax August 9, 2005.

192. Najmuddin Umar interview, August 18, 2006.

193. Interview, May 29, 2006.

194. Interview, May 18, 2007.

195. Kasturi Makota interview, Sweden, May 10, 2007. He argued that in the 1970s and 1980s, PULO was similarly "overcredited" with responsibility for attacks.

196. Runda Kumpulan Kecil.

197. Journalist interview with BA, May 3, 2006.

198. Anthony Davis, "Village Violence—Thai Insurgents Heighten Communal Tensions," *Jane's Intelligence Review,* June 1, 2007.

199. Personal communication, April 26, 2007.

200. Marshall and Pathan, "In Death's Shadow."

201. Don Pathan, "Old Separatists Still Dream of a Free Patani," *The Nation,* February 13, 2007.

202. Journalist, May 16, 2007.

203. Interview, December 3, 2005.

204. Najmuddin Umar interview, August 18, 2006.

205. Don Pathan, "Talks Vital to Restore Peace in the South," *The Nation,* November 27, 2006.

206. Marshall and Pathan, "In Death's Shadow."

207. Personal communication, April 27, 2007.

208. Personal communication, June 30, 2007.

209. Wattana, "Islam, Radicalism."

210. Connors, "War on Error," 160–62.

211. Don Pathan, "A Legacy of Failure in the Deep South," *The Nation*, August 6, 2004.

212. Colonel interview, March 13, 2006.

213. This view leaves open the question of how far the "new" BRN had any strategic overlap with the "old" BRN.

214. Another security official argued that the Patani sultanate could not really be seen as a state at all, let alone an Islamic state. Interview, May 19, 2006.

215. "We have been fooled that the glorious history of Patani was ruled by Muslim principles. In fact, the city was ruled by selfish Sultans, tunku, and their greedy relatives.... Can any religious expert prove that the governments of those Queens were Islamic ones?" Leaflet 124, undated, signed "The Alumni Association of Students in Thailand, Malaysia, and Indonesia." This leaflet could have been created by government officials. I have not found a deposition or leaflet source for the claim that Patani was previously an Islamic state; but the claim does appear on the PULO website (http://puloinfo.net/?Show=Patani), and the issue was raised by local academics at a seminar on Patani history held at PSU, August 4, 2006.

216. อิสมาอีล ลุตฟี จะปะกียา, อิสลามศาสนาแห่งสันติภาพ, [Ismael Lutfi Chapakia, *Islam, Religion of Peace*] (Yala: Social Service Center, Yala Islamic College, 2004), 81–82.

217. Leaflet 18, found Yaha, Yala, June 8, 2005.

218. One leaflet accused the Siamese government of ordering Islamic leaders such as the Chularajamontri to change Islamic doctrine and trying to amend the translations of the Koran and hadith in accordance with Thaksin's irresponsible desires (leaflet 11, found Mayo, Pattani, May 16, 2005). The point is addressed only rather obliquely in *Berjihad di Patani*, most of which is a generic tract on jihad, into which the word *Patani* has been occasionally inserted. Only in the appendices is this tract linked to the specific conditions of Patani.

219. Lawyer interview, June 18, 2006; journalist interview by BA, May 3, 2006.

220. Nidhi Aeusrivongse, "Understanding the Situation in the South as a "Millenarian Revolt,'" *Kyoto Review of Southeast Asia*, 6, 2005, http://kyotoreview.cseas.kyoto-u.ac.jp/issue/issue5/index.html.

221. Community leader interview, February 1, 2006.

222. On September 30, 2005, Thaksin Shinawatra had caused uproar when he referred to the construction workers at the new Bangkok airport as "coolies."

223. Journalist interview by BA, May 3, 2006.

224. On Nidhi's approach to history, see Chris Baker's "Afterword" in Nidhi Eoseewong, *Pen and Sail: Literature and History in Early Bangkok* (Chiang Mai: Silkworm, 2005), 361–84.

225. Najmuddin was charged with treason in 2004, for allegedly supporting the militants.

226. Najmuddin Umar interview, August 18, 2006.

Index

Numbers in italics indicate figures.